# BarnaTrends

## 2018

### What's New and What's Next at the Intersection of Faith and Culture

BakerBooks

*a division of Baker Publishing Group*

Published by Baker Books
a division of Baker Publishing Group
PO Box 6287, Grand Rapids, MI 49516-6287
www.bakerbooks.com

Printed in the United States of America

ISBN 978-0-8010-1864-0

Cover Design: Chaz Russo

# Table of Contents

132575

**Barna Trends** is an annual guide to the latest cultural, religious, and political trends designed to help you navigate a complex and ever-changing world.

**The *Barna Trends 2018* Team:**
**Roxanne Stone** Editor in Chief
**Alyce Youngblood** Managing Editor
**Chaz Russo** Creative Director
**Pam Jacob** Senior Research Director
**Brenda Usery** Production Manager
**David Kinnaman** President

**Contributors & Writers:**
Sarah Pulliam Bailey, George Barna, Mark Batterson, Katelyn Beaty, Francis Chan, Joyce Chiu, Jeremy Courtney, Andy Crouch, Inga Dahlstedt, Chuck DeGroat, Mark DeYmaz, Shani Dowell, Aly Hawkins, Brooke Hempell, Daniel White Hodge, Sharon Hoover, Cheryl Bridges Johns, Sharon Ketchum, David Kinnaman, Tom Krattenmaker, Cory Maxwell-Coghlan, Stanley McChrystal, Susan Mettes, LaTasha Morrison, Jonathan Morrow, Sarah Ngu, Svetlana Papazov, John Perkins, Mac Pier, Gareth Russell, Pete Scazzero, Caitlin Schuman, Amy Simpson, June Steckler, Roxanne Stone, Sara Tandon, Jamie Tworkowski, Alyce Youngblood

**Designers:**
Annette Allen, Judson Collier, Grant England, Chaz Russo

**The Barna Group Team:**
Chrisandra Bolton, Amy Brands, Matt Carobini, Joyce Chiu, Inga Dahlstedt, Bill Denzel, Aly Hawkins, Brooke Hempell, Traci Hochmuth, Rick Ifland, Pam Jacob, Elaine Klautzsch, Cory Maxwell-Coghlan, Steve McBeth, Susan Mettes, Josh Pearce, Gareth Russell, Lisa Schoke, Caitlin Schuman, Todd Sorenson, Roxanne Stone, Sara Tandon, Jess Turner, Todd White, Alyce Youngblood

**Barna Group** is a visionary research and communications company headquartered in Ventura, California, with locations in Atlanta and London. Widely considered to be a leading source for actionable insights on faith and culture, Barna Group has conducted more than one million interviews over the course of hundreds of studies. Since it was founded by George and Nancy Barna in 1984, Barna Group has carefully and strategically tracked the role of faith in America, developing one of the nation's most comprehensive databases of spiritual indicators.

**Barna Research** provides a clear view of your key audiences and actionable insights through custom research, consulting, and resources. To find out more, visit barna.com/services.

**Barna**
PO Box 1030
Ventura, CA 93002
805-639-0000
www.barna.com

**Stay Connected with Barna**
 @BarnaGroup
 @BarnaGroup
 @BarnaGroup
 Barna Group

# Data and Truth

*An Introduction by David Kinnaman,*
*President of Barna Group*

Welcome to *Barna Trends 2018*. Like the 2017 edition, this book is a compilation of our company's best research and most significant insights from the past year. In these pages, you'll find lots and lots of data (obviously) and also infographics, in-depth analyses, personal stories, and guest commentaries to tease actionable wisdom out of the information.

One of the differences in this edition of *Barna Trends* is a main feature in which we focus on "The Truth about a Post-Truth Society" (page 116). The phrase "post-truth" has caught on among political observers as a tidy encapsulation of our cultural moment, a time when it's hard for many people to tell the difference between facts and "alternative facts" or between truth and "my truth." Yes, it is glib, but post-truth is also a fair summary of broader cultural realities that have massive implications now and in the coming years for how Christians live, work, and serve. If there are no facts that everyone accepts as fact, is it possible to change anyone's mind—including our own? What does it look like to raise godly children in a culture where moral and ethical standards are based on what is fair to the exclusion of other considerations—such as what is *true*?

Barna's mission is to help spiritual influencers understand the times and know what to do. We believe that understanding the reality of this post-truth society and knowing how to wisely respond is more urgent than ever for Christian leaders, parents, and teachers—not just for ourselves but also as we raise up the next generation of Jesus followers.

Gen Z (teens born after 1998) pops up quite a bit in this new edition of *Barna Trends*, including what they believe and why (page 175), who they spend time with (page 106), how they use tech (page 84), who and what influences them (page 158), their involvement in community and church youth programs (page 145), and how they view the world and their place in it. What they tell us indicates that some of the trends we've long identified among Millennials—24/7 access to everything, alienation from institutions and tradition, distrust of external authority—are further amplified in Gen Z. Plus, we're uncovering perspectives and ideas unique to this upcoming generation; they're not just "little Millennials." For example, Gen Z is the first age cohort not to consider family as central to their sense of identity, even though the vast majority of them still lives at home. Mediated by social technologies, other influences exert enormous power to form young hearts and minds—and it's too early to say who these young people will become outside the formative structures that have shaped previous generations.

This is reality. What should the Christian community do about it?

In this post-truth moment lived both virtually and physically—of political and religious polarization (page 36), of too much information and too little understanding, of conversations that shed more heat than light—we want to say true things. More than that, we want to say true things that matter. The Barna team does this through well-designed research, obsessive number crunching, and careful analysis. Our hope is to wed data to truth in a union that bears the fruit of wisdom—on and offline, in ministry, in families, in churches, in schools, in businesses, and in communities—all to God's glory.

*Barna Trends* is part of that effort.

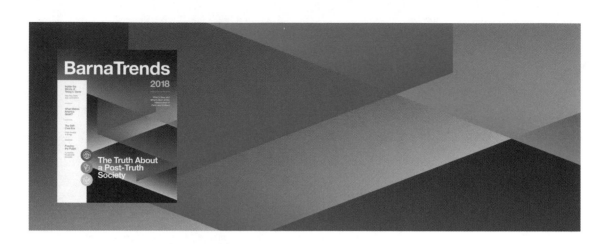

# How to Use This Book

*Barna Trends* is packaged to suit a variety of reading experiences: personal interest, group discussion, sermon preparation, academic study, market research, and so on. Its content is divided into three broad sections:

- **Culture** covers mindsets and movements within the broader public, from the internet to the voting booth.
- **Life** has a more personal lens, taking a closer look at our workplaces, homes, schools, and daily routines.
- **Faith** focuses on the state of our spiritual lives, individually and collectively, in America and around the world.

Each of these topics is divided further into additional subcategories, feature-length reports, fast facts, and eye-catching infographics, shaped by Barna's most recent and relevant research.

The Barna team or trusted experts sometimes share personal observations and predictions in **Barna Takes** or **Q&As**, while **At a Glance** sets the stage for each section with concise, easily digestible blurbs and quotes.

*Barna Trends* is bookended with a number of resources to aid your reading and learning experience. Over the next

*Interested in other projects from Barna Group? More information about Barna's research, services, speaking, books, and resources is available at barna.com*

few pages, a special **Behind the Scenes** section (page 9) will give you a peek into how our data are collected and analyzed. Then an introductory **Glossary** (page 13) will define key terms that are foundational to our reporting. At the end of the book, there is a breakdown of the **Methodology** (page 214) used for the surveys and studies that make up *Barna Trends*. (You'll also catch brief summaries of this information throughout the book; for example, *n=1,000 | December 2017* means the corresponding data is from the survey responses of 1,000 individuals in December of 2017. Unless otherwise stated, all percentages refer to nationally representative samples of U.S. adults.) If you're looking for a specific subject or statistic, the **Index** (page 220) will direct you to the major themes, contributors, and topics of *Barna Trends*.

Finally, if you want more information, definitions, or commentary, visit barna.com or follow us on social media for updates about current and upcoming projects.

# Behind the Scenes with Barna

As a religion and social research company, Barna has a mission to provide spiritual influencers with credible knowledge and clear thinking, enabling them to navigate a complex and changing culture through their ministry, work, or personal context.

That is *why* we do what we do—but along the way, we get a lot of questions about *how* we do it. For those curious about the nitty-gritty details of conducting research itself or about Barna's role in collecting and interpreting data, we put together the following FAQ.

### How does Barna choose topics to study and report on?

While Barna's researchers and writers sometimes explore questions in regular population surveys related to their own cultural or religious interests, the majority of the topics comes from partner organizations. Parachurch ministries, foundations, and private companies come to Barna with particular questions about trends in culture, ministry, politics, education, and so on, and we work with them to devise a research approach to effectively study that subject.

Occasionally, these studies become online reports or printed monographs, magazine-style research reports published by the Barna team and client partners. These projects provide a deep dive into the data, incorporating different types of research with expert interviews and infographics to provide a holistic picture of the findings and help a particular audience implement them.

### What do you mean when you refer to a "nationally representative sample"?

When surveying the general population, the goal of a nationally representative sample is to mimic the population among the U.S. as a whole. In other words, a completed survey is designed to represent the distribution of the U.S. adult population by region, ethnicity, age, gender, and educational attainment. We establish minimum and maximum ranges on respondents of various profiles. To make certain that the sample is representative of the general population, after completion of a survey, our researchers often apply minimal statistical weighting to balance those in categories with lower response rates.

Depending on the questions at hand, research can be focused organizationally—on an institution, network, or market—or geographically—on a city, region, nation, or even group of nations. Each type of research focus takes on different requirements for audience and data collection methods. For example, if we're doing internal research on an institution or network, we may not need or want the data to be representative of the nation but instead representative of that organization. Similarly, if we're studying a research question in a city or region, we may want to supplement research in the general population with research on local influencers or leaders to better understand and compare their experiences to the experience of the broader community.

### How do you find people to survey?

Due to an increasing number of households that do not have a landline telephone, at least half of a Barna phone survey includes adults interviewed on their cell phone. Telephone numbers are obtained through several reputable list brokers that offer consumer lists for purchase. Telephone samples include both listed and unlisted phone numbers. Interviewers place calls at various times of the day, various days of the week, and multiple times if necessary in order to minimize bias in respondents.

An increasingly common way that our team conducts research is via online surveys conducted with an online research panel. Our panel partners are carefully vetted to ensure we are finding "real people" to respond to our surveys. Participants in the panel are recruited using a controlled, invitation-only method and are then put through multiple identity checks. For example, they must have a physical address and a working email address. All panelists are also required to double opt in by confirming their interest through an additional email they receive. Digital fingerprinting collects data on their computer (operating system, browser version, etc.) that allows us to ascertain that they are a real person and that there are no duplicates in the file. Quality control checks are also included in the survey to make sure those who speed through the survey, give answers that don't make sense, fail trick questions, or appear unengaged are eliminated from our surveys, and, if multiple violations occur, from the research panel. Panelists are typically offered an incentive for their participation in the form of a gift certificate of some sort. Just as in telephone interviews, multiple reminders are sent to panelists to ensure that respondents are not just those who are the most eager to take the survey or who are more apt to check their email or answer the telephone often.

Using online and phone samples together allows the broadest distribution of individuals in the population an equal chance of participating in a survey, regardless of age, socioeconomics, geographical location, or other factors.

### What is the state of phone vs. online polling?

Almost all American adults (95%) own a cell phone, including more than three out of four (77%) who own a smartphone, according to Pew Research.[1] A study conducted by the Centers for Disease Control reports that as of May 2017, half of households (51%) did not have a landline telephone at home.[2] Additionally, more than one-third of households who own a cell phone and still have a landline (37%) say they answer all or most of their calls on their wireless phones. If combining cell phone–only households with the 15 percent of all households who have both a cell and landline phone but primarily or exclusively take their calls on their cell phone, nearly two-thirds of the adult population is considered unreachable by landline.

Barna found that the average adult cell phone user is 35 years old, compared to landline users, whose average age is 54. Cell users are also more likely to be male than female, more educated, a high earner, and an ethnic minority (though many of these numbers are also unlisted).

With declining response rates in telephone surveys (not as many people answer calls from an unknown caller or are willing to stay on the phone for a 15-minute survey) and rising costs of including cell phone interviews, researchers are finding the reliability of online surveys is increasing while the reliability of phone interviews is decreasing. Additionally, online surveys are less expensive to

run, offer the researcher the opportunity to show graphics or videos, and are easier for respondents to complete at their convenience when they are able to pay attention. The differences between data collected online and by telephone is relatively small, with a 3–5 percent difference in responses.

Of most importance, telephone surveys are more susceptible to "social desirability bias," meaning that people are more likely to give answers that paint them in a positive light when they are speaking with a live interviewer. Subjects covering sensitive topics are best conducted online, allowing people to answer anonymously or express negative attitudes. Barna's area of research—covering faith topics as well as some intimate subjects like financial giving or use of pornography—often lends itself to online surveys as a more appropriate channel.

### How do you go about interviewing pastors specifically?

Barna has developed a strong expertise in research with church leaders. Our participation rate in surveys with pastors is high; we've done over 14,000 interviews with pastors since 2006. Whether interviewed by phone or online, senior pastors are recruited from publicly available church listings covering 90 percent of U.S. churches that have a physical address and a listed telephone number or email address. Minimum and maximum ranges are placed on church size, denomination, and region to ensure representation. Minimum weighting is also used to match church characteristics from the National Congregation Study (by Association of Statisticians of American Religious Bodies).

Unlike the general adult population, senior pastors are often best reached by telephone. However, Barna also has recruited a pastor panel from its phone surveys, and these pastors participate in frequent online surveys as well.

## What is the significance of a survey sample's size? What is the potential for error?

Like most survey researchers, Barna uses polling that includes a minimum of 1,000 people in each survey for a general population sample. You may wonder, *Can only 1,000 people be representative of the entire U.S. population of 235 million adults?* The answer is yes! Because it is not physically possible to survey everyone in the U.S., researchers use a sample, or a small selection of the population as a whole, rather than a census.

Assuming that the respondents are chosen in a random, representative way, we know that with 1,000 interviews, the sample has a 95 percent chance of being accurate by plus or minus 3 percent. That means there is a 95 percent chance that the true percentage of the group being sampled is in that range. If we surveyed 1,000 new people and asked them the same questions, we would see similar answers varying by no more than 3 percentage points for any given question.

The larger the sample size, the lower the error rate. When comparing the results of two subgroups (e.g., men vs. women), a different statistical testing procedure is followed and usually requires a greater sample size.

## What is an "oversample"?

Sometimes Barna and its clients desire to target a specific demographic group and may conduct a larger portion of interviews among that group to look at subgroups within it. These additional interviews are conducted and combined with those who qualify naturally as part of the main sample (weighted to reflect the total population). Larger sample sizes allow us to improve the reliability of predictions of smaller subsegments. For example, if we wanted to more closely examine the results among women—say, younger vs. older women—we may survey a larger number of women to decrease the error rate.

## How does Barna approach analysis?

Albert Einstein said, "Not everything that can be counted counts, and not everything that counts can be counted." While making an "evidence-based" or "data-driven" decision is important, it's not just enough to have data; decision-makers need to have the right data in the right context. Today, people have more data at their fingertips than ever before, and yet we're starved for wisdom. Many of us are trying to understand how, on a fundamental level, what we know really changes what we do.

Analysis and interpretation are the heartbeat of Barna's work, and we hold up as our standard the tribe of Isaachar in 1 Chronicles 12:32 (KJV) who "had understanding of the times, to know what Israel ought to do." We rely on different elements to transform data from dry information into actionable wisdom by 1) committing ourselves to understanding the needs, pain points, and opportunities of our readers and partner(s); 2) exploring deeper insights through mixed methods and qualitative research; 3) employing advanced statistical analysis where needed to highlight relationships and interdependencies in the results; and 4) drawing on our experience of serving different ministries and arms of the Church for decades. Altogether, our team's goal is to help solve some of the most pressing problems and vexing concerns our partners and Christians face. Data are a foundational tool for understanding ourselves and our society, but it takes the in-depth relationships with our partners, our community, and our research topics to transform data into insight.

Because Barna has been working with churches and ministries for over 30 years, and because our staff is steeped in the Christian community, we are able to approach questions and topics of faith from an "insider" perspective. This means we don't just define someone's faith based on self-description ("I am an evangelical" or "I am a Christian") as mainstream research groups do, because we know that this can mean many things! Rather, we have a set of questions to assess both theological beliefs (such as "what will happen when you die?") and personal values ("my faith is very important in my life today"). Using a collection of questions we call Theolographics™, Barna has tracked specific Christian subsegments for three decades (see page 13 for a full Glossary). We have conducted analysis on hundreds of thousands of interviews to identify and understand the relationships between someone's faith and who they are demographically, as well as how they live out their faith.

# The Milestones of Research

### Conception

Barna spends weeks honing in on the key questions to be answered in a study. This is the most critical phase for keeping sight of objectives before diving into the logistics. Focus groups may also be helpful during this time to gain a better understanding of how the general public or a specific audience regards the subject at hand.

### Questionnaire Development

Our team uses a proprietary approach to map objectives to specific questions. Our editorial team, our researchers with various backgrounds, and even outside experts may add valuable insight at this stage, often in addition to a client's unique perspective. This phase sometimes takes longer for a really tricky topic (like Barna's study on pornography) or a unique approach (such as using visual polling to test emotional ideas).

### Analysis

Typically, it takes a few weeks to organize and analyze the data from a survey. This also involves data checks for quality control and to ensure that our data are reliable. The analysis phase can be shorter for a simpler survey, or longer for one in which we are using more advanced analytics (we love a good regression model!) or searching for relationships between different data or subgroups of the population.

### Fielding

Data collection usually takes one or two weeks for a broad sample of the population, or up to five weeks for a narrower or harder-to-reach audience, such as youth pastors.

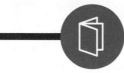

### Narrative Development

Finding the story (or stories) in a data set is the part our team loves most, as data never exist in a vacuum. Again, a variety of team members and stakeholders help offer a well-rounded interpretation of the findings, often referring back to the objectives mapped out prior to data collection.

### Reporting

If producing a printed monograph or online report, Barna may take up to a few months to write and depict the data and create infographics. Our team also may link a survey to other existing Barna research or secondary information about a particular market or issue. Though some research is commissioned only for clients' private use, we thrive on providing critical context that helps readers make use of it.

# Glossary—Theolographics

## Affiliation, Beliefs, and Practice

**Self-identified Christians** (sometimes called "all Christians" or just "Christians") choose "Christian" from a list of religious affiliations.

**Other faith** choose a faith other than Christianity from a list of religious affiliations.

**No faith** choose "atheist," "agnostic," or "none" from a list of religious affiliations.

**Born again Christians** are self-identified Christians who have made a personal commitment to Jesus that is still important in their lives today and believe that, when they die, they will go to heaven because they have confessed their sins and accepted Jesus Christ as their Savior.

**Non–born again (or notional) Christians** are self-identified Christians who do not qualify as born again.

**Practicing Christians** are self-identified Christians who say their faith is very important in their lives and have attended a worship service within the past month.

*Practicing Catholics* are practicing Christians who describe themselves as Catholic.

*Practicing mainline Protestants* are practicing Christians who attend a church affiliated with a mainline Protestant denomination: American Baptist Churches USA, the Episcopal Church, Evangelical Lutheran Church of America, United Church of Christ, United Methodist Church, and Presbyterian Church USA.

*Practicing non-mainline Protestants* are practicing Christians who attend a non-mainline church: charismatic/Pentecostal churches, churches in the Southern Baptist Convention, churches in the Wesleyan-Holiness tradition, and non-denominational churches, among others.

**Non-practicing Christians** are individuals who self-identify as Christian but do not qualify as practicing.

**Churched adults** have attended church, other than a special event such as a wedding or funeral, in the past 6 months.

**Unchurched adults** do not report attending a church service in the past six months.

**Dechurched adults** previously attended church but now qualify as unchurched.

**Never churched** adults have never attended church.

**Evangelicals** meet nine criteria, which include having made a personal commitment to Jesus Christ that is still important in their life today and believing that, when they die, they will go to heaven because they have confessed their sins and accepted Jesus Christ as their Savior. The seven other conditions include saying their faith is very important in their lives; believing they have a personal responsibility to share their religious beliefs about Christ with non-Christians; believing that Satan exists; believing that Jesus Christ lived a sinless life on earth; asserting that the Bible is accurate in all that it teaches; believing that eternal salvation is possible only through grace, not works; and describing God as the all-knowing, all-powerful, perfect deity who created the universe and still rules it today. Being classified as an evangelical is not dependent on church attendance or denominational affiliation, and respondents are not asked to describe themselves as "evangelical."

To qualify as **post-Christian**, individuals must meet nine or more of the following factors: do not believe in God; identify as atheist or agnostic; disagree that faith is important in their lives; have not prayed to God in the last week; have never made a commitment to Jesus; disagree that the Bible is accurate; have not donated money to a church in the last year; have not attended a Christian church in the last 6 months; agree that

Jesus committed sins; do not feel a responsibility to share their faith; have not read a Bible in the last week; have not volunteered at a church in the last week; have not attended Sunday school in the last week; have not attended a religious small group in the last week; rank low on the Bible engagement scale; are not born again. Highly post-Christian individuals meet 13 or more of these 16 factors.

An **orthodox view of God** is the belief that God is the all-powerful, all-knowing, perfect creator of the universe who rules the world today.

A **biblical worldview** is defined as believing that absolute moral truth exists; the Bible is totally accurate in all of the principles it teaches; Satan is considered to be a real being or force, not merely symbolic; a person cannot earn their way into heaven by trying to be good or do good works; Jesus Christ lived a sinless life on earth; and God is the all-knowing, all-powerful creator of the world who still rules the universe today (used in worldview research).

**Interested Christians** are self-identified Christians, excluding those who have never been to a worship service and those who disagree that their faith is very important for their lives (used in generosity research).

**Active Christians** are those actively engaged in churchgoing, Bible reading, and prayer at least monthly (used in United Kingdom research).

**Engaged Christians** are self-identified Christians who are churched and agree strongly with the following statements: that the Bible is the inspired word of God and contains truth about the world; that they have made a personal commitment to Jesus Christ that is still important in their life today; that Jesus Christ was crucified and raised from the dead to conquer sin and death; that their religious faith is very important in their life today; that they have a responsibility to tell other people their religious beliefs (used in Generation Z research).

## Relationship to Scripture

**Bible engagement definitions** are based on data collected for American Bible Society's annual State of the Bible study. Barna created a typology based on people's view of and level of engagement with the scriptures:

*Bible engaged* means that people have a "high" view of the scriptures and read the Bible four or more times per week. They view the Bible as a) the actual or b) the inspired Word of God with no errors, or as c) the inspired Word of God with some errors. They must also read, use, or listen to the Bible four times a week or more to be considered Bible engaged.

*Bible friendly* people also have a "high" view of the scriptures but read it fewer than four times in a week.

*Bible neutral* people have a lower, but not negative, view of the Bible. Those in this group choose neither of the top two definitions of the Bible (i.e., the "highest" views) nor the most skeptical statement. They tend to pick "middle options" and rarely or never read the Bible.

*Bible skeptics* believe the Bible is just another book of teachings written by men. The Bible skeptic selects the statement in the survey that reflects the "lowest" view of the Bible and rarely or never reads the Bible.

*Bible hostile* is a subset of Bible skeptics. They view the Bible as a book of teachings written by men that's intended to manipulate and control other people.

**Bible-minded** people believe the Bible is accurate in all the principles it teaches and have read the scriptures within the past week.

**Bible readers** read the Bible at least three to four times a year outside of a worship service, Mass, or church event.

## Generosity Groups

**Givers** are motivated by "others-focused" goals: to provide for their family, to give charitably, to serve God with their money, or to leave a legacy for others (used in generosity research).

**Keepers** are motivated by "self-focused" goals: to support the lifestyle they want, to be content, to be debt-free, or to earn enough to show how hard they work (used in generosity research).

Please see page 217 for a summary of Barna's **risk metric** for pastors (used in *The State of Pastors* research).

# Glossary—Demographics

## Generations

**Generation/Gen Z** were between ages 13 and 19 at the time of the study.

**Millennials** were born between 1984 and 2002.

**Generation/Gen X** were born between 1965 and 1983.

**Boomers** were born between 1946 and 1964.

**Elders** were born prior to 1946.

**Young adults** refers to ages 19–25 and **teenagers** refers to ages 14–18 (used in Ireland research).

**Ethnicity** is based on respondents' self-descriptions of their ethnicity. Those who describe themselves as Hispanic plus another ethnicity are coded as Hispanic only. To ensure adequate sample sizes, Barna usually segments the population only by the three largest ethnic groups:

> *White/Caucasian*
> *Black/African American*
> *Hispanic/Latino*

Data about *Jews* include American adults who consider themselves to be "Jewish," have at least one parent who is 100 percent Jewish, or both of their parents are no less than half Jewish (used in Jewish Millennials research).

## Region

**Northeast** are residents of CT, DE, MA, MD, ME, NH, NJ, NY, PA, RI, VA, VT, WV, and Washington, DC.

**Midwest** are residents of IA, IL, IN, KS, KY, MI, MN, MO, ND, NE, OH, SD, and WI.

**South** are residents of AL, AR, FL, GA, LA, MS, NC, OK, SC, TN, and TX.

**West** are residents of AK, AZ, CA, CO, HI, ID, MT, NM, NV, OR, UT, WA, and WY.

## Political Affiliation and Ideology

**Democrats** are registered as a Democrat at their current address.

**Independents** are registered as non-partisan at their current address.

**Republicans** are registered as a Republican at their current address.

**Conservatives** identify as "mostly conservative" when it comes to political issues.

**Liberals** identify as "mostly liberal" when it comes to political issues.

# Trending in ...
# Culture

While hot topics and hashtags change every day (or sometimes multiple times a day), it can be tough to keep up—let alone to feel informed about the issues, movements, and mindsets that make up our communities.

For this reason, *Barna Trends* begins with a cultural primer, in hopes that readers might engage intelligently and compassionately with the world around them (yes, maybe even with the online trolls). This opening section offers an in-depth overview of Americans' foundational beliefs about people and policy.

In CULTURE, Barna looks at trends such as:
- the presence of faith in the military
- America's current attitude toward refugees
- the factors (and scandals) that shaped the 2016 election
- pastors' cultural credibility crisis
- what people really think about "fake news"

 Media

Politics

Perspectives

Featuring:

Sarah Pulliam Bailey, Mark Batterson, Joyce Chiu, Jeremy Courtney, Susan Mettes

# At a Glance: Culture

## Goodnight, TV

What is the last thing the American parent does before bedtime? In a Barna survey for *The Tech-Wise Family*, the top response was "watch TV or a movie" (31%). Next up, more than one in five (22%) spend time with their spouse or significant other. Though 70 percent of parents admit to sleeping with their phone next to them, just 10 percent say checking social media is the last thing they do before going to sleep.

*n=1,201 U.S. parents of children age 4–17 | January 25–February 4, 2016*

# Married with Children? You Might Like Trump    *n=1,109 | May 15–19, 2017*

The GOP calls themselves the "family values" party, and whether or not you feel their policies back up this claim, the current GOP president certainly appeals to families. Mid-2017 Barna data revealed that stage of life and family seems to have a significant impact on whether an individual approves of President Donald Trump. For example, married U.S. adults are three times more likely than single adults to say he is doing a great job (23% vs. 7%), while those who have never been married are more inclined to think he is doing a poor job (37% vs. 24%) or worse than expected (35% vs. 26%). Married Americans are also more trusting of Trump (30% vs. 8% of never married Americans say "definitely"), yet a majority of single people says they don't trust him at all (80% vs. 42% of married adults). To a lesser though still significant degree, being a parent of young children is connected to greater approval of and trust in Trump; more than a quarter of parents of minors say Trump's performance has been great (26% vs. 10% of those with no kids under 18), and one in three definitely trusts him (31% vs. 15%).

## Undocumented Questions

More than half of American adults (52%) disagree that amnesty and/ or citizenship should be granted to undocumented immigrants under 18 (32% strongly, 20% somewhat). Thirty-nine percent agree with offering amnesty to minors (14% strongly, 25% somewhat), while 9 percent are unsure where they stand on this issue. A majority of Hispanic (55%) and black (50%) Americans supports this amnesty provision at least somewhat, compared to 32 percent of white Americans.    *n=1,097 | April 7–14, 2016*

One in four married U.S. adults says Trump is doing a great job

**One in five prayerful Americans prays most often for global injustices**

# Christian Values and Criminal Justice

*n=1,015 | June 5–9, 2017*

The vast majority of Americans (87%) feels that the primary goal of the justice system should be restoration for all involved. Christian beliefs seem to encourage this hope for holistic justice. For example, according to a Barna study in partnership with Prison Fellowship, practicing Christians (35%) are more likely than the national average (23%) to strongly agree that, because of their values, it is important to care for prisoners. Evangelicals are most convinced (44% strongly agree). Yet more than half of practicing Christians (53%) still agree at least somewhat that "it's important to make an example out of someone for certain crimes, even if it means giving them a more severe punishment than their crime deserves." When asked if their values make them willing to advocate for criminal justice reform, all Americans (24% strongly agree) and practicing Christians (29% strongly agree) are more in sync.

## Nation, World Rank Low on Prayer Lists

Among American adults who report praying at least once in the past three months, one in four (24%) says the content of their prayers most often pertains to the nation or government. One-fifth (20%) most often prays for global problems and injustices. These broader petitions, however, rank much lower than other more personal issues. Before global and national interests, prayerful Americans cover: giving thanks (62%), family and community needs (61%), guidance in crisis (49%), health and wellness (47%), confession (43%), safety (41%), peace (37%), and blessings for meals (37%).

*n=794 U.S. adults who've prayed in the last three months | June 5–9, 2017*

I think that the time and era we are in is ripe for engagement with intercultural ministry. I use the term *intercultural* because it is more about the interweaving of cultures into a particular ethos rather than simply having multiple cultures. In other words, it is too simple to have 'many cultures' present, without ever interweaving them into the church or ministry. Moreover, interculturalism is about removing hegemonic authority and disrupting dominance from one group. Thus, the term is much more appropriate and applicable."

—*Daniel White Hodge, director of the Center for Youth Ministry Studies and associate professor of youth ministry at North Park University in Chicago, in Barna's* The State of Youth Ministry

**Half of American adults say the government should not fund organizations that promote abortion**

# Examining Abortion Funding

*n=1,097 | April 7–14, 2016*

One of President Trump's first acts was to sign an executive order barring United States aid from any nongovernmental organization that also provides abortion counseling or services internationally. Since then, his administration has taken other bold measures to restrict abortions, such as aiming to cut federal funding for Planned Parenthood. These moves have had a predictably polarizing affect on both pro-life and pro-choice camps within the country, and Barna observed this divide when asking American adults whether they feel government funding should go to organizations that promote abortion. Roughly half (49%) say it shouldn't, 10 percentage points more than those who say such funding should be permitted (39%). The groups are split by 12 percent of adults who are unsure if this is an appropriate use of government aid. Democrats are less certain that the government should support these organizations (25% absolutely, 30% possibly) than Republicans are certain that it shouldn't (58% definitely not, 15% probably not). Evangelicals are the group most opposed (78% definitely not), while liberals are the group most in favor (39% absolutely).

I believe that God is the God of all life, and that his Word reveals the most inspiring model for thriving economies. To separate biblical principles such as creativity, just wages, human dignity, and stewardship from the workplace is to set our societies up for failure. Only holistic Christianity that incorporates faith into the whole life—uniting work, ministry, worship, and family—will succeed in bringing the reality of God's presence to the professional realm. When believers engage vocation as an act of worship to God (see Colossians 3:23–24), they introduce the strongest work ethics into the marketplace. They become modern, Spirit-filled Bezalels (see Exodus 31:1–5) who are noted for their skill and knowledge in all kinds of work, modeling righteous living in their local cultures and pointing their neighbors to hope-filled community in Christ."

*—Svetlana Papazov, founder of Real Life Church and Real Life Center for Entrepreneurial and Leadership Excellence in Richmond, Virginia, in* Barna's The State of Pastors

# A Political Snapshot of Faith Segments

Barna's research reveals much about the politics of America's five dominant faith segments (see Glossary on page 13 for full definitions). Here's how they differ in meaningful ways when it comes to their views on some of the most contentious issues of the day.

- Almost half of religious skeptics (48%) see themselves as environmentalists. Several groups—adherents of other faiths (43%), notional Christians (39%), and non-evangelical, born again Christians (36%)—are clustered pretty closely in claiming this label. Nearly one in five evangelicals (18%) identifies as an environmentalist.
- A majority of skeptics supports the Black Lives Matter movement (53%), the most of any segment, followed by adherents of other faiths (51%), notionals (38%), and non-evangelical born agains (36%). Evangelicals are the holdout here; just 18 percent identify with Black Lives Matter.
- Skeptics are also the group with the highest percentage of LGBT advocates (66%), with a notable drop before those of other faiths (47%). Four in 10 notionals (39%) and more than a quarter of non-evangelical born agains (27%) support LGBT rights. A small minority of evangelicals takes this commonly liberal stance (4%).
- Evangelicals are actually as likely as notional Christians to own a gun (30% each), and non-evangelical born agains top them with 37 percent. About one in five skeptics (22%) is a gun owner, and adherents of other faiths have the smallest percentage in this category (10%). *n=1,097 | April 7–14, 2016*

## Few Trust Hollywood for Headlines

When celebrities lend their voice to discussing a particular cause, policy, or current event, it can occasionally provide a helpful push for awareness. But often—and all over the internet—it simply prompts pleas for entertainers to "stick to their day jobs." The bottom line? Americans don't trust big Hollywood names on the issues. Just 6 percent say celebrities are a credible source of news. (Politicians don't fare much better, with trust from just 7 percent.) Millennials (14%) are the group most likely to give celebrities the benefit of the doubt. Those with full-time jobs (11%), higher salaries (11% of those making $50K+ annually), or college degrees (9%) are also fairly willing to trust celebrities for news. *n=1,021 | February 8–14, 2017*

**53%** of religious skeptics support the Black Lives Matter movement

# Media

Key information about an age
of information overload

# 3 Top Stories about Modern News Media

The media world is rapidly changing. Traditional news organizations are struggling to find their footing as financial challenges, technological shifts, and quickly changing consumer behaviors force them to reinvent themselves—and often. Free content is disrupting traditional pay models, the increasing use of smartphones is opening up new channels for consumption, the low barriers to entry for content producers have overpopulated the news space, and younger audiences are overturning reliable indicators of consumer behavior. Add to this a growing suspicion about institutions and the ongoing assault on truth (or, at the least, on facts), and you have a recipe for a volatile relationship between "the media" and "the audience."

What role does news media play in informing the public? Which outlets are earning trust (and clicks)? Drawing from a number of Barna studies, here's a look at this complex media moment in American history.

### Media's Impact on the Election

The fairness of the media's 2016 election coverage was frequently called into question throughout the campaign by now-President Trump, who continues to label the mainstream press as "fake news." (For more on this phenomenon and how Americans feel about it, see page 26.) Though not all Americans would go to the same extremes, they are, for the most part, sympathetic to his broader sentiment. More than twice as many believe the media were completely unfair and subjective about the presidential race than completely fair and objective (16%, compared to 7%) and almost four in 10 (38%) believe the media were at least inconsistent. Despite this deep level of distrust, the news media had the most decisive influence over personal decisions to support a certain candidate in the 2016 election (60%), especially compared to other types of media, such as TV (50%), social media (40%), campaign advertising (39%), and political commentators on radio (34%). Despite the large amounts of money poured into campaign advertising, Americans are still more likely to depend on a third party.

### The Sources Americans Trust

It's increasingly difficult for credible voices to cut through the noise in the new democratic, fast-paced digital age. Yet, even in a skeptical climate, people still turn to traditional media outlets for new information. TV news (69%) remains the

## Where Do You Get Your News?

n=1,021 | February 8–14, 2017

*How often, if ever, do you personally use each of the various media listed below to learn something new or to get new information? (% who answered "ongoing throughout the day")*

**33%** Internet websites

**24%** Mobile or smartphone

**20%** Social media websites

**14%** Cable television

**12%** Network television

**8%** Radio

**4%** Books

**4%** Newspapers

**3%** Magazines

**3%** eBooks

most trusted source for getting information about what is going on in the world, followed by local (50%) and national (44%) newspapers. Trump himself is known for his cable news obsession and seems to trust some sources, especially Fox News, so it's not a stretch to assume public opinions about dishonest media are aimed only at some news outlets.

Rates of reported usage of internet searches (44%) and reading online news/content sources (42%) prove that web-based content is competing with local and national papers as a trustworthy source. (Granted, almost all national and local papers now have an online presence, so there is likely some significant overlap in these categories.)

When it comes to gaining perspective or information on moral and religious issues, however, American adults look to their family members, especially over online sources. For these kinds of topics, they are more likely to trust a parent (66%) than Google (34%) or to listen to a relative (61%) over a friend (39%). In addition to family, traditional sources still pull an eager audience; for example, most American adults turn to a book (85%) over a medium like YouTube (15%) when learning about more complex topics of morality and religion.

### The Media Americans Consume

How do these feelings align with Americans' actual media consumption habits?

Live broadcasts remain the news media Americans are most likely to consume (54%), with traditional reporter-written articles not too far behind (44%). Social media posts are popular among one-third of adults (34%), proving the increasing influence of these platforms.

As content is now being delivered and shared through multiple platforms, two-thirds of American adults (66%)

## Trusted News Outlets
n=1,557 | November 9–16, 2016

*Which sources do you trust for getting news or information about what's going on in the world?*

| | |
|---|---|
| TV news | 69% |
| Local newspapers | 50% |
| National newspapers | 44% |
| Internet searches | 44% |
| Online news/content sources | 42% |
| Social media news | 34% |
| Magazines | 25% |
| None of the above | 10% |

use social media to get the headlines, and one in five (20%) uses social media sites throughout the day to "learn something new or get new information." For the most part, Americans are just finding what they need across the web: one-third (33%) uses specific websites on an ongoing basis to glean fresh information and one-quarter (24%) scrolls their mobile or smartphone for this purpose.

Interestingly, though TV news had the strongest influence over decision-making for the 2016 election and live broadcasts continue to be a popular format, Americans actually spend much less time watching TV than browsing the web. With streaming services and highlight reels being shared on social media, having a physical television to consume—or critique—TV news is perhaps less of a necessity.

"This democratization of the media landscape has also challenged notions of authority—of who is allowed to generate the news," Barna editor in chief Roxanne Stone says. "The traditional gatekeepers, all of whom have their own biases and privileges, are no longer the only purveyors of news. There is good here: stories from minorities and those long ignored by mainstream media are now gaining a platform. Yet there is also a negative side: with fewer gatekeepers, it's become increasingly hard to discern what's trustworthy. Which presents a growing need for leaders—at church, in the media, in schools—who can help others make sense of the world in generous and discerning ways."

# The "Fake News" Phenomenon

In 2016, "fake news" emerged into the public vernacular, first in connection to Facebook's inability to keep misleading articles from going viral. Post-election, accusing reports of being fake news has become a political weapon wielded by all sides. This indiscriminate application has made the meaning of *fake news* difficult to discern, promoting a sense of mistrust among politicians, pundits, and the public alike. Barna's own research suggests the divisive nature of fake news may have more to do with murky definitions than media's clear deceptions.

Three in 10 (31%) say the problem of fake news lies in reader error—"misinterpretation or exaggeration of actual news on social media"—not factual mistakes in reporting itself. From there, the blame shifts left; a quarter (24%) says the source is mainstream liberal media, while just 13 percent point the finger at mainstream conservative outlets. Nearly one-fifth (18%) "don't know much" about fake news, while 9 percent fault bloggers and independent journalists.

Many segments—particularly the unemployed (41%), Millennials (38%), non-white Americans (37%), Catholics (36%), and women (35%)—maintain that misinterpreting news via social media is the primary issue.

Evangelicals (51%), Republicans (46%), practicing Christians (40%), and Elders (37%) feel strongly that liberal journalism is the trouble. This isn't surprising given that these groups are likely to have voted for President Trump, whose administration consistently expresses animosity toward the press, especially non-conservative outlets. What is surprising is that Democrats (20%), liberals (23%), and those of no faith (22%) are not as willing to arraign right-wing media. The top response from each of these groups is that fake news stems from mishandling on social media. Further, they are more inclined to examine the culpability of like-minded media camps. For example, just 6 percent of Republicans say fake news is a problem in mainstream conservative media, while 11 percent of Democrats say it occurs in mainstream liberal media.

## What's to Blame for "Fake News"?

- Republicans
- Democrats
- Evangelicals
- No faith
- All adults

**Misinterpretation/exaggeration of actual news on social media**

31% · 21% · 35% · 25% · 33%

**Mainstream liberal media**

24% · 46% · 11% · 51% · 14%

**Mainstream conservative media**

13% · 6% · 20% · 2% · 22%

**Bloggers and independent journalists**

9% · 8% · 11% · 1% · 12%

*n=1,097 | April 7–14, 2017*

# Where the Trolls Are

Internet comment sections have become known for bias and bitterness. Thankfully, not too many Americans reside in these dark corners of the digital world—or, at least, do not admit to it. When Barna asked U.S. adults if they ever get in arguments on social media, more than half (55%) say never. A quarter (24%) says it's a rare occurrence, while one in five (21%) argues online at least sometimes.

Millennials, given their dependencies on devices and bent toward online activism, seem like possible candidates for digital skirmishes and are indeed more likely than other generations to butt heads (33% "sometimes" + "often"). Still, two-thirds of Millennials (67%) say they rarely, if ever, take their disagreements to social media. A majority of Elders (80%), who perhaps don't spend as much time online, avoids altercations entirely.

Along party lines, Republicans (8%) and Democrats (5%) report frequent disagreements more than Independents (.4%), who don't have a stake in as many political fights.

Parents with young children at home are five times as likely as those with no children under 18 to report often clashing with a cyber friend (11%, compared to 2%).

Sixteen percent of practicing Catholics say they frequently argue on social media, the highest percentage of any faith segment. Practicing Protestants, however, are pretty conflict averse, with six in 10 saying they never have this experience (compared to 41% of practicing Catholics). Evangelicals, though often caught in the crosshairs of internet controversy, claim to bite their tongues; 70 percent say they never argue on social media.

What's the most common reason for social media spats? "They started it!" Among those who argue at least rarely, more than one-quarter (26%) credit an argument to a stranger who didn't like what they posted, while one in five (22%) says someone they know challenged them. From there, percentages are fairly split among those who have defended someone else who was embroiled (19%) or took issue with something a peer or stranger shared (17% each).

Curious power dynamics seem to motivate confrontation. For example, men, college graduates, conservatives, and those of no faith demonstrate a willingness to pick fights with people they don't know. Meanwhile, black adults, women, notional Christians, and those with a high school education or less are prone to go to battle in defense of others.

*n=1,021 | February 8–14, 2017*

## Reasons People Argue on Social Media

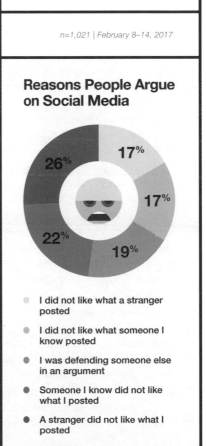

- I did not like what a stranger posted
- I did not like what someone I know posted
- I was defending someone else in an argument
- Someone I know did not like what I posted
- A stranger did not like what I posted

*n=455 adults who have gotten into arguments on social media | February 8–14, 2017*

# Our Daily Habit: Television

By now you might have heard critics hail this era as the "golden age" of television. Thanks to the advent of streaming services, such as Netflix, Hulu, HBO Go, and Amazon, more series than ever are being produced, and with unprecedented budgets and quality. But even though there has never been a better time to be a couch potato, some predict the TV bubble will burst and that the mass disruption of cable and network channels isn't sustainable. For now, though, the reason the medium is growing remains certain: Americans love watching TV—and a lot of it.

For example, almost seven in 10 American adults (68%) turn on their sets on a daily basis. The next highest response is among the 8 percent of Americans who watch TV five days a week. Small percentages have more limited or moderate TV engagement, turning them on one (2%), two (4%), three (4%), four (5%), or six (4%) days a week. Elders (83%) and Boomers (80%) are avid daily TV viewers, compared to Generation X (61%) and Millennials (57%).

Interestingly, being employed full-time compared to being unemployed makes very little difference regarding the number of days people use their TVs, although retirees are the most likely to keep the screen lit all week.

In terms of the actual time American adults spend watching TV shows in a typical day (including forms like streaming), the average is four hours. The most common range is between two and five hours, which constitutes 65 percent of responses. Only 8 percent watch just one hour a day, while 15 percent watch between six and eight hours a day. Another 12 percent veer into excess, watching 10 hours or more on a daily basis. At least some claim to glean something out of all this TV time: Despite the growing popularity of online services and content, more than half of U.S. adults (56%) still use network stations to learn something new or to get new information at least daily. Around half (48%) use cable TV for the same purpose.

## How Many Days of the Week Do Americans Watch TV?

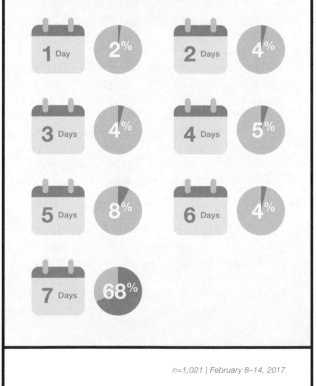

1 Day — 2%
2 Days — 4%
3 Days — 4%
4 Days — 5%
5 Days — 8%
6 Days — 4%
7 Days — 68%

*n=1,021 | February 8–14, 2017*

# This American Podcast Audience

The popularity of podcasts has risen in recent years, most notably due to the success of hits like *Serial* and *S-Town*, multiple new networks, and increased interest in public radio "classics." As everyone from comedians to pastors takes to podcasting, the medium has evolved from an affordable "side project" to an innovative format that allows for cult followings (and creative advertising).

Even so, the podcast heyday has perhaps not yet arrived; six in 10 American adults (61%) say they never even listen to them. A combined 25 percent tune in frequently, on at least a monthly basis (5% "once a month," 10% "once a week," 10% "daily"). Fifteen percent listen to them rarely, less often than once a month.

Millennial listening habits far surpass their older peers'. More than four in 10 among this generation (42%) enjoy podcasts at least once a month, including 17 percent on a daily basis. The employed are more likely to be daily listeners (15% full-time and 12% part-time, compared to 6% unemployed). Presumably, workers are listening during commutes (or are at least looking for audio diversions on the job). There could be a class connection too, as those with greater education or higher salaries are also more avid listeners.

Barna asked what types of podcasts listeners gravitate toward, and the most popular themes and genres include news and politics (35%), comedy (31%), and technology (30%). Roughly one-quarter puts their earbuds in for interviews (26%) or health content (24%). Podcasts on business (19%), games/hobbies (17%), and true crime (13%) rank lower on the list. Together, religion and spirituality programs (21%) and sermons (14%) account for a decent audience, and they're hitting their target market within the Church: Practicing Christians are fans of the

podcast medium in general—17 percent are listening daily, compared to just 6 percent of non-Christians—and many prefer faith content (37% religion and spirituality, 31% sermons), especially among practicing non-mainliners (45% religion and spirituality, 39% sermons).

When it comes to using podcasts for news media specifically, just 11 percent say they're likely to do so—mainly Millennials (20%), college graduates (18%), and liberals (17%).

## Who's Embracing Podcasts?

*(% U.S. adults who listen to podcasts at least once a month)*

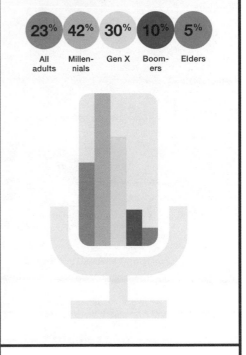

| 23% | 42% | 30% | 10% | 5% |
|---|---|---|---|---|
| All adults | Millennials | Gen X | Boomers | Elders |

*n=1,021 | February 8–14, 2017*

# From Sofas to the Silver Screen

When it comes to cinema, many Americans still love to get out of the house, grab some popcorn, and make a night of it. Two-thirds of American adults (67%) say they saw at least one movie at the theater during the past year. A plurality saw one or two movies in a cinema (21%). Percentages decline from there; a small and eager 5 percent saw 21 films or more at a theater during the past year. Exactly one-third (33%) didn't make it to a theater at all in 2016, a five percentage point increase from 2015 (28%).

Even though Americans are still hitting the cinema with enthusiasm, they watched more movies on video, DVD, Blu-ray, or streaming during the past year than at the theater. Another convenience of staying home is the option to watch via cable, broadcast, or satellite TV. Though this is a less popular form of movie-watching than DVDs or streaming online, more movies are still watched this way than at the theater. The number of movies watched on cable, broadcast, or satellite TV are evenly spread across the spectrum from one to two movies (12%), three to five (11%), six to 10 (17%), 11 to 20 (18%), and 21+ movies (22%). One in five (20%) didn't watch any movies on TV in 2016.

### Faith on Film

When it comes to Hollywood's treatment of Christianity, audiences are often conflicted, believing it is either generally negative (11%) or generally positive (13%). Similar amounts believe the portrayal is neutral (15%). The largest contingent (28%) believes Christianity gets a mixed treatment: sometimes negative, and sometimes positive. Interestingly, despite the split in opinion, at least one in 10 (10%) believes Hollywood relies heavily on stereotypes. This aligns with the fact that in the last two years, only 5 percent of American adults have watched any movies that caused them to change a belief about the Christian faith. However, 16 percent thought more seriously about religion, spirituality, or their faith after seeing certain movies.

## Americans Still Love Going to the Movies

*(amount of movies seen in the last year)*

● Theater   ● VHS, DVD, Blu-ray, or streaming   ○ Cable, broadcast, or satellite television

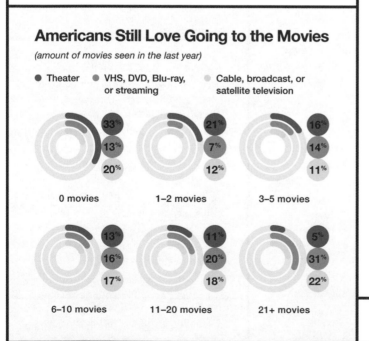

0 movies: 33% / 13% / 20%
1–2 movies: 21% / 7% / 12%
3–5 movies: 16% / 14% / 11%
6–10 movies: 13% / 16% / 17%
11–20 movies: 11% / 20% / 18%
21+ movies: 5% / 31% / 22%

*n=1,021 | February 8–14, 2017*

# A Q&A on Consuming News

## with Sarah Pulliam Bailey

*Bailey is a religion reporter for the* Washington Post *and runs the* Post's Acts of Faith. *She was previously a national correspondent for* Religion News Service *and spent four years as online editor for* Christianity Today. *She lives in New York City with her daughter and husband, an editor at the* New York Times.

*How would you encourage consumers to continue the process of fact-checking as they digest news?*

Humans, especially Christians, have a desire to know the truth, whether in our everyday lives or in bigger questions about life and death. Journalists—usually people who are trained and follow ethical codes—are generally the closest we can get to the truth of our everyday lives for questions such as "What is the crime rate in my area?" or "How are my tax dollars being spent?" We can handle criticism, and sometimes we deserve it, but I encourage people not to make sweeping claims about "the media." A news reporter (as opposed to an opinion columnist) builds a piece on facts, quotes, description, interviews, and research. Is something incorrect? Don't be afraid to pass that feedback on to the reporter and perhaps the editor. They can write a correction or clarification, or it can be helpful if they pursue follow-up stories.

*What would you recommend as a "balanced diet" when it comes to consuming news?*

I love my TV journalist friends, but I don't recommend consuming most of your news through TV because it generally encourages passive instead of active participation. TV is also a visual medium, often with a bias toward visual-driven stories instead of idea-driven stories. Fifty years ago, more people got their information from major newspapers, networks, and radio outlets like NPR, so Americans heard the same thing across the country. Now people tailor their news to specific needs and habits, so they aren't getting the same news as their neighbors. As news organizations compete for attention online, it's often harder for quality journalism to break through. Whatever news you consume, I recommend being picky about the quality like you would be picky about your food. Don't just pick from the trays that pass by you; pick from places that carefully write and edit their journalism.

You don't need to spend hours of your day consuming news to be informed. If the news gives you anxiety or mental health distress, you certainly don't need breaking alerts on your phone. Scroll through a newsletter or roundup to see headlines and read a few stories that seem interesting or useful. I'd recommend subscribing to at least one or two magazines for longer, in-depth pieces that take time and careful writing and editing. I read some blogs, download a lot of podcasts, and surf social media, but again, it's important to remember to consume content that has been carefully edited. If you like Twitter, follow journalists you trust and see what they read and share.

# TECH AROUND THE CLOCK

On average, parents say their children spend five hours using an electronic device on a typical weekday.

## GOOD MORNING

**62%** of parents check their phone within the first hour of the morning. *And what are they doing on the phone in that first hour of the day?* Select all that apply.

**74%** CHECKING EMAIL

**51%** SENDING OR READING TEXTS

**48%** CHECKING SOCIAL MEDIA

**36%** READING THE NEWS

**24%** CHECKING/ORGANIZING CALENDAR

**17%** USING A BIBLE OR DEVOTIONAL APP

**10%** WATCHING VIDEO

**6%** LISTENING TO AUDIOBOOK OR PODCAST

**6%** NONE OF THESE

## GOOD AFTERNOON

*After school, kids spend most of their time . . .*
Select all that apply.

**65%** DOING HOMEWORK

**64%** WATCHING TV OR MOVIE

**56%** ENGAGING WITH FAMILY MEMBERS

**42%** PLAYING VIDEO GAMES

**39%** INFORMAL PLAY OR ACTIVITY

**32%** READING OTHER THAN FOR HOMEWORK

**27%** ON SOCIAL MEDIA OR TEXTING WITH FRIENDS

**25%** DOING EXTRACURRICULAR ACTIVITIES OR CLASSES

**25%** ONLINE OTHER THAN FOR HOMEWORK

**23%** PLAYING ORGANIZED SPORTS

**22%** HANGING OUT WITH FRIENDS

**8%** READING THE BIBLE/ DEVOTIONS/PRAYER

## GOOD EVENING

More than four in 10 parents say electronic devices are a significant disruption to family meals.

**24%** STRONGLY AGREE

**18%** SOMEWHAT AGREE

**14%** NEITHER AGREE NOR DISAGREE

**17%** SOMEWHAT DISAGREE

**27%** STRONGLY DISAGREE

## GOOD NIGHT

*What's the last thing parents do before bed?*

**31%** WATCH TV

**10%** CHECK SOCIAL MEDIA

**3%** SPEND TIME READING ONLINE

**2%** PLAY A VIDEO GAME

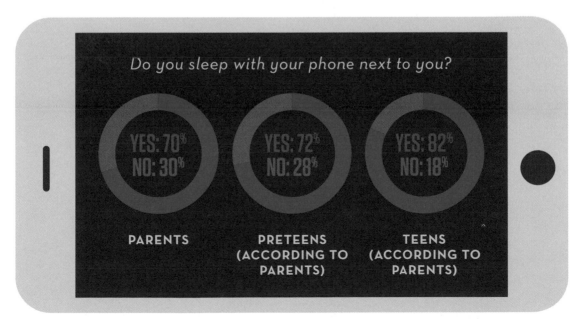

*Do you sleep with your phone next to you?*

YES: 70%
NO: 30%

YES: 72%
NO: 28%

YES: 82%
NO: 18%

PARENTS

PRETEENS (ACCORDING TO PARENTS)

TEENS (ACCORDING TO PARENTS)

*n=1,021 U.S. parents of children ages 4–17 | January 25–February 4, 2016*

# Politics

What drives and divides the Left
and the Right in the United States

# The 2016 Election: A Recap

The 2016 presidential election cycle was a dramatic one, culminating in a Republican victory that surprised political pundits and millions of Americans alike. More than a year later, armed with concrete post-election data, Americans have a better grasp on the factors that allowed Donald Trump to best Hillary Clinton and claim the Oval Office—as well as a keener awareness of the difficulty of accurately predicting elections. (For more on the nature of political polling, see page 122.)

With insight from special analyst George Barna, Barna's election recap specifically sheds light on the significant role of religion and the meager influence of the media in the historic 2016 vote.

### Faith Trends among Voters

Evangelicals emerged as one of Trump's most ardent bases of support. Nearly four out of five (79%) voted for Trump, compared to 18 percent who sided with Clinton, providing the Republican candidate with better than a four-to-one margin. Non-evangelical born again Christians also gave the 45th president a comfortable margin (56% Trump, 35% Clinton). Among non-Christian groups, Clinton was the clear preference. When it comes to the voters who associated with a non-Christian faith, 71 percent selected her, while only 20 percent backed Trump. Skeptics also preferred Clinton, but by a smaller margin (60% Clinton, 27% Trump).

Barna's research indicates that perhaps the most significant faith group in relation to the Trump triumph was notional Christians. These individuals have supported the Democratic candidate in every election since 1996. On average, notionals have given the Democratic candidate 58 percent of their votes. That trend was broken in 2016 as Clinton took just 47 percent of the group's votes, while Trump earned 49 percent. Given that notionals are by far the largest of the five faith segments, that transition was a game-changer for the Republicans.

While the evangelical vote for Trump was significant, Barna definitions and data do not show it was unusually large. The 79 percent that evangelicals awarded to the GOP nominee was actually the lowest level of evangelical support for a Republican candidate since Bob Dole lost to Bill Clinton in 1996, garnering 74 percent of their support, and was slightly lower than the 81 percent

given to Mitt Romney in 2012. The Barna survey also revealed that Protestants gave Trump 58 percent of their votes and Clinton only 36 percent. Catholics split their vote, awarding 48 percent to each candidate. This is the first election in the last 20 years in which the Democratic candidate did not win the Catholic vote.

### Two Months Made All the Difference

After comparing the data from Barna's national poll in early September 2016 with an election survey from November 2016, it's clear that even two months made a big difference in voters' minds.

Minor movement toward Trump occurred during those two months among both evangelicals (an 8-percentage-point gain in his lead over Clinton) and non-evangelical born again Christians (a 3-percentage-point increase in his lead). Trump's biggest jump in support during the home stretch came from notional Christians. While that segment preferred Clinton by 12 points in September, they wound up siding with Trump by a 2-point differential. That represents a 14-percentage-point gain in the final two months among the numerically largest pool of religious voters.

Clinton finished strongly and secured the popular vote, partially because of a huge rise in support among people aligned with non-Christian faiths. Her margin of preference increased among that group from 7 points in September to a whopping 51 points on Election Day—a 44-point climb in eight weeks. Unfortunately for her campaign, this particular segment was the smallest of the five primary faith segments.

Another shocking twist during the last two months was the shift of allegiance to Trump among atheists and agnostics; Trump gained 10 percentage points on Clinton among this group.

One telling factor in the election, according to Barna: "There has been no discussion about the fact that the skeptic vote really kept Hillary Clinton in the race. The 33-point margin she retained with that one-fifth slice of the voting population was her primary faith base. The size of the skeptic population continues to grow, while the born again community continues to shrink. That is a trend that will be a major challenge for conservative and Republican candidates in the future."

## Major Headlines Had Little Impact

When Barna examined people's reactions to several of the campaign-related headlines that received substantial

attention, just less than half of the voters interviewed (46%) said the media had been fair and objective in its handling of campaign news. Even so, other data indicates that bias has more sway than fairness, as groups already compelled to vote for Clinton brushed off many of her negative stories yet were enraged by Trump's—and vice versa.

Voters report being most significantly impacted by Trump's comments about Mexican immigrants. More than one-third of voters (36%) said this made a major impression on them. Nearly as many voters (33%) identified his plan to temporarily halt the flow of Muslim refugees into the United States. The next three events on the list include: the recording of Trump boasting about making unwanted sexual advances toward women (29%), insulting or derogatory names that Trump called his political opponents (28%), and his refusal to release income tax statements (24%). The least impactful situation of those evaluated in the survey was the number of Republican leaders who said they would not vote for Donald Trump, which made a major impression on one-eighth of voters (13%).

The event that affected Clinton's campaign the most was also the longest-lasting of the media emphases and the one some theorize lost her the election: her use of a private email server for transmitting classified documents and related efforts to destroy the evidence. Overall, one-third of voters (33%) says that situation had a major impact on their voting decisions. One out of four voters (25%) says the revelation that Clinton received numerous six-figure speaking fees from Wall Street firms, foreign governments, and special interest groups had a major impact on them. The same proportion (25%) mention the discovery of large contributions made by foreign governments to the Clinton Foundation during Clinton's tenure as secretary of state. Roughly one out of five voters admits their voting decision was influenced by Clinton's support of late-term, partial-birth abortion

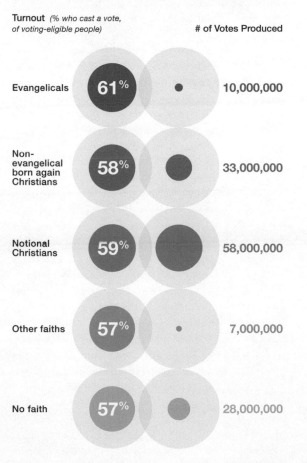

## Voter Turnout Among Faith Segments

**Turnout** *(% who cast a vote, of voting-eligible people)*

**# of Votes Produced**

| | Turnout | # of Votes Produced |
|---|---|---|
| Evangelicals | 61% | 10,000,000 |
| Non-evangelical born again Christians | 58% | 33,000,000 |
| Notional Christians | 59% | 58,000,000 |
| Other faiths | 57% | 7,000,000 |
| No faith | 57% | 28,000,000 |

*n=1,023 registered voters | September 2016*

## Political Party Reactions to Campaign Headlines

● Democrat ● Independent ● Republican

*(% that says story had a major impact on their voting decision)*

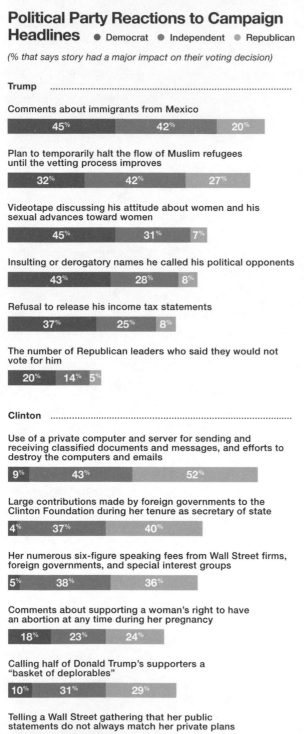

**Trump**

Comments about immigrants from Mexico

45%  42%  20%

Plan to temporarily halt the flow of Muslim refugees until the vetting process improves

32%  42%  27%

Videotape discussing his attitude about women and his sexual advances toward women

45%  31%  7%

Insulting or derogatory names he called his political opponents

43%  28%  8%

Refusal to release his income tax statements

37%  25%  8%

The number of Republican leaders who said they would not vote for him

20%  14%  5%

**Clinton**

Use of a private computer and server for sending and receiving classified documents and messages, and efforts to destroy the computers and emails

9%  43%  52%

Large contributions made by foreign governments to the Clinton Foundation during her tenure as secretary of state

4%  37%  40%

Her numerous six-figure speaking fees from Wall Street firms, foreign governments, and special interest groups

5%  38%  36%

Comments about supporting a woman's right to have an abortion at any time during her pregnancy

18%  23%  24%

Calling half of Donald Trump's supporters a "basket of deplorables"

10%  31%  29%

Telling a Wall Street gathering that her public statements do not always match her private plans

4%  29%  32%

(22%), her calling half of Trump's supporters a "basket of deplorables" (22%) and her comment at a private Wall Street gathering that her public statements do not always match her private plans (20%).

There were substantial differences in the impact of these stories based on voters' party identification and political ideology. Three of Trump's situations had a major impact on more than four out of 10 Democrats: his comments about Mexican immigrants (45%), the lewd *Entertainment Tonight* videotape (45%), and his insults of political opponents (43%). Meanwhile, even the least influential Clinton situation for Republicans was still listed by about one out of four of them, and the other alleged scandals had a major impact on as many as half of the GOP voters.

"Voter reaction to these negative stories was based more on whether they planned to support the candidate in question than on the basis of an objective response to the behavior in question," Barna states. "In the end, the revelations about the unfortunate behavior of each candidate had a surprisingly limited impact on people's voting choices." Barna also indicates surprise in finding that only 5 percent of evangelicals say the videotape of Donald Trump discussing his sexual advances toward women had a major impact on their thinking.

"That is the very type of event about which evangelicals typically express concern. Their muted reaction in this case seems like a political rather than spiritually driven response. After all, the least impactful of the Clinton scandals had more than five times as many evangelicals citing it as a major factor than was true for the Trump sexual scandal. That conflicts with the usual evangelical point of view."

*n=1,281 | November 4–16, 2016*

# Crossing the Divide

Joyce Chiu
Barna Group
Business Development
Manager

It is no secret that our country's racial divide extends into the Church. Interestingly, this divide exists even though most self-identified Christians say they hold similar theological views. Barna found that the majority of both white and black self-identified Christians says they believe in absolute moral truth (69% vs. 62%) and hold a biblical worldview (50% vs. 53%). Although most Christians describe their views similarly, the implementation of such views is often vastly different, as is apparent in the Church's racially disparate political identities.

The majority of white Christians (50%) prefers a less active and far-reaching government (vs. 15% of black Christians who agree). The same Barna study showed almost twice as many white Christians as black Christians see themselves as fiscally (50% vs. 28%) and socially (46% vs. 27%) conservative. Dif-ferences in party lines are also stark: only 6 percent of black Christians align with Republicans compared to 37 percent of white Christians. Meanwhile, seven out of 10 black Christians (71%) think of themselves as Democrats, while only about one-third of white Christians (31%) aligns with this party.

Why is there such an extreme political divide between black and white Christians, despite their equal claims to a biblical worldview? The answer requires an understanding of the different contexts in which most black and white Christians reside, as politics are the complex by-product of not only our theologies but also our personal experiences and cultural makeup.

Consider that black Americans are almost twice as likely as white Americans to reside in urban city centers, as opposed to suburban or rural areas.[3] The effects of good government can be more obvious in the city—an environment that emphasizes interdependence with the government, from its mass transit to its community programs—than in the self-reliant culture of suburbs or rural areas. The socioeconomic implications of living in urban areas also includes living in closer physical and financial proximity to poverty. Indeed, one in every three black children in the U.S. lives in poverty—almost three times higher than the rate for white children.[4] All of these could be reasons that black Christians are more likely than white Christians to embrace big government. Different patterns in the home and family may also influence politics: for example, a higher likelihood of single parents, teen mothers,[5] and female-headed households among black Americans[6] correspond with more socially liberal stances on issues such as the gender pay gap or abortion, even for Christians.

Having a less divided Church doesn't mean we agree on everything, but it does mean—as followers of Jesus—we leave our microcultures to empathize with one another in patience, compassion, and love. Christena Cleveland writes, "People can meet God within their cultural context but in order to follow God, they must cross into other cultures because that's what Jesus did in the incarnation and on the cross."[7] How will you cross over the divide?

# Responses to the Start of Trump's Term

In the months leading up to and following President Donald Trump's inauguration, there has been a cycle of conflict between political parties—and, as Barna's research has found pre- and post-election, the ensuing responses in the United States' deeply divided political system could almost be scripted. Most events or decisions seem only to reinforce the commitment of Trump supporters and stir the wrath of Trump opponents.

Barna wanted to know, how do citizens really feel about the 45th president's performance thus far? Are they comfortable expressing those opinions in public forums or at demonstrations? What level of trust does Trump and his team inspire? And—despite the often vitriolic discourse of the day—do people, particularly Christians, pray for Trump? Granted that the political climate and the news cycle in turn shift frequently and rapidly, here's how Americans responded in a survey as of mid-2017.

## What People Think—and Say—about Trump

A plurality of Americans believes President Trump's performance has been worse than they expected (30%) or at least a poor one (27%). However, 15 percent feel he is doing a good job, and one in 10 (11%) says his performance has exceeded their expectations.

The reviews are predictably warm among Trump voters. Four in 10 (39%) feel his leadership has been great thus far and almost one fifth (18%) views it as better than they expected. Though some liberals may search for Trump supporters turned sour, a minority of Trump voters says his leadership has not lived up to their hopes (12%) and just 7 percent call his performance poor.

Accordingly, Republicans in general are ready to praise Trump's term as great (35%) or better (16%). Some Republican outliers feel he's doing poorly (9%) or falling below expectations (16%). Meanwhile, a plurality of Democrats (40%) characterizes his term thus far as worse than they expected. Independents, though perhaps less invested in Trump's leadership than the other parties, lean toward saying he is performing worse than they expected (34%).

As expected, given their high voter turnout for Trump, evangelicals are also on board with Trump's presidency and are the only faith segment among whom the top responses are positive. More than half (54%) say his term has been at least great, if not further

impressive. Practicing Christians and active church attenders, however, are fairly split between approving of his performance (28% and 23%, respectively) or feeling it has been subpar (25% each).

While white Americans are the ethnicity that most approves of Trump's performance (21% say he's doing a great job, 14% say he's doing better than they expected), a plurality still feels he is leading poorly (23%) or not meeting standards (24%). More than four in 10 among Hispanic (43%), Asian (43%), and black (42%) Americans believe he is doing worse than they anticipated, and less than 6 percent of each of these groups call his performance great.

Do people feel comfortable going public with their praise or critique? Those disappointed in Trump don't seem to be shy: many U.S. adults say they've openly expressed disapproval of Trump, either with people they know (39%) or online (22%). Americans with positive opinions may be less forthcoming in the current political climate; one in five (21%) has gone so far as discussing their approval of Trump with others they know and 16 percent have done so on the internet.

Trump voters specifically are more willing to publicly convey their satisfaction (47% with people they know, 38% online). Similarly, evangelicals are fairly forthright about their continued support, both in person (33%) and online (25%).

Looking at ethnicities, all are more likely to proclaim disapproval than approval of Trump, especially in conversation. Online, black adults are most vocal with disappointment (31%), and white adults are most vocal with praise (21%).

Six in 10 Democrats (58%) bring up Trump frustrations in conversations. While Republicans are slightly less forward about their approval of Trump in personal discussions (41%), the internet perhaps provides some camaraderie or confidence; they are as likely to post positively about Trump online as Democrats are to post negatively (35% and 36%, respectively). While almost half of Independents (47%) have expressed neither approval nor disapproval of Trump, four in 10 (40%) have spoken negatively about Trump with people they know.

Despite the great focus on attendance at Trump's campaign rallies or at the marches opposing him, Barna found few Americans say they have actually participated in demonstrations concerning Trump. Overall, as of mid-2017, just 7 percent had protested him, and 6 percent had rallied for him. Even among those who voted for Trump, just 15 percent attended his rallies. Those who do take such actions are typically young: one in 10 Millennials have either gone to a public protest (11%) or supporter rally (11%). Looking at party affiliation, and as with other expressions of approval or disapproval, Republicans are as likely to show up for Trump rallies as Democrats are to show up for Trump protests (10% each).

## Levels of Trust in Trump

More than half of Americans (56%) say they do not trust Trump—at all. Meanwhile, more than two in five are willing to trust him either somewhat (23%) or definitely (21%), percentages that double among his voters (51% "definitely" and 43% "somewhat").

Beyond Trump himself, one in three (33%) says they trust none of the cabinet members or key officials Trump has appointed in his administration, matching the combined percentage of those more inclined to trust these leaders (11% all of them and 21% for the most part). Nearly one in five, however, admits to not knowing enough about the people Trump has appointed (18%), a sentiment likely

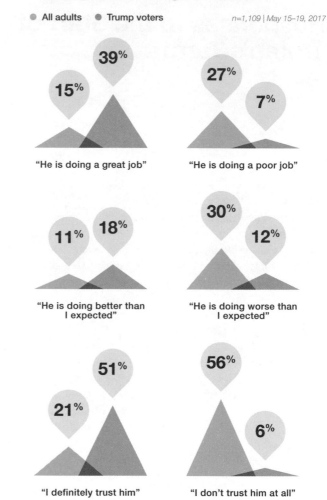

**Trump Voters Remain More Optimistic, Trusting than Average Americans**

● All adults ● Trump voters     n=1,109 | May 15–19, 2017

15%   39%
"He is doing a great job"

27%   7%
"He is doing a poor job"

11%   18%
"He is doing better than I expected"

30%   12%
"He is doing worse than I expected"

21%   51%
"I definitely trust him"

56%   6%
"I don't trust him at all"

fostered by the notable turnover rate of high-ranking officials early in Trump's term.

A large majority of Republicans (84%) trusts Trump, including 44 percent who do so without reservation, and one in four Republicans (24%) trusts all of the people Trump has appointed. At the other extreme end, a majority of Democrats has absolutely no trust in Trump (81%) or his cabinet and administration (53%). While most Independents (63%) also don't trust Trump, they are the group most likely to acknowledge not being well-informed when it comes to the key roles surrounding him (32%).

# Who Prays for Donald Trump?

n=1,109 | May 15–19, 2017

**37%** All adults

**41%** White

**44%** Black

**18%** Hispanic

**69%** All Practicing Christians

**27%** All Democrats

**53%** Democrat Practicing Christians

**60%** All Republicans

**82%** Republican Practicing Christians

There are significant trust deficits among groups who feel less represented by Trump and his cabinet. For example, women are typically less confident in Trump (61% "not at all") than are men (50% "not at all"), a feeling that extends to his administration (37% of women vs. 29% of men trust none of them). Black and Hispanic Americans put little trust in Trump (90% and 77% "not at all," respectively) or his staff (61% and 46% "none of them," respectively), while white voters have at least some faith in the president (29% "somewhat," 28% "definitely") and the key players in his administration (16% "all of them," 28% "for the most part"). Those with lower incomes (under $50,000 annually) also struggle to trust Trump (70% "not at all") and his administration (44% "none of them"), especially in comparison to those earning between $50,000 and $100,000 (54% trust Trump at least somewhat, 43% trust his administration at least for the most part) or higher (57% trust Trump at least somewhat, 45% trust his administration at least for the most part).

## Praying for the President

A majority of Americans—nearly two-thirds (63%)—does not pray for the new president, while 37 percent say they do. Evangelicals (88%), both very religious and very supportive of Trump, are the most likely to support him in this way. Other groups who were likely to vote for Trump—including practicing Christians (69%), active church attenders (60%), and conservatives (54%)—are also prayerful for the new president. Despite their high levels of disapproval and low levels of trust in Trump, black Americans are almost as likely as white Americans to pray for him (41% and 44%, respectively).

Regardless of affiliation, an active faith increases the chance that someone prays for Trump. While just 27 percent of all Democrats pray for the president, that percentage doubles among Democrats who are also practicing Christians (53%). Among Republicans, six in 10 (60%) include Trump in prayer, a number that again climbs significantly among practicing Christians in the party (82%).

n=1,109 | May 15–19, 2017

# What Makes America Great?

We've heard a lot lately about "making America great again," particularly during the 2016 election when red hats bearing this slogan were practically ubiquitous. But what, exactly, do people believe makes America great? Well, it depends who you ask.

The "American dream"—that you have the opportunity to become whomever you want to be—encapsulates the pride of one in four (24%) Americans. Other top responses include the Constitution (21%), free speech/free press (21%), freedom of religion (20%), and democracy (20%).

The Constitution and Bill of Rights are more revered among older generations than Millennials and Gen X. Freedom of religion is almost twice as likely to be a source of pride among Elders than any other generation, while a "melting pot" society is almost four times less valuable for Elders. Millennials esteem U.S. technology and innovation at a percentage almost three times higher than other age groups. Younger generations are also more likely than older citizens to take pride in American arts and culture.

White Americans are almost twice as likely as any other ethnic group to say the Constitution is foundational to U.S. greatness but are less likely than any other ethnic group to feel this way about America's diverse society, freedom of religion, and arts and culture.

Evangelicals take little pride in the Bill of Rights or free speech/free press, but they do esteem freedom of religion and America's Christian roots at a significantly higher rate than any other group. Practicing Christians similarly value religious freedom and Christian heritage but share more pride in the Bill of Rights and free speech/free press.

A notable divide exists between political ideologies. Conservatives value the Constitution, military strength, and America's Christian values more than liberals, who are more inclined to take pride in free speech/free press and a multicultural society.

## Sources of American Pride

n=1,015 | June 5–9, 2017

*As an American, what are you proud of in your country? What, in your opinion, makes America great? (top two choices)*

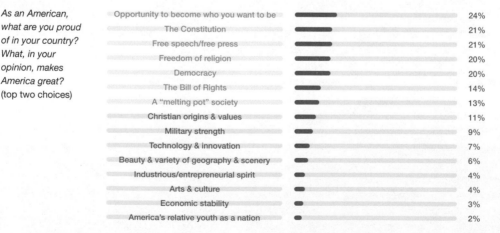

| | |
|---|---|
| Opportunity to become who you want to be | 24% |
| The Constitution | 21% |
| Free speech/free press | 21% |
| Freedom of religion | 20% |
| Democracy | 20% |
| The Bill of Rights | 14% |
| A "melting pot" society | 13% |
| Christian origins & values | 11% |
| Military strength | 9% |
| Technology & innovation | 7% |
| Beauty & variety of geography & scenery | 6% |
| Industrious/entrepreneurial spirit | 4% |
| Arts & culture | 4% |
| Economic stability | 3% |
| America's relative youth as a nation | 2% |

# A Q&A on Leading in Divided Times

## with Mark Batterson

*Batterson serves as lead pastor of National Community Church (NCC), which has eight locations throughout Washington, DC, including theaters and the largest coffeehouse on Capitol Hill. He holds a doctor of ministry degree from Regent University and is the* New York Times *bestselling author of 11 books.*

***How do you lead and unite your congregation without shying away from complex issues of today?***

We live in a culture where it's wrong to say something is wrong, and I think *that* is wrong. That said, the Church should be more known for what we're for than what we're against. That's a good starting point. Because our church is in the epicenter of politics, it can be challenging to discern between "political" and "biblical" issues, and they often overlap. And if I have to choose between political correctness and biblical correctness, I'll choose biblical correctness seven days a week and twice on Sunday!

We made a decision on day one that we would strive to be nonpartisan. In other words, we don't endorse candidates or parties. Galatians says there is neither Jew nor Greek, slave nor free, male nor female in Christ. We add Democrat and Republican to the list. But we're not afraid of tackling tough issues that may be perceived as leaning right or left. For example, we believe it's our biblical mandate to care for refugees. We have not publicly commented on the policies related to that issue, and honestly some of those things are past my pay grade. But we have 250 people on our refugee care team, and we're actively making a difference in the metro DC area on that front.

***Barna's data show Christians, especially evangelicals, have a hard time talking to people who*** are unlike them. How can pastors better address difficult topics and help Christians overcome their conversational barriers?***

Let's be honest: if you have a good friend who is gay, you approach that "issue" differently because it's not an "issue" anymore; it's a person. It doesn't have to change your theology, but it will change your heart. We have a saying at NCC: a church that stays within its four walls isn't a church at all. We desperately need relationships with people who aren't like us. Fortunately, that's easy in our urban environment—just one of our eight campuses has 60 different nationalities represented. But we've had to be intentional too. We challenge people to be friends with those who have a different skin color, political affiliation, or sexual orientation. And it's not about having an "agenda" for them; our agenda is love. Sure, love is truth. We want others to be transformed by the truth, just like we need to be. But it's more about asking questions than offering answers. I believe the key to any healthy relationship is grace and truth. According to John 1:14, Jesus was full of both. Grace means *I'll love you no matter what*. Truth means *I'll be honest no matter what*. The combination of grace and truth makes for transformation.

# Perspectives

A closer look at viewpoints that
are shaping our culture

# Energy Solutions Fuel Confusion

A majority of American adults (71%)—including most faith segments (with the exception of evangelicals)—believes humans have caused climate change. However, there remains a lack of public consensus on the best way to fight it.

A plurality (37%) agrees that establishing renewable energy sources is the most effective solution for climate change. This is also the top choice among those who believe humans are responsible for climate change. It's notable that the top two direct approaches—renewable energy and technological advancement (14%)—require little constraint on behalf of Americans, in contrast to options that require more intention or sacrifice, such as "recycling or composting" (12%), "implementing a carbon tax" (2%), or "becoming a vegetarian" (1%). Small percentages point vaguely to "something else" (7%) or suggest "expanding public transportation" (3%).

The big story is that roughly one in four Americans (23%) is simply "not sure" what to do. "Uncertainty about the best path forward, particularly among skeptics of human-caused climate change, exemplifies the complexity and ambiguity that plague the issue," says Cory Maxwell-Coghlan, a senior writer for Barna Group. Education and class may act as compounding factors here. Adults with a high school education or less are more likely to be unsure than those with a college degree (32% vs. 13%), as well as those making less than $50,000 compared to those making over $100,000 (27% vs. 14%). Even people who firmly believe humans are catalysts of climate change are unclear about how to best address it. For example, black adults overwhelmingly affirm that humans are catalysts for climate change (72%) but are some of the most unsure about solutions (40%).

Political ideology makes just a slight difference as to what solutions people prefer. Despite the differences in political views on market regulation, only a sliver of respondents across the board believes in implementing a carbon tax. Moderates and liberals tend to gravitate toward using renewable energy sources (49%), while conservatives remain split between renewable energy (24%), development of technology (21%), and uncertainty about solutions (23%). The ambivalence of conservatives may be due to the fact that they are split on whether humans cause climate change in the first place (47% agree, 46% disagree).

## What Is the Best Way to Fight Climate Change?

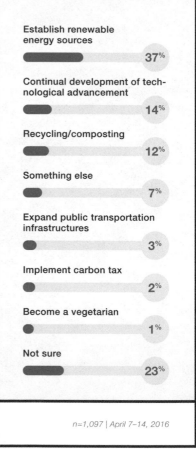

Establish renewable
energy sources

37%

Continual development of technological advancement

14%

Recycling/composting

12%

Something else

7%

Expand public transportation
infrastructures

3%

Implement carbon tax

2%

Become a vegetarian

1%

Not sure

23%

*n=1,097 | April 7–14, 2016*

**"I Agree That the Police Unfairly Target People of Color and Other Minority Groups"**

79% 63% 33%

Liberals          Moderates          Conservatives

# Perspectives of Police Brutality

More than half of Americans (53%) agree at least somewhat with the idea that "the police unfairly target people of color and other minority groups." Yet Barna's data show that opinions divide starkly along generational, racial, political, and religious lines. For example, one-third of Millennials (32%) strongly agrees—9 percentage points more than the average and a full 22 points more than Elders.

Combined, non-white groups overwhelmingly affirm that bias affects police treatment of minorities (75% "strongly" + "somewhat" agree), while the majority of white Americans disagrees (54% "strongly" + "somewhat"). Black adults are also the most likely to say they live in fear of the police (56% "absolutely" + "possibly"), almost twice the proportion of Latinos (29%) and Asians (28%), and more than four times the percentage of white adults (15%).

Looking at political ideology, the majority of moderates (63%) and liberals (79%) agrees at least somewhat that police unfairly target minorities, as opposed to one-third (33%) of conservatives. This ideological gap exists despite the fact that a majority of conservatives (87%), moderates (81%), and liberals (67%) appears to live without personal fear of police brutality.

When it comes to religion, evangelicals are much less likely to agree even somewhat that the police are unfair compared to the national average (29% vs. 53%). As a whole, self-identified Christians are split—47 percent agree and another 47 percent disagree that prejudice toward minorities influences police—though non-Christians (66%) feel firmly that authorities are guilty of unfair targeting.

Overall, class differences such as one's level of education and household income do not seem to factor into a fear of police brutality: having a college degree or an income over $100,000 did not significantly lower respondents' likelihood to express concern. It's notable, however, that having a child under 18 makes one more likely to say they fear police brutality (31% vs. 19% without young children).

*n=1,097 | April 7–14, 2016*

# Americans Shift on Immigration Issues

The ongoing conflict in the Middle East, the refugee crisis across Europe, and the amount of terror attacks both abroad and at home have raised the stakes on the already heated topic of immigration. In addition, President Trump's rhetoric, both on the 2016 campaign trail and since taking office, has leaned toward a tougher stance on border protection, informed by an "America first" philosophy that prioritizes opportunities for U.S. citizens. What do American adults think of those policies? Looking at both pre-election

## Do you agree with Donald Trump's executive order to block individuals from Muslim-majority nations from entering the U.S.? n=1,019 | May 2017

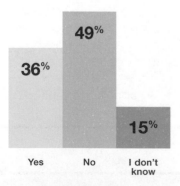

| | | |
|---|---|---|
| 36% | 49% | 15% |
| Yes | No | I don't know |

and post-election data, Barna found that the public sentiment has shifted radically toward a softer view of immigration and of the plight of refugees.

At the time of this writing, Trump's executive order to block individuals from certain Muslim-majority nations from entering the U.S. has seen numerous drafts and legal challenges. The controversy reflects a country-wide uncertainty about the order. Almost half—a plurality—of American adults (49%) disagrees with Trump's order, while just more than one-third (36%) agree. A small 15 percent don't know where they stand. White Americans (47%) are much more likely than Hispanic (18%), black (7%), or Asian (19%) Americans to agree with the order. Republicans (72%) agree more than Democrats (16%), and evangelicals (60%) agree more than those with "other" faiths (16%), a category that includes Islam.

According to Trump, and made clear by the title of the order, its intended purpose is "Protecting the Nation from Foreign Terrorist Entry into the United States." Trump's focus on Muslim-majority nations in this executive order is based on the belief that Muslims perpetrate the majority of terrorism. But the American public is still making up its mind. For example, in 2016, 16 percent of Americans strongly disagreed that Muslims perpetrated the majority of terrorism, compared to one-quarter (25%) only one year later in 2017. The vast majority of the shift occurred among those who were previously unsure (21% in 2016, now 11% in 2017).

These shifts and the pushback on Trump's executive order point to a broader softening on immigration policies in America. In just the past 12 months, sentiments have changed on the overall value of diversity. For instance, in 2016, 37 percent of American adults strongly agreed that people from different cultures enrich America, shooting up 10 percentage points in 2017 to almost half (47%). These changes occur across every segment with jumps of 10 percentage points on average among age groups, ethnicities, and faith tribes, with the exception of conservatives, who have only shifted 3 percentage points.

Americans are also more open to allowing immigrants into the country. In 2016, when asked if they agree or disagree with the statement "we allow too many immigrants into the country," three in 10 (30%) strongly agreed. But only one year later, less than one quarter (23%) strongly agrees, a shift of 7 percentage points. The drops are particularly significant among the older generations, with Boomers seeing a 16-percentage-point drop and Elders a 17-percentage-point drop from 2016 to 2017. Again, much remains unchanged when looking at ideological differences. Conservatives (45% to 39%) still feel strongly about limiting the immigrant flow into the United States, while liberals remain just as open as they

# Terrorism, Immigration, and Refugees

n=1,097 | April 2016; n=1,019 | May 2017

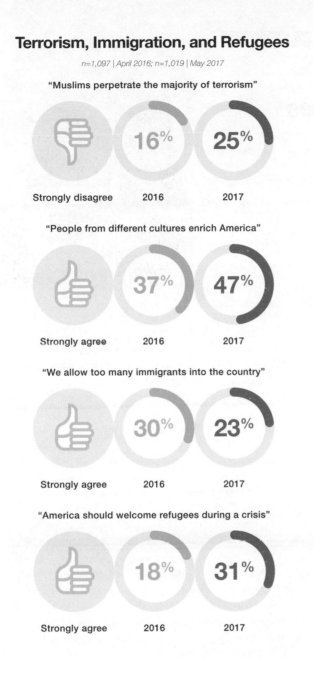

**"Muslims perpetrate the majority of terrorism"**

16%    25%

Strongly disagree    2016    2017

**"People from different cultures enrich America"**

37%    47%

Strongly agree    2016    2017

**"We allow too many immigrants into the country"**

30%    23%

Strongly agree    2016    2017

**"America should welcome refugees during a crisis"**

18%    31%

Strongly agree    2016    2017

that those who were most opposed to immigration are the ones who have also had the biggest change of heart.

At the core of these shifts is a more open attitude toward refugees. The number of adults who strongly agree that America should welcome refugees during a crisis has almost doubled in a single year, from 18 percent in 2016 to 31 percent in 2017. Images of the Syrian Civil War and stories of the trials of refugees across Europe have likely had a dramatic impact on the perspective among American adults in a very short period, counterbalancing—and even eclipsing—bold national rhetoric on border protection

However, not every segment has been as quick to change their minds on accepting refugees: evangelicals, for instance, held steady with a statistically insignificant difference between 12 percent in 2016 and 16 percent in 2017. By comparison, the percentage of practicing Christians who say they want the U.S. to welcome refugees in a time of crisis grew from 16 percent to 36 percent in the same time period.

As the public revisits their feelings on immigrants and refugees, it remains a secondary priority from the pulpit, at least alongside more local or parochial issues. When U.S. Protestant pastors were asked to identify national issues they are most concerned about, comprehensive immigration reform (9%) was relatively low on the list, compared to protecting programs that help hungry people and poor people in this country (20%), job creation and unemployment (18%), and balancing the budget and ending deficit spending (17%).

were in 2016 (15% to 14%). Though white Americans are still less inclined than others to be open to immigration, the percentage that feel the U.S. welcomes too many immigrants also dropped 11 percentage points, from 39 percent who strongly agreed in 2016 to 28 percent in 2017. Additionally, evangelicals dropped 11 percentage points from 42 percent to 31 percent. These trends show

n=1,097 | April 2016; n=1,019 | May 2017; n=600 U.S.
Protestant pastors | October 27 – November 17, 2016

# A Q&A on Welcoming Refugees

## with Jeremy Courtney

*Courtney is founder & CEO of Preemptive Love Coalition, a community of peacemakers who provide frontline relief and long-term development in areas of polarizing conflict. He is the author of* Preemptive Love *and the forthcoming* Love Anyway. *Courtney lives in Iraq with his wife and two children.*

***One in four Americans believes most terrorism is perpetrated by Muslims. How do you address this fear?***

Media over-reporting on Islamist terror and wars in Muslim countries gives a distorted view of reality. When we hear about Muslim terror four times more than it deserves, I'm not surprised by this negative perception. But "facts" don't compel us to take great risks. So I share stories from my 15 years in Muslim countries from Iraq, Syria, Egypt, Somalia, and Sudan. I have friends among the wealthiest and the poorest. We've been guests in the homes of the world's top Islamic leaders. When I share about how I stopped living in fear of "radical Islamic extremists," I'm speaking from experience. The only way through fear is to step toward whatever scares us most.

***To what would you attribute Americans' softening on immigrants and refugees between 2016 and 2017?***

If the change had happened over several years, a softer stance might be attributed to media coverage of babies drowning, ISIS beheadings, or chemical attacks, but, in my estimation, that peaked in 2013–2015. To explain a push toward compassion in the past year, I think one theory towers over the others: Trump has a "liberalizing" effect on certain Americans. A more unifying president could have led the country toward conservative positions, but Trump's bombast drives many away, even well-known conservative leaders. To some, being contra-Trump is a knee-jerk way to be "moral." The political climate of late has also caused others to more closely examine their responsibilities to their neighbors.

***Why do you think evangelicals remain unlikely to believe America should have more open borders?***

I'm not sure it is a moral imperative for America to open its borders; good people hold different views. However, the unassailable moral imperative of the Church is to welcome those who are on the run. The barrier for evangelicals is the way they map alongside conservative politics. Competing political visions are normal, but we should be more honest about when we are pursuing the kingdom of America or the Kingdom of God. Thankfully, these stats don't tell the whole story: individuals and churches from all sides are helping organizations like Preemptive Love serve refugees. If you are more conservative, we give you ways to work at the headwaters of conflict on root problems so people don't have to flee in the first place. If you're more liberal, we provide a framework to welcome refugees in your own home while actively acknowledging terrorism. "Conservative" doesn't mean not wanting to be helpful. "Liberal" doesn't mean being soft on security.

# Dealing with Domestic Poverty

Perhaps bolstered by progress since the United States' 2008 economic downturn, less Americans express concern about domestic poverty today than they did 10 years ago. Even so, according to the most recent Census Bureau data, the U.S. poverty rate stands at 13.5 percent, affecting more than 43 million people.[8] Based on a Barna study conducted in partnership with Compassion International, here's a glimpse into what the nation believes about its poverty problem.

### Is U.S. Poverty Serious?

Almost half of Americans today (46%) feel domestic poverty is one of the most serious social problems in the U.S. One in ten (11%) goes so far as to call it the most serious issue—though this is half the percentage of U.S. adults who said the same in 2007 (21%). Another four in 10 (38%), though they acknowledge it as a problem, wouldn't count it among the most dire. Only 2 percent don't feel it is a problem at all.

Elders are the generation least concerned about domestic poverty; more than half (53%) say it is not among the country's serious problems, while Millennials and Gen X are more than three times as likely to regard it as the greatest problem (14% and 13% vs. 4% of Elders).

Personal income level seems to have some connection to concern about domestic poverty. Adults making less than $50,000 a year (52%) are more likely than higher earners (44% of those making between $50,000 and $90,000, 38% of those making $100,000 or more) to feel poverty in the U.S. is among the most important issues facing the country.

A liberal viewpoint perhaps fosters interest in addressing national poverty. More than half of those who identify as political liberals (54% vs. 38% of conservatives) see this as one of the country's significant problems, and they are twice as likely as conservatives to call it the most serious one (15% vs. 8%).

Global compassion also typically translates into interest in poverty in the U.S. One in five of those who express extreme concern about global poverty (21%) calls domestic poverty the nation's most serious problem, and half (50%) see it as at least among the most serious. In addition, more than a quarter of those who believe they could personally have a major influence on global poverty (27%) view poverty as the nation's biggest problem.

### Caring for the Country's Poor

So whose job is it to address poverty in the U.S.? A plurality of American adults says it should be the task of the government, either federal (31%) or state and local leadership (30%). From there, they rely on humanitarian organizations (17%) or individual citizens (12%). Just five percent say it's the Church's role to help the nation's poor, slightly more than those who say it's the responsibility of businesses (2%).

Unsurprisingly, a liberal ideology supports the idea that federal government should deal with the country's poverty problems (42%), something only 16 percent of conservatives believe. Conservatives are more likely than liberals to trust domestic poverty in the hands of nonprofit organizations (22% vs. 11%) or citizens (16% vs. 10%). Boomers (22%) also exhibit a unique trust in the ability of nonprofit organizations to address poverty compared to younger generations (14% of Millennials and Gen X). Those with a high school education or less (38%) are also prone to say it's the job of state and local governments.

While self-identified Christians (8%) and practicing Christians (15%) lean a little more on the local church in this regard, they still see the government as being primarily responsible for dealing with domestic poverty. Almost no Americans who are atheist or agnostic (1%) feel U.S. poverty falls within the church's purview. Only those who qualify as evangelical depend most on the church to deal with local poverty; one in three (32%) says it's the responsibility of places of worship, even more so than nonprofits (22%) or state (18%) or federal (14%) governments.

More than half of those who say the local church is responsible for dealing with global poverty (53%) believe the church is also responsible for domestic poverty, while four in 10 of those who trust federal (40%) or local governments (40%) to address global

poverty in turn say these entities should handle domestic poverty. Those who think nonprofits should handle global poverty, however, shift toward government resources when it comes to domestic needs: one in three (32%) says it's the federal government's responsibility, and they are just as likely to say it's the role of state governments (27%) as nonprofit organizations (27%).

### If You Had $100 . . .

If presented with the opportunity to donate $100 to help a poor child, almost two-thirds of American adults (64%) would prefer to give their money to help a child in the U.S. Eight percent would offer it to an organization aiding children overseas, while one in four (23%) says it wouldn't matter to them.

Notable differences are evident here among generations: Millennials (17%) are most likely to give their hypothetical $100 to help a child in another country (compared to 7% of Gen X, 2% of Boomers, 3% of Elders) and least likely to say they'd give it to address child poverty in the U.S. (46% vs. 64% of Gen X, 77% of Boomers, 73% of Elders). Liberals are also twice as likely as conservatives to have interest in financially helping kids in global poverty (15% vs. 7%), while conservatives would prefer to donate within the U.S. (70% vs. 54%).

Those who are extremely concerned with global poverty (16%) or are optimistic about their ability to majorly affect global poverty (21%) are willing to put their money where their mouth is, preferring to donate their $100 to a nonprofit helping children overseas rather than in the U.S.

## Whose Problem Is American Poverty?

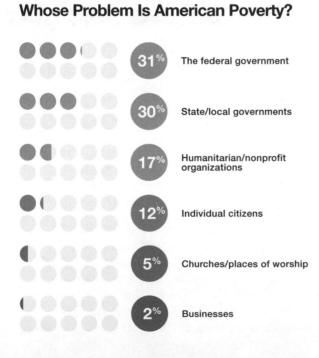

31% The federal government

30% State/local governments

17% Humanitarian/nonprofit organizations

12% Individual citizens

5% Churches/places of worship

2% Businesses

*n=1,001 | May 2017*

# An Examination of "In but Not of the World"

Susan Mettes
Barna Group
Research Manager

You won't find chapter and verse for the command "Be in the world, but not of the world" since this phrase isn't in the Bible. It isn't entirely made up though. Throughout the New Testament, advice to Christians warns about the world.

The picture these passages paint, however, is not of a family friendly enclave of Christians doing Christian things and watching and listening to Christian things; it's of a courageous resistance to the misrule of selfish values.

Unfortunately, many Christians do seem to live in a "Bible bubble." In research Barna conducted in partnership with Bible Study Fellowship, practicing Christians show signs of isolating themselves. Just under half (47%) select "I believe it is important to maintain a safe distance from 'the world'" rather than "I believe it is important to be actively 'in the world.'" A series of questions along similar lines determined that 68 percent of practicing Christians espouse a more culture-opposed than culture-embracing attitude.

In his book *Culture Making*, Andy Crouch describes this as a posture—a default attitude—of condemnation toward culture. It would be more appropriate as a gesture—an occasional, situation-specific attitude, Crouch explains—toward certain aspects of our culture, such as online pornography or blatant dishonesty.[9]

It doesn't seem that Jesus or his apostles encouraged a "safe distance" when they encouraged holiness. When they became Jesus's friends, respectable fishermen found themselves dining with the town pariahs (see Mark 2:15). Safety, Jesus indicated, comes from cooperating with the Holy Spirit, not from physical or cultural separation.

"The world" Christians are warned against refers to the values Christians shouldn't take on, not a culture Christians should entirely avoid. Corruption comes from believing you are entitled to a more comfortable life than your friends, not from looking at their polished photos on Facebook. It comes from valuing sexiness above all else, not from listening to music with a strong beat. In short, the world's harm stems from the inside out, not the outside in.

The world God loves includes all he created, especially people. In fact, God seems to value cultural treasures enough to give them a place in heaven (see Revelation 21:26). That's a strong case for staying involved in engineering and science innovation, the taxpayer base, education policy, film, fashion, music, and art.

Christians, as part of God's beloved created world, have been challenged to enter an environment with corrosive values. Even though withdrawing is much simpler, committed Christians need to approach human traditions and creations without a default posture of opposition.

# Majority of Christians Influenced by New Spirituality

In an increasingly globalized and inter-connected world, Christians are more aware of (and influenced by) competing ideas and worldviews than ever. But just how much have other ideas crept their way into the Christian perspective? Barna's research shows that only 17 percent of Christians who consider their faith important and attend church regularly actually have a biblical worldview (see Glossary on page 13 for definitions).

So, if Christians are open to nonbiblical perspectives, what *are* they believing? In partnership with Summit Ministries, Barna conducted a study among practicing Christians in America to gauge how much the tenets of other worldviews influence Christians' beliefs about God, meaning, and eternity. The competing worldview that practicing Christians most embrace is new spirituality. Six in 10 (61%) agree with at least one of its key ideas, perhaps because it holds a positive view of religion, emphasizes the supernatural, or feeds into a growing dissatisfaction with institutions.

The statement that resonates most relates to ethical behavior: one-third of practicing Christians (32%) strongly agrees that "if you do good, you will receive good, and if you do bad, you will receive bad." This karmic statement, though not explicitly from scripture, appeals to many Christians' sense of

## Which Ideas Appeal to Christians?

"If you do good, you will receive good, and if you do bad, you will receive bad."

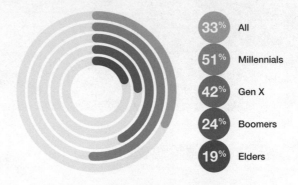

| 33% | All |
| 51% | Millennials |
| 42% | Gen X |
| 24% | Boomers |
| 19% | Elders |

"All people pray to the same god or spirit, no matter what name they use for that spiritual being."

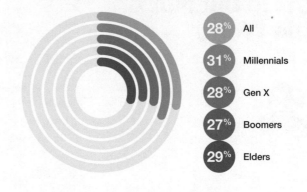

| 28% | All |
| 31% | Millennials |
| 28% | Gen X |
| 27% | Boomers |
| 29% | Elders |

ultimate justice. For example, another Barna study found that 52 percent of practicing Christians strongly agree that the Bible teaches "God helps those who help themselves." Having come of age in a less Christianized context, practicing Christian Millennials (51%) and Gen X (42%) are more likely than Boomers (24%) and especially Elders (19%) to find resonance with this view. Also, practicing Christians who live in cities (43%), which are often melting pots of ideas and cultures, are more accepting of these views than their suburban (28%) or rural counterparts (26%).

Another common view among almost three in 10 practicing Christians (28% strongly agree) is that "all people pray to the same god or spirit, no matter what name they use for that spiritual being." Again, those in cities, more often sites of religious plural-ism, are significantly more likely (39%) to find truth here than

*% among practicing Christians who strongly agree*

**"Meaning and purpose come from becoming one with all that is."**

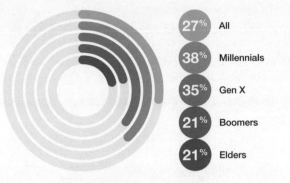

| | |
|---|---|
| 27% | All |
| 38% | Millennials |
| 35% | Gen X |
| 21% | Boomers |
| 21% | Elders |

**"Many religions can lead to eternal life; there is no 'one true' religion."**

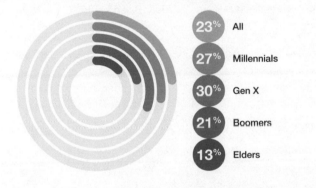

| | |
|---|---|
| 23% | All |
| 27% | Millennials |
| 30% | Gen X |
| 21% | Boomers |
| 13% | Elders |

those in more religiously homogenous suburbs (25%) or small towns (22%). Interestingly, the generations agree on this one, with no statistical significance among them.

Further, the belief that "meaning and purpose come from becoming one with all that is" has captured the minds of more than one-quarter of practicing Christians (27% strongly agree). Millennials and Gen X especially resonate with this view of unity (38% and 35%), twice as many as either Boomers or Elders (both 21%). City dwellers again are more open to this view, and black (35%) and Hispanic (34%) Americans are significantly more likely than white Americans (25%) to believe meaning and purpose come from becoming one with all that is.

Another popular tenet of new spirituality that resonates with a little less than one-quarter of practicing Christians (23% strongly

agree) is that "many religions can lead to eternal life; there is no 'one true' religion." This universalist view again finds more traction among Millennials (27%) and Gen X (30%), compared to Boomers (21%) and Elders (13%), and is twice as common in a city (33%) than in a small town (14%)

Though less common, 8 percent of practicing Christians believe "everyone is God" and another 8 percent say they are "part of a larger 'mind' that encompasses the universe." These responses crystallize what Barna has been tracking as an ongoing shift away from Christianity as the basis for a shared worldview. Barna has observed and reported on increasing pluralism and relativism, corresponding with a moral decline among Americans in general and even in the Church. Nevertheless, it is striking how pervasive some of these beliefs are among people who are actively engaged in the Christian faith, particularly in the younger generations.

"The challenge with competing worldviews is that there are fragments of similarities to some Christian teachings, and some may recognize and latch on to these ideas, not realizing they can be distortions of biblical truths," says Brooke Hempell, senior vice president of research for Barna.

"The call for the Church, and its teachers and leaders, is to help Christians dissect popular beliefs before allowing them to settle in their own ideology. Informed thinking is essential to developing and maintaining a healthy biblical worldview and faith as well as being able to have productive dialogue with those who espouse other beliefs."

*n=1,456 U.S. practicing Christians | March 2017*

# The Pastoral Credibility Crisis

Just one in five U.S. adults (19%) believes Christian ministers are very influential in their community, according to Barna research in partnership with Pepperdine University. One-quarter says pastors' influence is minimal (24% "not very" + "not at all" influential), while a lukewarm plurality (40%) says they are somewhat influential. Not surprisingly, church leaders' more captive audiences—such as practicing Christians (44%), evangelicals (42%), and weekly churchgoers (37%)—are more apt to esteem them as very influential.

Those of no faith are most likely to believe pastors hold negligible local influence (44%), but this view may have more to do with indifference than disdain. One-third of the religiously unaffiliated (33%) admits they are simply "not sure" whether clergy play an influential role in their community, which is twice the national average (17%).

## The Pastor's Benefit to Community

Four in 10 U.S. adults (40%) assert the presence of pastors is "a significant benefit" to their community, and one in four (26%) says it's "a small benefit." In a sign of stiffer headwinds to come, however, Millennials are less inclined than older Americans to say pastors are a significant benefit (29%), especially when compared to Elders, who tend to be quite convinced of the significant benefits pastors bring to their city or town (60%).

A small minority of U.S. adults (5%) feels that ministers pose a disadvantage to their community. As one might predict, this view is concentrated among adults with no religious faith (12% "small" + "significant" disadvantage) or who identify with a religion other than Christianity (9%). Again, however, a majority of both groups is more likely to feel neutral on the question than to be actively negative. One-third of those with no faith and one-quarter of adherents to another faith judge pastors to be "neither a benefit nor a disadvantage" and one in four among both groups is just not sure.

The public's neutral or noncommittal responses concerning ministers' influence are reflected in pastors' perceptions of their place within community life. When asked how satisfied they are with the respect pastors are afforded by their surrounding community, about one in five (22%) says it's "excellent." Just about half (48%) say it's "good," and another one in five (21%) rates community respect for clergy as "average."

## The Pastor's Voice in Culture

The majority of practicing Christians (51%) says pastors are "very credible" sources of wisdom "when it comes to the most important issues of our day." But among the broader population, one in five (21%) believes pastors are very credible sources of insight on today's issues; one in four thinks pastors are "not very" (14%) or "not at all credible" (11%); and 15 percent are "not sure." The plurality of Americans once again occupies a noncommittal middle: two in five (39%) say pastors are "somewhat credible" in this area.

People do trust pastors when it comes to overtly "spiritual" topics but are less confident in their counsel on more everyday, "close-to-the-ground" issues. For instance, one-third of all adults considers ministers very reliable counsel when it comes to "how the church can help people live according to God's will" (36%) and "God's will for human beings and the world" (35%). Fewer believe pastors are very reliable, however, when it comes to "how relationships work and how to make them better" (26%) and "how people can live out their convictions privately and publicly" (23%).

People are most skeptical about pastors' insights when it comes to "how Christianity should inform our political and justice systems." Just one out of eight adults (17%) believes pastoral wisdom on this topic is very reliable, half the proportion of those who say pastors are not very (20%) or not at all reliable (19%). And even though practicing Christians are among the most convinced of pastors' wisdom in the political realm, fewer than half (40%) say ministers are very reliable in this regard.

*n=1,025 | April 29–May 1, 2015*

# IMPRESSIONS
## POP-CULTURE PASTORS

In partnership with Pepperdine University, Barna asked, are media portrayals of pastors—as heroes, villains, and everything in between—similar to Americans' personal experiences?

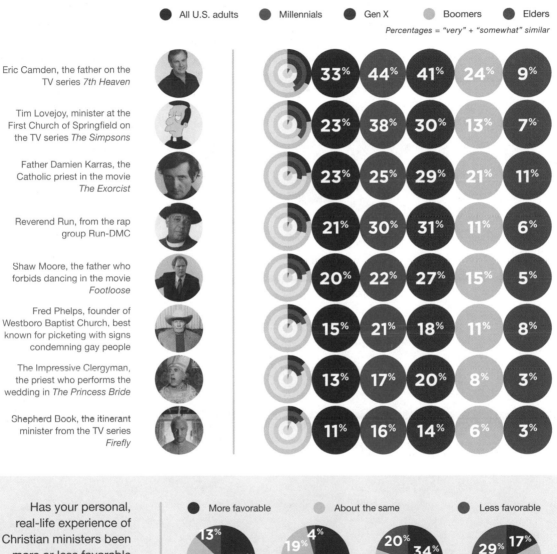

● All U.S. adults   ● Millennials   ● Gen X   ● Boomers   ● Elders

*Percentages = "very" + "somewhat" similar*

| | All U.S. adults | Millennials | Gen X | Boomers | Elders |
|---|---|---|---|---|---|
| Eric Camden, the father on the TV series *7th Heaven* | 33% | 44% | 41% | 24% | 9% |
| Tim Lovejoy, minister at the First Church of Springfield on the TV series *The Simpsons* | 23% | 38% | 30% | 13% | 7% |
| Father Damien Karras, the Catholic priest in the movie *The Exorcist* | 23% | 25% | 29% | 21% | 11% |
| Reverend Run, from the rap group Run-DMC | 21% | 30% | 31% | 11% | 6% |
| Shaw Moore, the father who forbids dancing in the movie *Footloose* | 20% | 22% | 27% | 15% | 5% |
| Fred Phelps, founder of Westboro Baptist Church, best known for picketing with signs condemning gay people | 15% | 21% | 18% | 11% | 8% |
| The Impressive Clergyman, the priest who performs the wedding in *The Princess Bride* | 13% | 17% | 20% | 8% | 3% |
| Shepherd Book, the itinerant minister from the TV series *Firefly* | 11% | 16% | 14% | 6% | 3% |

Has your personal, real-life experience of Christian ministers been more or less favorable or about the same as how the media portrays pastors, priests, and other ministers?

● More favorable   ● About the same   ● Less favorable

**All U.S. adults:** 48% / 39% / 13%

**Practicing Christians:** 77% / 19% / 4%

**Dechurched adults:** 47% / 34% / 20%

**No religious affiliation/"nones":** 54% / 29% / 17%

*n=1,025 | April 29–May 1, 2015*

# Trending in ...
# Life

Many of Barna's most recent and impactful studies look at the ways people learn, work, consume, relax, and relate on a daily basis. This is the realm of life, from your office hallways or neighborhood sidewalks to your living room sofa or, well, your therapist's couch.

The research consistently points to a modern obsession with staying busy, but we hope the following pages—including *Barna Trends*' featured report on how to filter news and views in today's post-truth climate—challenge you to slow down, think deeply, and connect intentionally.

In LIFE, Barna looks at trends such as:
- perceptions of and experiences with counseling
- Americans' assessments of their alcohol habits
- the rise of the self-care era
- what people believe causes school violence
- how young generations are building a diverse future

 **Vocation & Education**

**Habits**

**Relationships**

**Community**

Featuring:

Katelyn Beaty, Andy Crouch, Shani Dowell, Brooke Hempell, David Kinnaman, Tom Krattenmaker, Jonathan Morrow, John M. Perkins, Mac Pier, Roxanne Stone, Sara Tandon, Jamie Tworkowski, Alyce Youngblood

# At a Glance: Life

# Gen Z Views on Sexuality

*n=1,450 teens ages 13–19 |*
*November 2016*

According to a Barna study in partnership with Impact 360 Institute, a majority of teens ages 13–19 (68%) says their gender and sexuality are very important to their sense of self. So what do teens actually believe regarding traditional views of sexuality? A slight majority (54%) agrees that marriage should be a lifelong commitment between a man and a woman, though one-third (31%) disagrees, 21 percent of whom do so strongly. Among teens who are engaged Christians, almost all (91%) strongly support this idea of marriage. A majority of teens (55%) feels there is nothing wrong with homosexual relationships—interestingly, roughly the same percentage who agrees marriage is meant to be a lasting commitment between spouses of the opposite sex. Young people's thinking on the morality of sex before marriage is varied; overall, 46 percent of teens disagree that sex outside marriage is immoral, one in five (21%) is unsure, and one-third (32%) agrees that it is wrong. Monogamy is something almost all young people can get behind; 89 percent agree that it is immoral to cheat on a spouse.

## Moms and Dads Find Time to Relax

It might be easy to assume that parents have less time to invest in self-improvement or spiritual routines, but Barna's data show that, among adults who self-identify as Christians or spiritual, those who have children under 18 are actually more likely than those without young children to practice yoga (18% vs. 9%), journal (18% vs. 12%), or read spiritual books (25% vs. 18%).

*n=1,091 | November 4–15, 2015*

**54%** — More than half of parents make decisions based on developing children's character

## Decisions, Decisions

More than half of U.S. parents (54%) determine what their family does with their time (projects, activities, commitments, etc.) by first considering what is good for developing their children's character. Almost half (46%) make decisions based on what makes them happy. Thirty-seven percent are motivated by what is good for their children's achievements in life and one-third (33%) is concerned with what makes most financial sense.

*n≈1,201 U.S. parents of children ages 4–17 |*
*January 25–February 4, 2016*

**One in three women and one in five men start seeing a counselor because of a trauma**

**40%** of parents talk to kids about friendship, forgiveness, and work ethic

# Catalysts for Counseling Vary by Gender

When presented with a list of reasons that prompted them to see a mental health counselor, men and women differ in their answers. Men are more likely to decide to visit a counselor on a doctor's recommendation (36%)—the top response among male respondents—compared to just one in four women (24%) who chose this option. Men are twice as likely as women to report beginning counseling when their marriage faced trials (19% vs. 9%). They are also more than three times as likely (10% vs. 3%) to report going to a counselor because they were simply curious about the process. However, trauma is the most common reason for women to start therapy; one in three women (33%) says the loss of a loved one or a job, divorce, an accident, or some other crisis pushed them to talk to a professional, compared to one in five men (21%) who points to a similar incident as the motivation for seeking mental health treatment.

n=420 U.S. adults who have seen a counselor or therapist | February 8–14, 2017

# The Topics of Character-Driven Parenting

If you're a parent of young children, how often do you talk to them about self-control? If you're like 50 percent of U.S. parents of children ages 4 to 17, you do so daily. In fact, as Barna found in research for *The Tech-Wise Family*, families often discuss topics related to character building. Nearly half talk about patience (49%) or happiness (49%) with their children. Fairness (43%), being a good friend (40%), forgiveness (40%), work ethic (40%), and reliability (38%) are also common subjects. More than one-third (36%) cover conflict resolution and more than one-quarter (27%) talk to their kids about serving others.

n=1,201 U.S. parents of children ages 4–17 | January 25–February 4, 2016

Many churches are built around a family model. They are most comfortable ministering to families and have developed an infrastructure to support couples and children. Single and dating young adults move around more often, they switch jobs more frequently, and their social lives often take precedence over institutional commitments. Yet if young adults are waiting longer to get married, the church can't afford to simply hope they'll come back once they get married and settle down. People's twenties are a critical part of their formation—people shape identity, habits, and beliefs during those years. They are important years to be part of a church community. Pastors and spiritual leaders must take a look at the ways they are reaching out to young adults." —*Roxanne Stone, Barna Group editor in chief*

# One in Three Teens Is Cyber Bullied

While a slight majority of young people ages 13 to 19 (55%) has not experienced bullying on social media, one in three (33%) says this has happened to them, 11 percent of whom agree strongly. There's an interesting uptick among teens of no faith who have been mistreated on social media (27% agree somewhat, 14% agree strongly), compared to engaged Christians (16% agree somewhat, 12% agree strongly). Another 13 percent of teens are unsure if they have been victims of online bullying. Social media can negatively impact teens in other ways, of course, including making them feel bad about a lack of excitement in their lives (39% agree at least somewhat) or breeding insecurities about the way they look (31% agree at least somewhat). Whatever their online encounters, however, a majority of teens regards their usage as moderate; 52 percent agree at least somewhat that they use social media less than friends.

*n=1,450 teens ages 13–19 | November 2016*

# Life Happens in the Living Room

In his book *The Tech-Wise Family*, Andy Crouch writes, "Fill the center of your life together—the literal center, the heart of your home, the place where you spend the most time together—with the things that reward creativity, relationship, and engagement." Barna's research conducted for Crouch's book shows just how well parents are doing with this task. Most families do almost everything together in their family or living room. Two-thirds of parents (64%) say they spend the most time as a family in this space. Families are most often participating in leisure or entertainment activities in the family room (79%), but it's also the place where families say their creative activities happen (51%). Bedrooms come in second for leisure hours (24%), followed by the outdoors (20%) or the kitchen (18%). Given the hands-on nature of cooking and table tasks, parents also say they spend creative time in the kitchen (33%) and dining room (28%). Just more than a quarter (26%) head outdoors to exercise their creativity.

*n≈1,021 parents of children ages 4–17 | January 25–February 4, 2016*

# Religious Reasons to Teetotal

*n=1,281 | November 4–16, 2016*

One in three adults over age 21 (33%) does not consume alcoholic beverages of any kind, 14 percent of whom credit this decision to religious reasons. Though evangelicals are one of the groups most likely to be religiously motivated to avoid alcohol (28%), they are more likely to refrain because they don't like putting intoxicating substances in their body (51%). Meanwhile, more than four in 10 of those who practice religions other than Christianity (43%) say they abstain because of their faith. But what about people of no faith who don't drink alcohol? Among this segment, the top reason hits close to home: three in 10 (30%) have witnessed negative effects of drinking on their family or friends.

> People want to give time to outreaches that make an impact. Connect with your mission partners to learn their needs, both locally and globally, then explore ways to meet the needs through the abilities and passions of your congregation. Be open to new expressions of outreach as well as reruns of older yet still-needed projects. When we create opportunities that matter, people are willing to join in the work.
>
> "Congregation members/attendees have a wide range of financial and time availability. Whether a single mom or an empty nester, people want to serve. To best engage them, offer a variety of outreach options. Not only will a range of opportunities provide ways to explore the members' best fit and calling, they will allow a natural progression for your church family to deepen their connection with your mission partners. For example, in your partnership with a local homeless shelter, a member could donate a dozen oranges, bake a hot casserole, join the rotation to serve breakfast monthly, contribute to their building fund, join their social media team to raise awareness about local poverty or lead the shelter's weekly Bible study. From an addition on the grocery list to weekly engagement, these types of opportunities offer numerous ways to engage with your mission partners."
>
> —*Sharon Hoover, director of missions at Centreville Presbyterian Church in Centreville, Virginia, in Barna's* The State of Pastors

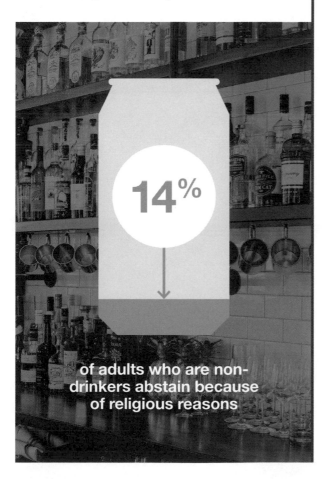

**14%**

of adults who are non-drinkers abstain because of religious reasons

# Vocation & Education

The ways we learn, work, and pursue purpose

# What Parents Look for in Schools

In early 2017, education policy, particularly school choice, was at the top of U.S. news sites. Senate hearings for the confirmation of Betsy DeVos as secretary of education were contentious, partly because DeVos, an alumna of a private Christian school, supports alternatives to public schools. In her opening statement, DeVos said, "Parents no longer believe that a one-size-fits-all model of learning meets the needs of every child, and they know other options exist, whether magnet, virtual, charter, home, religious, or any combination thereof."[10]

Though her eventual confirmation was regarded by some as controversial, her statement matches the perspectives among parents of current and prospective students of Christian schools, according to a Barna study conducted in partnership with the Association of Christian Schools International (ACSI). The landscape of religious schools and parent preferences is shifting in some significant ways.

## The Changes Christian Schools Face

Christian education is currently serving a small group of American families. For example, ACSI, one of the biggest Christian school associations, includes just 1 percent of U.S. children ages 5–19. Macro trends suggest that figure is at risk of shrinking (except in school voucher states), and anecdotal evidence from schools suggests that many are already experiencing the challenge of gaining and retaining families.

The first and most important macro trend impacting the landscape for Christian schools is the changing faith profile of American adults. Barna finds the proportion of adults who affiliate with Christianity at all or cite an active faith is shrinking precipitously, with the sharpest decline among Millennials. In this context, choosing Christian education will become increasingly exceptional. Simultaneously, Christian parents may be more motivated to enroll their children in Christian education if other school options prove increasingly hostile to Christian beliefs and values.

The second trend concerns the proliferation of school options. An increase in public charter and magnet schools offers higher quality options to families at no cost. Under DeVos, these and other education options may be even more competitive.

In addition to these direct forces, a cultural shift toward personalized experiences also affects school choice. The individualized approach to schooling, where each child has his own customized weekly schedule of activities and often even a separate school, comes from parents putting a high value on finding the "best fit" for each child's unique needs and gifts.

Finally, the experiences of Millennials, whose children are currently in preschool or early grades, will almost certainly change how schools interact with families. More school-switching in younger parents' backgrounds has given them firsthand experience with a wider range of school types than earlier generations and primed them to move their own children from school to school as needed. In addition, delayed parenthood for Millennials means that the next generation of students will come from different family structures and parents in different life stages.

## What Parents Want in Schools

Barna surveyed a group of current parents of ACSI school students as well as a group of parents whose children attend elsewhere but are open to an ACSI school. Given that a parent would consider a Christian school, what is it that they think a school should have?

### 1) Safety

Safety is an essential school characteristic for more than 90 percent among the parent groups Barna surveyed. Safety can mean anything from a toxin-free building or a padded playground to bullying prevention. However, it can also include "cultural safety," such as feeling safe to ask questions or express doubt, learning to work through differences, or a general sense of belonging and respect.

Based on findings from qualitative research, prospective Christian school parents are thinking of their children's physical and

# What Do You Hope Your Child Will Obtain from Their Education?

● Current parents   ○ Prospective parents

| | Current | Prospective | | | Current | Prospective |
|---|---|---|---|---|---|---|
| Strong principles and values | 68% | 53% | Practical life skills | 32% | 51% |
| Love for God and people | 65% | 33% | Increased opportunities in life | 29% | 45% |
| Wisdom (ability to apply knowledge) | 60% | 47% | Fulfilling career | 22% | 38% |
| Faithfulness and obedience to God | 54% | 21% | Good relationships | 22% | 29% |
| Leadership skills and abilities | 52% | 46% | Independence from parents | 12% | 22% |
| Spiritual maturity | 36% | 17% | Financial success | 10% | 28% |
| Discovery of calling or purpose | 33% | 19% | Increased social status or mobility | 1% | 4% |

emotional safety from other children in the school. However, current Christian school parents are more likely to be thinking of the freedom to ask questions or raise doubts, like those related to their religious faith.

### 2) Academic excellence

Academic excellence is a top priority for both current and prospective Christian school parents. A large majority of current Christian school parents (95%) says it is essential. For prospective parents, that percentage is slightly lower, at 88 percent. Surprisingly, parents do not consider academic excellence more important as their children grow older and closer to the window for college admissions.

### 3) Values and spirituality

Character development is a high priority for all parents, but some parents select a specific area of character as most important: spiritual development.

While all of the parents Barna surveyed place emphasis on character development, ACSI parents indicate that they believe education is primarily for developing a child's character and spirituality, before academics and career preparation.

Prospective parents, on the other hand, put spiritual purposes of education on equal standing (in terms of the number of times selected) with social skills and personal achievement.

### 4) Warm and communicative teachers

Children experience a wide range of relationships at school, but the core ones are with peers and teachers. Parents want warm teachers who they can reach easily. "Teachers who really care about their students" is the aspect of schools that ACSI parents

are most likely to say is essential (tied with safety at 98%), followed closely by "accessible teachers," which slightly fewer (94%) said was a necessity.

Likewise, almost all prospective parents believe caring and accessible teachers (91% and 80%, respectively) are essential to schooling.

Parents—especially ACSI parents—generally want small class sizes for their children. It is likely this aspect of a school might indicate to parents that their child will get the personal attention from teachers that nearly all deem crucial.

Parents whose children are in private Christian schools tend to rank their experience with the schools very highly. It may be that Christian schools meet this cluster of all-important school characteristics in a unique way—even as choices for elementary and secondary schooling go through radical change.

*n=400 U.S. parents | September–October 2015; n=971*
*U.S. parents of students in ACSI Christian schools |*
*November–December 2015*

# What Causes School Violence?

It's a dilemma that dominates media coverage of tragedies and keeps parents and teachers up at night: Why is there so much violence in our nation's schools? In a Barna survey of U.S. adults, in partnership with MJM Entertainment Group, the most commonly selected factors are difficult family situations, such as divorce or absent parents (51%), followed by untreated mental illness (43%) and easy access to guns (40%). These top reasons indicate a noteworthy mix of concerns related to both means and motive.

Along generational lines, there are few variations from the average answers, though older respondents are more likely to view violence in video games (36% Boomers, 43% Elders) or TV (24% Boomers, 33% Elders) as contributing factors to school violence.

Family trouble, mental health, and gun access are again identified consistently across faith segments, with the exception of evangelicals. While evangelicals' first selection also pertains to problems at home, they next choose lack of religion in school (58%), ahead of mental illness (34%) and gun accessibility (26%).

Race plays some role in how adults rank the primary reasons for school violence. For example, black adults are more likely to select access to guns (54%) or neglected mental health (48%) over trouble at home (40%).

Republicans are more likely to blame violence on a lack of religion in school (31% vs. 13% Democrats) and Democrats are much more likely to blame easy access to guns (55% vs. 28% Republicans). Both parties weigh family conflicts heavily (46% and 58%, respectively) and, to a lesser extent, untreated mental illness (48% and 35%). Independents are more likely to agree with Republicans on guns (30%), but they are on a similar page with Democrats when it comes to mental illness (47%). While gun control remains a polarizing policy conversation, the data point to common ground for all parties to come together to prevent school violence.

## What Americans Believe Contributes to School Violence

| | |
|---|---|
| Difficult family situations | 51% |
| Undiagnosed/untreated mental illness | 43% |
| Easy access to guns | 40% |
| Violence in video games | 27% |
| Violence on TV | 22% |
| Lack of religion in school | 20% |
| Violence in film/movies | 15% |
| Violence in music | 14% |
| Other | 10% |
| Lack of armed guards in schools | 7% |
| Not sure | 3% |
| Don't believe any factors lead to violence in schools | 3% |

*n=1,281 | November 4–16, 2016*

# Higher Ed Primarily Seen as Career Move

What is the point of going to college?

It's a valid and popular question these days—and one Barna posed to U.S. adults in a recent survey in partnership with the Association for Biblical Higher Education. From a list of options, respondents could select as many as they believe apply. The results are indisputable: Seven in 10 adults 18 and older believe the primary purpose of a college education is to prepare for a specific job or career, and just over half say it is to increase financial opportunities. About half think the goal is to stay competitive in today's job market.

Now compare the top choices with the bottom three options: learning how to make a difference in the world, developing moral character, and encouraging spiritual growth. In the prevailing views of Americans today, ethical, moral, and spiritual goals are less important than career objectives when it comes to college.

Falling between job-focused highs and spiritual lows are aims related to personal growth and practical skills: strengthening critical thinking and writing skills, growing in leadership skills, discovering who you are, and learning about academic interests. These mid-list items could be understood as the "soft skills" that support a career-driven focus or personal goals oriented toward self-improvement.

Self-identified Christians are just as likely, and in some cases more likely, to hold the college-is-about-career perspective. Christians agree with the general population that college is primarily about preparing for a specific job or career, increasing financial opportunities, and staying competitive in today's job market. One of the most significant findings is Christians' overall disassociation of higher education with spiritual and moral development. In lockstep with all U.S. adults, only 7 percent of self-identified Christians say college is for encouraging spiritual growth, and just 14 percent say it's for developing moral character. Unexpectedly, those of no faith are statistically tied with self-identified Christians in saying that spiritual growth is the purpose of college.

## What's the Purpose of Going to College?

● all U.S. adults
● self-identified Christians

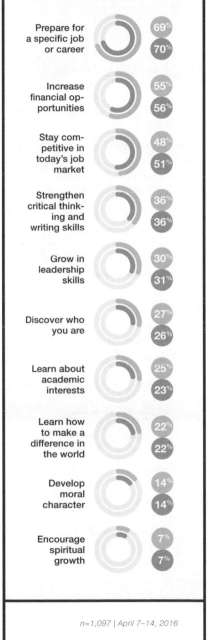

| | all U.S. adults | self-identified Christians |
|---|---|---|
| Prepare for a specific job or career | 69% | 70% |
| Increase financial opportunities | 55% | 56% |
| Stay competitive in today's job market | 48% | 51% |
| Strengthen critical thinking and writing skills | 36% | 36% |
| Grow in leadership skills | 30% | 31% |
| Discover who you are | 27% | 26% |
| Learn about academic interests | 25% | 23% |
| Learn how to make a difference in the world | 22% | 22% |
| Develop moral character | 14% | 14% |
| Encourage spiritual growth | 7% | 7% |

*n=1,097 | April 7–14, 2016*

# A Q&A on Academic Opportunity

## with Shani Dowell

*Dowell is a graduate of Howard University and holds an MBA from Stanford University. Her career in education includes work with the Posse Foundation, Bridgespan Group, KIPP Foundation, and Teach for America. She's currently the executive director of Teacher Pathways for Relay Graduate School of Education.*

***How can education play a unique role in a student's character formation or community development?***
I observed a focus group with college students where they had to rank what mattered most to them in their post-college job. Most cited "having an impact." While adults citing the purpose of college as "preparing for a job" or "increasing financial opportunities" sounds less idealistic than we may want to hear, it's understandable. One-third of incoming freshman will be the first in their family to attend college.[11] Only one out of three students graduates in four years.[12] A strong majority is working their way through college and navigating new environments on campuses as well as personal and academic challenges. The work to simply graduate from college becomes one of character formation. Further, as one out of three adults themselves has a college education,[13] I imagine that for many it would seem a luxury, and an impractical one, if it isn't offering professional or financial opportunities.

Even more than education playing a role in formation of character or community, people of faith can consider what they can do to make the education system more just— where [currently] less than half of even the highest scoring low-income students graduate college[14]—especially if most believe college increases financial opportunities. In the immediate term, educators and parents play an important role in displaying justice in their schools, curriculum, and community. [Ask yourself,] *Does the school reflect the diversity of the city? Are educational opportunities being extended to all? How are we helping students who are financially wealthy or from historically dominant groups understand their privilege? How are we helping students who are historically disenfranchised understand that they are entitled to the same quality of schools and opportunities as others?*

***For those who are neither parents nor teachers, why might they have a responsibility, even a Christian one, to be informed and concerned about the state of education?***
Micah 6:8 tells us to seek justice and love mercy. Not only are kids denied academic skills in many schools, but our schools can also be places that break the spirit and humanity of students. More heartbreaking, it is specifically directed at African American, Latino, and poor kids. We are all complicit in this because we either choose not to know or not to engage. This is where students across our country spend most of their days. We should all feel a charge to make those days ones filled with growth, learning, wisdom, and a spirit of hope and possibility.

# What America Thinks of Women in Power

The makeup of the American workplace is transforming. According to the Department of Labor, the number of women in the labor force has grown from 27 percent in 1948 to 57 percent in 2016.[15] Barna found that the majority of Americans (77%) is comfortable with the future possibility of more women than men in the workforce, including both men (75%) and women (78%). But the younger generations are more open than their older peers: Millennials, many of whom have come of age in the wake of third-wave feminism, are the most comfortable (84%) compared to Elders (57%). Though a majority of evangelicals is comfortable (52%), they remain the most hesitant, perhaps due to a more traditional interpretation of women's roles as primary caregivers in the home. More working women means couples with children are approaching childrearing in a variety of ways. This includes, of course, the more recent phenomenon of the "stay-at-home dad," a scenario with which most American adults say they are comfortable (82%).

From accounts of women receiving sexist treatment in the technology industry to celebrities calling out the Hollywood wage gap, the national conversation about the limits that still exist for women in the workplace (even for A-list actors) has received renewed attention in recent years. Most Americans share the concern that significant obstacles still make it harder for women to get ahead than men (53%). Three in 10 (30%) believe those obstacles are largely gone. Women are more likely to believe those obstacles exist than men (59% vs. 46%). Interestingly, Boomers are just as likely as Millennials to believe obstacles still exist (58% and 57%), suggesting that little has changed between the generations. Evangelicals are the most skeptical of the existence of barriers for women in the workplace; less than one-third (32%)—fewer than any other segment Barna studied—believe significant obstacles still exist.

When asked about these hurdles, women believe that fair pay (67%), equal opportunity for promotion (56%), and maintaining a work-life balance (41%) are the most important issues facing working women. This makes sense considering three-quarters of adults (74%) believe employers should always be required to pay men and women the same salary for the same job. However, only two-thirds of men (65%) believe equal pay should always be required, compared to 82 percent of women.

Despite these difficulties, the large majority of American adults (94%) is comfortable with a female CEO. Again, women are more welcoming of the idea than men (97% vs. 90%). Evangelicals exhibit the lowest level of comfort with this reality (77%).

How do those comfort levels play out day to day, in real offices and working relationships? Most Millennials (89%) believe men and women can have a healthy working relationship, but with some caveats. Though a plurality (40%) doesn't see the male-female dynamic as a problem, just as many (38%) believe the relationship should be limited to the context of an office or workspace, with some (11%) even believing company rules should regulate those relationships.

Millennials are uniquely accepting of women in the workplace. When Millennials were asked how they think women can make a workplace better, the most popular response was that men and women are equal and gender should not even be a consideration (55%). Just as important to them is having diverse perspectives (53%), and as many as two in five (40%) believe women should be represented in the workplace by virtue of the fact that they represent half the population. Smaller percentages select responses suggesting women are kind (26%) and nurturing (19%).

Despite their optimism, Millennials still say they face gender-related challenges in the workplace. For instance, almost one-quarter (22%) believes they have been treated differently at work because of their gender, an experience more resonant with women than men (25% vs. 19%). One in 11 women (9%) believes they have been held back at work because of their gender. The good news is that most (64%) have experienced neither of these challenges.

Though Hillary Clinton failed to become the first female U.S. president, the vast majority of American adults (85%) is comfortable with the possibility of a female in the White House. This is equally true among men (85%) and women (86%). Democrats (98%) are much more supportive of the idea than Republicans (65%). When it comes to gender balance in Congress, the support is even more unanimous. Almost all American adults (95%) are comfortable with an equal number of women and men in Congress, though women are more comfortable

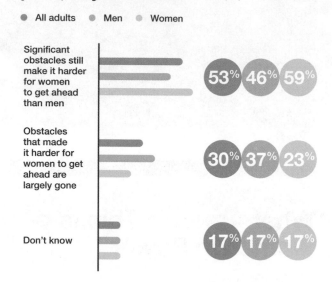

## When it comes to women in the workplace, do you believe:    n=1,023 | September 12–19, 2016

● **All adults**  ● **Men**  ● **Women**

| | All adults | Men | Women |
|---|---|---|---|
| Significant obstacles still make it harder for women to get ahead than men | 53% | 46% | 59% |
| Obstacles that made it harder for women to get ahead are largely gone | 30% | 37% | 23% |
| Don't know | 17% | 17% | 17% |

than men (98% vs. 91%). The gap between those on either side of the political spectrum is smaller when it comes to Congress (96% among Democrats, 86% among Republicans).

But despite widespread support for women in politics, two-thirds of American adults (67%) still believe it is easier for a man than a woman to get elected to high political offices. Women are more likely than men (72% vs. 63%) and Democrats are more likely than Republicans (79% vs. 51%) to believe this is the case. Though a majority of evangelicals (94%) are also on board with gender balance in Congress and most (73%) would be comfortable with a woman in the White House, they are more skeptical than other segments of the challenges for women (58%), with two in five (42%) believing it's just as easy for women as it is for men to get elected to high political offices.

"This study—and the cultural realities it uncovers—are imminently significant for the Church," Barna editor in chief Roxanne Stone says. "More than half of most congregations are women. They are increasingly part of the workforce, they are rising in the ranks at work, and they are finding immense value in their jobs. How can the Church offer vocational discipleship for women (and men) that includes both occupation and parenting?"

*n=1,023 | September 12–19, 2016; n=803 Millennials | February 2–10, 2016*

# A Q&A on Women at Work

## with Katelyn Beaty

*Beaty is editor at large for* Christianity Today, *where she was the youngest and first female managing editor. She is the author of* A Woman's Place *and has commented on faith and culture for the* Washington Post, *the* Atlantic, *the* New York Times, *CNN, ABC, NPR, Religion News Service, and more.*

### *What are some less frequently discussed examples of potential hurdles for working women?*

Since most companies still feature more men than women in positions of top leadership, women rising through the ranks lack role models and mentors. Many women find they are spoken over in meetings, their ideas are ignored, or their displays of confidence may be perceived as bossy or too dominant. Women also experience competition with other women due to a sense that only one can win a seat at the table of leadership. Even in organizations with proactive policies, interpersonal politics can prevent women from staying in the game.

### *What is missing from a church in not supporting or reaching out to working women?*

Most Christian women work in some capacity, full-time or part-time, at the office or at home. When local churches do not speak meaningfully about professional work, they miss a huge opportunity for discipleship and spiritual formation. Some women could easily walk away with the sense that the church is only for full-time mothers, but I believe churches can be prime places where all women's work is seen and celebrated. Further, workplaces will suffer when Christian women are not supported, because Christians at their best bring excellence, compassion, and creativity to their daily work. Integrating faith and work often means doing one's work with all your heart, as if it has eternal significance (see Colossians 3:23), so workplaces only stand to gain better work and workers when they support Christian women in their ranks.

### *Why is there lingering tension in Christian communities around women and work?*

Among all Christians, evangelicals are typically the most likely to hold to traditional gender roles: men in positions of formal leadership or economic provision in the home and women in positions of support, domestic care, or childrearing in the home. We're talking about centuries of cultural norms being upended in the past 100 years, and many evangelicals believe these norms are dictated in scripture, so it's no surprise that this is a lingering barrier among Christians. What's exciting to me is to see so many Christian women thrive in the workplace despite these norms—to see them excel in positions of influence, finding support from their spouses and friends and Christian communities. As with all cultural shifts, Christians have to figure out how to adapt while staying faithful to scripture. I happen to think this particular cultural shift—of women entering and thriving in the workforce—is a shift evangelicals can firmly get behind.

# PREPARING PASTORS

Pursuing higher education remains a popular choice for pastors, a Barna study in partnership with Pepperdine University shows.

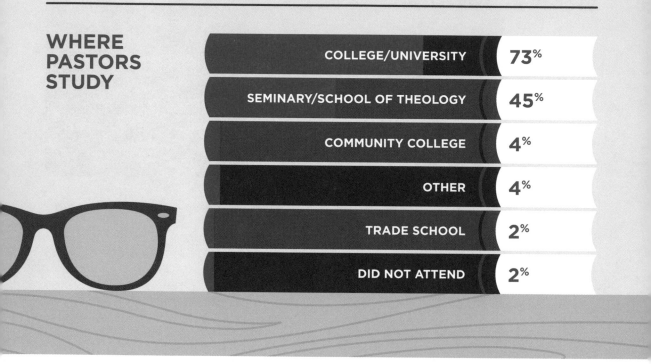

## WHERE PASTORS STUDY

| | |
|---|---|
| COLLEGE/UNIVERSITY | 73% |
| SEMINARY/SCHOOL OF THEOLOGY | 45% |
| COMMUNITY COLLEGE | 4% |
| OTHER | 4% |
| TRADE SCHOOL | 2% |
| DID NOT ATTEND | 2% |

The most common degrees among pastors include a Bachelor of Arts/Science (70%) and a Master of Divinity (49%)

One out of five pastors (21%) has received a doctoral degree of some kind, most often a DMin (14%)

## FIRST-CAREER DEGREES

A significant number of today's pastors didn't start out that way. Here are some of the degrees they earned before becoming "second-career clergy."

Juris Doctor

Botany

Physical Therapy

Public and International Affairs

Music Education

# DEGREES OF PREPARATION

*n=824 U.S. Protestant pastors | April–December 2015*

Nearly three-quarters of pastors rate their ministry training as excellent or good.

When it comes to how well seminary prepares people for effective church leadership, pastors offer mixed reviews.

| | |
|---|---|
| **8%** | very well |
| **50%** | somewhat well |
| **34%** | not too well |
| **8%** | not at all well |

---

The top three things pastors wish they had been better prepared for:

**29%** counseling burdens or solving people's problems

**29%** administrative burdens

**27%** handling conflict

---

Pastors at high risk of burnout (see page 217) feel underprepared in all aspects of ministry, particularly relational responsibilities.

**50%** handling conflict

**38%** administrative burdens

**37%** the importance of delegation and training people

**34%** church politics

**34%** challenges in leadership

Some factors feel especially challenging for specific segments of pastors.

**Pastors under 50:**

administrative burdens — **34%**

that ministry "never gets easier" — **9%**

**Female pastors:**

high expectations — **18%**

the sense that they "must do everything" — **15%**

**Seminary attendees:**

handling conflict — **36%**

church politics — **24%**

**Pastors in churches with high annual budgets ($1M+):**

the importance of delegation and training people — **39%**

challenges in leadership — **28%**

# Habits

The routines (and screens) that
make up our modern lifestyles

# The Buzz about Alcohol

Since the end of Prohibition in the 1930s, alcohol has enjoyed a unique legal and cultural legitimacy in the United States, second only to America's caffeine habit. Spearheaded by pietistic denominations such as the Methodists, Prohibition was part of a larger temperance movement that sought to curb the moral aberrations and harmful health effects of excessive consumption. Though Prohibition limited alcohol use for a time, it ultimately failed in its larger mission to shift cultural attitudes and arguably ended up exacerbating the very problems it sought to resolve. Almost a century later, Barna wondered, what do American adults believe about drinking and its excesses?

### America's Drinking Habits

Most Americans are very comfortable with drinking alcohol. Two-thirds of adults ages 21 and older (67%) drink at least occasionally. While Elders (77%) are more likely than Millennials (65%) to say they drink alcohol, Millennials who drink actually consume more than other generations, with an average of three drinks per week, compared to the average adult, who consumes two drinks a week.

Though most Americans are comfortable with drinking, three in 10 admit they sometimes drink more than they should. Larger quantities of Millennials (43%) and Gen X (38%) who drink at least occasionally report that they sometimes overdo it, compared to just 15 percent of older generations (Boomers and Elders) who say they sometimes consume too much liquor.

Religious faith may play a key role in one's decision-making about alcohol consumption. For instance, evangelicals (46%) and practicing Christians (60%) are less likely to partake in drinking alcohol, and if they do drink, they consume less than the average adult in a given week. Just 2 percent of evangelicals acknowledge that they sometimes consume too much alcohol. One-third of U.S. adults 21 and older (33%) says they do not drink alcoholic beverages of any kind.

### A Glass Half Empty

The temperance movement stressed the ambivalent feelings Americans held about the effects of alcohol—feelings which still exist today. For instance, among those of legal drinking age who do not drink, the most common reason given is seeing the negative effects drinking has on family members and close friends (27%). Another one-quarter (25%) says they don't like the taste of alcohol. People also choose not to drink for health reasons (21%) and a dislike for putting intoxicating substances of any kind into their

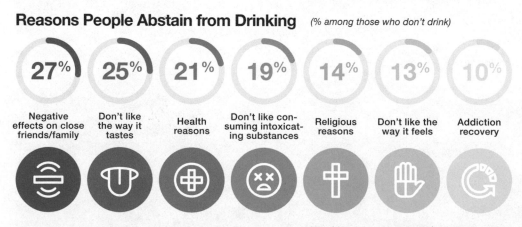

## Reasons People Abstain from Drinking   *(% among those who don't drink)*

| 27% | 25% | 21% | 19% | 14% | 13% | 10% |
|-----|-----|-----|-----|-----|-----|-----|
| Negative effects on close friends/family | Don't like the way it tastes | Health reasons | Don't like consuming intoxicating substances | Religious reasons | Don't like the way it feels | Addiction recovery |

*n=394 adults age 21+ who don't drink | November 4–16, 2016*

# Drink and Be Merry:
# Most Americans Embrace Alcohol

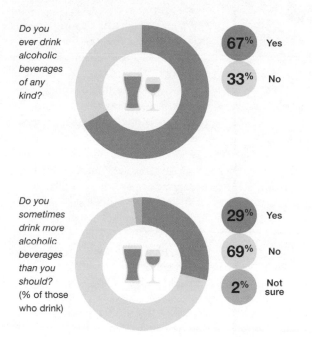

*Do you ever drink alcoholic beverages of any kind?*

**67**% Yes

**33**% No

*Do you sometimes drink more alcoholic beverages than you should?*
*(% of those who drink)*

**29**% Yes

**69**% No

**2**% Not sure

---

bodies (19%). Just one in 10 (10%) says they have an addiction and are in recovery. In addition to this, more than four in 10 adults (41%) say drinking has been the cause of trouble in their family. Gen X (46%) are more likely to have seen alcohol cause a problem in their family compared to the other generations. Interestingly, though evangelicals are the least likely to drink or overdrink, they are more likely than average to say alcohol has caused a problem in their family (54%).

## Last Call

Promoting moderation is considered one way to reduce alcohol abuse. How do Americans regard moderate drinking habits (that is, having one or two drinks a day, as defined by the Dietary Guidelines for Americans[16])? Most adults agree that drinking in moderation is either good for your health (23%) or makes no difference (39%). Slightly more than one in five (22%) believes it is bad for your health and another one in six adults (16%) doesn't have an opinion on the matter. Twice as many men than women think having just a drink or two a day has health benefits (32% vs. 14%). Gen X are also more likely to believe it is good for your health (28%).

Other segments more likely than average to perceive moderate drinking as being beneficial include married adults (27%), those with children under 18 (29%) living at home, and high-income households (34%). Half of all Elders (49%) believe moderation doesn't make any difference.

Another hotly debated approach to curbing alcohol abuse has to do with lowering the drinking age from 21 to 18. The rationale is that allowing 18- to 20-year-olds to drink in regulated environments with supervision would decrease unsafe drinking activity in the future, especially considering that most teens drink already, and in unsupervised environments. The majority of adults (60%), however, opposes such a law, compared to the one in four (24%) who is in favor of it. Sixteen percent do not have an opinion on the issue.

Opposition to lowering the drinking age increases with age. Nearly half of Millennials (48%), six in 10 Gen X (58%), seven in 10 Boomers (69%), and nearly three in four Elders (74%) oppose lowering the drinking age. Evangelicals (86%) and practicing Christians (68%) are more likely to oppose changing the current law compared to just over half of non-Christians (52%). Women are more likely than their male counterparts to oppose reducing the legal drinking age (67% vs. 53%).

For an optimistic opinion about alcohol, talk to adults who do drink at least occasionally. They are more likely than nondrinkers to believe moderate drinking has health benefits and that the legal drinking limit should be lowered to 18. They are also less likely to say drinking caused trouble in their family.

---

*n=1,281 adults age 21+ | November 4–16, 2016*

# On Our Bookshelves

Despite the inundation of potential distractions in our oversaturated (and often very visual) media landscape, Americans remain committed to digging their noses into the pages of a book: almost half of American adults (45%) read at least five books in the past year. Even so, almost one-fifth (18%) still didn't read any books at all in that time. A plurality (37%) reads somewhere between one and five books. Almost one-fifth (17%) exceeded 15 books annually; women (27%) and college graduates (21%) are among these most prolific readers.

Even with these fairly high levels of reading, most Americans (58%) would still like to read much more. Women (63%), Millennials (75%), and Gen X (69%) are among the most enthusiastic to increase their book reading. For most (55%), however, the amount of books read this year remained consistent with the total of the previous year. Almost equal amounts say their book reading has increased (23%) or decreased (21%) in that time. Millennials (33%) and Gen X (26%) report the highest levels of increase, while men are some of the most likely to report a decrease (18%).

For those whose book reading has been on the decline, the main factor is that life has become busier (48%). Others (35%) say they find it harder than it used to be to focus on books. Though one-quarter (25%) says they read more content online, Americans are just as likely to blame other non-digital diversions, such as working too much (22%) or handling the demands of family (23%).

The primary reason for an increase in reading? Simply enjoying and desiring time in the written word (76%). Having more spare time made it easier for more than two-fifths (38%) to work through some titles, and others cited school (18%), a new book club (14%), or required reading for work (10%) as boosts to their book reading.

*n=1,021 | February 8–14, 2017*

## What Helps People Read More Books?

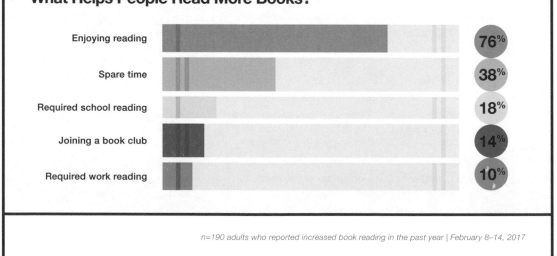

| | |
|---|---|
| Enjoying reading | 76% |
| Spare time | 38% |
| Required school reading | 18% |
| Joining a book club | 14% |
| Required work reading | 10% |

*n=190 adults who reported increased book reading in the past year | February 8–14, 2017*

# Busyness:
# A New Family Tradition

What most hinders the effectiveness of youth ministry? According to the youth pastors that Barna surveyed in partnership with Youth Specialties and YouthWorks, teens' busy lives top the list (74%). No other issue even comes close. Parents, however, aren't as concerned with their kids' packed schedules. In fact, only one out of nine U.S. parents (11%) says their child is "way too busy." About six in 10 (58%) say the balance of activities "is good" and three in 10 (31%) even think their teen "needs more to do."

According to the parents of teens, activities are many and varied. Beyond classes, more than half (48%) are involved in sports of some kind and about two in five (37%) are in school band or another musical discipline. One-fifth of teens has jobs (19%) or is involved in art, photography, or filmmaking (20%), while somewhat fewer are in drama, theater, dance (17%), or an academic club (16%).

Perhaps parents are unfazed by how busy their children are because they are hustling so much—and resting so little—themselves. More than one-third (34%) say time management is one of the most difficult things about family life and raising children. A quarter struggles to find time for personal priorities and activities outside work or home (23%) or maintain time for healthy relationships with their spouses (24%). Only one in seven adults (14%) sets aside a day a week for rest or Sabbath. Even then, they are probably working. More than four in 10 say they do enjoyable work, and an additional nearly four in 10 (37%) say they'll do nonenjoyable tasks if they need to be done. Only one in five (19%) takes a real break from working on their day of rest. Even fewer Americans commit to daily time alone (16%), with God (21%), doing activities that recharge them (12%), or not using electronics at all (12%).

Somehow, families still manage to prioritize sharing meals together, Barna's *The Tech-Wise Family* research shows. On average, families eat together at least six times a week. But it's not quite a Norman Rockwell painting. Other things—or screens— still compete for attention at the table; 42 percent agree devices are at least somewhat disruptive to dinner time.

n=1,400 | June 2013; n=606 U.S. parents of teens | February 2016; n=352 U.S. youth pastors | February 2016; n=1,021 | November 2016

# After-School Activities

Between the school dismissal bell and the call for dinner, how do kids fill their time? If you picture an idyllic afternoon of bike rides, playgrounds, and ice cream trucks, think again. A device-free afternoon is now unusual for children who have come of age in a tech-saturated world. In fact, most of the after-school activities of children involve technology, research for *The Tech-Wise Family* shows. A significant majority of children (64%) watches television or movies after school, regardless of their age group. More than four in 10 (42%) play video games, but this is much more common among children ages 9–12 (48%) and 14–17 (49%). More than one-quarter (27%) spend their free time on social media or texting with friends, though this is primarily an activity among the 14–17 age group (48%). Half as many 9–12-year-olds (25%) do the same, as well as only 13 percent of those eight or younger. One in four (25%) spends time browsing online, another activity dominated by teens.

Screen time is not the only activity that consumes the afternoon and evening hours of children. In fact, the most common activity for any child is still doing homework (65%) (though certainly this now sometimes requires engagement with technology) and watching television or movies (64%). The third most common activity is interacting with family members, an after-school reality for over half (56%) of American children. But unsurprisingly, teenagers (54%) and 9–12-year-olds (57%), having formed more non-familial relationships, are less likely to spend time with their family than the two younger age groups (60% of 5–8-year-olds and 69% of those under the age of 5). Around four in 10 kids (39%) engage in some kind of informal play or activity, an activity those under 5 do twice as much as teenagers (56%, compared to 28%). Reading books beyond schoolwork is still fairly popular (32%)—but mostly among those without schoolwork (42% under age 5). Activities outside the house, like extracurricular activities or classes (25%), playing organized sports (23%), or hanging out with friends (22%) are much less common. The least common of all after-school activities is reading the Bible/devotions/prayer (8%).

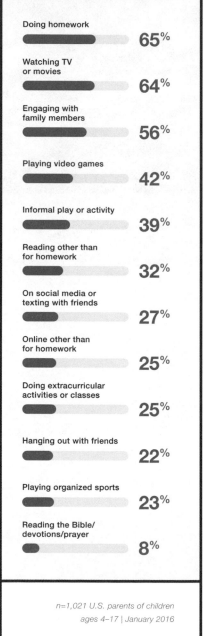

## School's Out, Screens On

*On a typical weeknight, how do your child(ren) generally spend their time?*

Doing homework
**65**%

Watching TV or movies
**64**%

Engaging with family members
**56**%

Playing video games
**42**%

Informal play or activity
**39**%

Reading other than for homework
**32**%

On social media or texting with friends
**27**%

Online other than for homework
**25**%

Doing extracurricular activities or classes
**25**%

Hanging out with friends
**22**%

Playing organized sports
**23**%

Reading the Bible/devotions/prayer
**8**%

*n=1,021 U.S. parents of children ages 4–17 | January 2016*

# Counseling Experiences and Perceptions

Professional counseling is a tool for helping people heal from trauma, facilitate mental health, build strong relationships, and change destructive patterns of thinking. While the internet has promoted the discussion about and availability of counseling options, our high-tech, always-on culture also highlights the importance of these therapeutic relationships. The Substance Abuse and Mental Health Services Administration reports 18 percent of U.S. adults experience mental illness each year.[17] With this in mind, Barna wanted to know just how many American adults are engaging in counseling and how they feel about it.

Overall, four in 10 American adults (42%) have utilized counseling at some point. Thirteen percent say they are currently seeing a counselor or therapist, while more than a quarter (28%) say they have seen a counselor or therapist in the past. Encouragingly, another 36 percent say they're at least open to it, although almost one in four (23%) says they never would go to counseling.

### Younger Generations Are More Open
By all measures, Millennials and Gen X have more interest in counseling than Boomers and Elders. One-fifth of Millennials (21%) and 16 percent of Gen X are currently engaged in therapy. By comparison, only 8 percent of Boomers and 1 percent of Elders are presently working with a counselor or therapist. Generally, Boomers and Elders are far less open to the experience. While just 15 percent of Millennials and 18 percent of Gen X say they never would go to counseling, 30 percent of Boomers and 34 percent of Elders feel this way.

Younger adults are also more likely to report that someone in their immediate family has seen a counselor, particularly Gen X. While 17 percent of adults say a family member is currently seeing a counselor, one in five Millennials (21%) and one in four Gen X (24%) say the same. These numbers far exceed reports from Boomers (11%) and Elders (5%). This difference could be connected to younger adults having a greater willingness to recommend counseling to their friends and family members. While 42

**What Is Most Important When People Pick a Counselor?**    n=1,021 | February 8–14, 2017

| 46% | 42% | 34% | 22% | 18% |
|---|---|---|---|---|
| Affordability (including insurance coverage) | Specialization or expertise | Years of experience | Positive reviews from people I know | Proximity or convenience |

| 13% | 9% | 8% | 6% | 3% |
|---|---|---|---|---|
| Education level | Someone similar to me (such as same age, gender, background, etc.) | Similar religious background | Someone with more/different life experience than me | Accolades or awards |

percent of all adults say they have made such a recommendation, close to half of Millennials (49%) and Gen X (51%) have done so.

## Affordability Is Important

When asked which two attributes are most important to them in choosing a counselor, the plurality selects affordability (46%) and specialization or expertise (42%). Predictably, the importance of affordability changes by income level. Those earning $100,000 or more each year strongly favor specialization or expertise (48%) more than any other factor, including affordability (22%). For those whose annual salary is $50,000–$90,000 (47%) or less than $50,000 (52%), affordability is the number one factor.

While only 8 percent of U.S. adults say a similar religious background is one of the most important factors, this is much more essential to some. For example, among conservatives, one out of five (20%) indicates a similar religious background matters greatly to them, far more than the 3 percent of liberals who say the same. Among evangelicals, almost half (47%) also list this factor among their top two, a striking comparison to the few of no faith (1%) who look for a therapist with a similar faith experience.

## Why People Seek Counseling

Among adults who have seen a counselor, three in 10 (30%) say a doctor's recommendation prompted them to begin counseling. Another 28 percent say it was a traumatic experience, such as the loss of a loved one, loss of a job, disease, accident, or divorce. Men are more likely to report the former (36%, compared to 24% of women), while women are more motivated by the latter (33% compared to 21% of men). Another one in four (25%) says they went to receive treatment for a mental illness.

Pastoral recommendations rank low as catalysts to begin counseling, although this is unsurprisingly somewhat more likely for practicing Christians (14%) than it is for nonpracticing Christians (3%) and non-Christians (1%). These numbers may reflect pastors' habits rather than individuals' lack of willingness to seek or act on a pastoral recommendation. For example, a 2003 study published by Health Services Research reported that when people came to clergy for help for mental illness—historically, the number one place they turn—clergy referred less than 10 percent to mental health care providers.[18]

Almost one in 10 married people (9%) says they attended required premarital counseling—half the percentage (21%) who have sought therapy when their marriage faced a trial.

Millennials are the generation most likely to begin counseling as treatment for mental illness, with more than one-third (34%) doing so. This is followed by 23 percent of Gen X and 21 percent

of Boomers. These statistics may point to decreasing stigma around mental illness among younger generations, who have grown up with more open or public conversations about mental health.

Additionally, one in three non-Christians (33%) acknowledges seeking treatment for mental illness, more than twice the percentage of practicing Christians (15%) who have gone to counseling for this purpose. While there's a chance the faithful experience stronger mental health—after all, science confirms that religious belief and a loving, stable community can be healing and have psychological benefits—this may also reflect the strength of stigma within Christian circles, as many churches have been slower to accept mental illness as a legitimate struggle requiring professional help.

## Americans Feel Good about Counseling

Though their reasons for visiting a counselor may vary, Americans consistently indicate the experience was very positive (47%). Another 29 percent say it was somewhat positive, with a small minority calling it somewhat (5%) or very negative (1%). The remaining 17 percent rate their experience as neutral.

For the Christians who do pursue professional counseling, it's highly rewarding; more than half (54%) call it very positive (vs. 36% of non-Christians). Practicing Protestants (69%) and Catholics (77%) are particularly upbeat about their time in therapy. Perhaps this higher level of satisfaction explains why practicing Christians (52%) are more likely than non-Christians (43%) to recommend counseling to friends and family.

*n=1,021 | February 8–14, 2017*

# The Importance of Opening Up

Alyce Youngblood
Barna Group
Managing Editor

When I was younger, I sometimes heard well-meaning, exhausted adults talk about sending an unruly child to a counselor, in the same tone they reserved for threatening detention or removing phone privileges. Particularly in the Church, I gleaned this sense that counseling should be pursued quietly and only as a last resort, when prayer and sheer will proved too slow to "fix" an individual.

Over time, people close to me challenged these ideas. A roommate studying psychology told me how a childhood experience in therapy shaped her life and career. Online, I encountered information about the prevalence of mental illness, as well as solidarity for those facing it. Some of my peers, I learned, had been in therapy for years, in both good times and bad. Eventually, I sat down with counselors myself. After doing so, I too began to talk about it openly. And beyond the health benefits, I saw the beautiful ways counseling fit within spiritual growth. It wasn't a punishment; it was an invitation.

Barna has found that ideas about mental health are often nurtured by relationships. Most of those who are seeing or have seen a therapist have family members who have done the same. A majority of those who would at least consider counseling feels their family is also open to it (and vice versa—almost three-quarters of those who would never be open to counseling say their relatives share this sentiment). People are more likely to recommend therapy to friends and family if they've engaged in it themselves. Further, those who report having a good experience with counseling point back to a community that actively participates in it.

Close relationships can even be persuasive in helping someone *choose* their counselor. Roughly one in five says it's important to them that a counselor has positive reviews from someone they personally know, and a similar proportion found theirs through a friend or family member's recommendation.

It's not newsworthy that people tend to embrace ideas or habits that are modeled for them. But as I consider these statistics and my own story, I'm reminded that any growth is a shared endeavor, profoundly dependent on the right mix of external influence and internal response. On "a word fitly spoken" (Proverbs 25:11 KJV) meeting a heart applied to understanding (see Proverbs 2:2 KJV).

If your personal circle helps form your perceptions of mental health, it's worth measuring its diameter. Reframing ideas about mental illness, and even taking part in counseling, may require an "outside-the-comfort-zone" vulnerability. What do we stand to miss when these conversations occur in an echo chamber? How many people who desperately needed counseling haven't sought it out because no one in their circle recommended it?

At the right times, I was inclined to hear the wisdom of compassionate, informed, and diverse voices on the subject of mental health. I'm grateful for it, and I feel I have to talk about it, especially as a Christian. The well-being of any individual or community is an exchange, a holy balance of listening up and speaking out.

# A Q&A on Counseling

## with Jamie Tworkowski

*Tworkowski is the founder of To Write Love on Her Arms, a nonprofit movement dedicated to presenting hope and finding help for people struggling with depression, addiction, self-injury, and suicide. He is the author of the* New York Times *bestselling book* If You Feel Too Much.

***Though most U.S. adults either have seen a counselor or would be open to it, one in four people says they would never see a counselor. What are reasons people say or assume they never would be open to therapy? Is counseling for everybody?***

The stigma suggests mental health is something we aren't supposed to talk about. As for counseling specifically, being willing to go to counseling means being willing to admit there's a problem. When we admit there's a problem, when we bring that out into the open, then we have to deal with it. And we're talking about things people are often afraid to deal with, because there's often pain and shame associated and this stuff takes people out of their comfort zone.

To answer the second question, yes, we believe counseling is for everyone. It doesn't mean every *counselor* is for everyone; it may take time to find someone who feels like a good fit, but we do believe counseling works. It's not an easy step to take, but we do believe it's worth it.

***Barna research indicates that Elders are much less likely than other generations to have seen a counselor. Though a plurality***

***is open to it, more than one-third say they never would consider this. What has changed over time? How have their circumstances been different, as well as the conversation or stigma surrounding mental health, when compared to younger generations, particularly Millennials?***

Over time, I think people have learned that mental health is real and that seeing a counselor works. So we're seeing younger people become more open, not only when it comes to talking about mental health, but when it comes to believing it's OK to ask for help.

We believe honesty is contagious. We're certainly seeing more and more young people speak openly and honestly about their mental health, and that invites other people to do the same. Also, a case can be made that Millennials have grown up in a world where it's easier to talk about their feelings, because these folks have grown up with social media.

***Only small percentages of people connect with a counselor either through their church or on a pastor's recommendation. Why do you think this is?***

The Church has not done a great job of leading the discussion about mental health, and the Church has not done a great job of pointing people to mental health professionals. As a result, it's easy to think that if someone is struggling,

their needs will simply be met by God and/or the people of the church. I think that when it comes to mental health issues, a lot of Christians think about taking their pain to God through scripture and prayer, but they don't think about connecting with a mental health professional.

I tend to compare it to a broken arm; if your friend breaks their arm, it's totally fine to pray. But your friend would probably like for you to pray on the way to the hospital, where broken arms get fixed. Mental health should be approached in the same way. When something breaks, you take it to an expert.

***When choosing a counselor, people are most concerned about affordability—more than the therapist's education, age, background, proximity, and so on. What are some ways to remove this barrier? In addition, does the Church have a part to play in increasing accessibility and affordability of mental health care?***

There's certainly a need for affordable mental health care. It's important to stay informed and to communicate with elected officials. Oftentimes, there are affordable options people aren't aware of. People should start by learning what their insurance company covers. Beyond this, it's important to note that many counselors are willing to work on a sliding scale. And mental health counselor interns are required to do hundreds of hours of free or discounted counseling as part of becoming licensed.

I love the idea of the Church being part of the solution when it comes to mental health. One example is churches designating funds to help people pay for counseling. In addition, I would love to see churches hire licensed mental health counselors so they can offer more than just pastoral counseling.

# Take Care

*How Americans better themselves and breathe easy*

*n=1,089 | November 2016*

Recently, conversations about "self-care" have entered the mainstream as people seek out ways to unplug, relax, and pursue personal health and growth. In an effort to see how Americans are being mindful of their well-being, Barna asked people to identify practices they participate in on a regular basis—some more spiritual in nature, some that could be more broadly categorized as self-help or self-improvement.

## One in Four Adults Finds Time to Get Outside and Think Deeply

| Spending time in nature for reflection | Reading books on spiritual topics | Meditation | Practicing silence and/or solitude | Journaling or writing your thoughts | Yoga | Attending groups or retreats |
|---|---|---|---|---|---|---|
| 25% | 21% | 19% | 16% | 14% | 12% | 12% |

## Generations Unwind in Different Ways

Younger generations are open to a variety of ways of investing in themselves. Millennials gravitate toward getting everything out on paper. Yoga is a fairly common practice among both Millennials and Gen X, though much rarer among older generations. Though Boomers and Elders are hesitant to participate in some of the activities listed, they most enjoy spiritual reading and time spent in nature.

● Millennials ● Gen X ● Boomers ● Elders

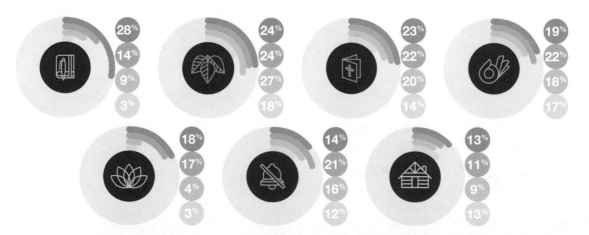

# The Class Factor in Self-Care

High- and middle-income earners take advantage of practicing yoga, reading spiritual books, or attending retreats—forms of self-improvement that usually require some kind of financial investment.

● $75K+  ● $40–75K  ● Under $40K

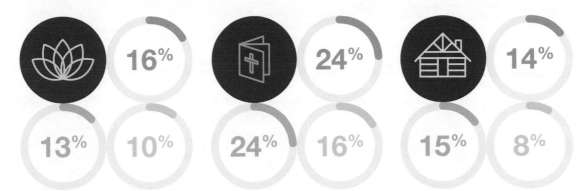

| | | |
|---|---|---|
| 16% | 24% | 14% |
| 13% | 24% | 15% |
| 10% | 16% | 8% |

More learned adults are drawn toward cerebral expressions, such as silence or solitude.

● College graduate  ● Some college  ● High school or less

20% 21% 11%

21% 23% 16%

Regardless of income or education level, spending time in nature or journaling are similarly appealing to adults.

| | $75K+ salary | $40–75K salary | Under $40K salary | College graduate | Some college | High school or less |
|---|---|---|---|---|---|---|
| | 27% | 22% | 26% | 27% | 27% | 22% |
| | 13% | 12% | 17% | 12% | 18% | 13% |

# Relationships

An intimate overview of
Americans' love lives

# America's Relationship Status

According to decades of Barna's demographic data on the American public, the segment of American adults who are currently married—though fluctuating slightly over the last 16 years—remains steady at just over half of all adults (52% in 2000, 52% in 2016). The percentage of those who are currently divorced also remains steady at about one in 10 (10%), from 11 percent in 2000. Because of the reality of remarriage, the currently divorced rate does not take into account past divorce, which, when accounted for, brings the proportion of American adults who have ever been divorced to one-quarter (25%), a rate that has remained steady since 2000 (when it was 24%). The percentage of single people (never married), however, has increased from just over one-quarter (27%) to three in 10 (30%). This uptick is the big story here, particularly when looking closely at different age groups.

For instance, in the 16 years since 2000, the proportion of single people in the 25–29 range rose 9 percentage points (from 50% percent to 59%) and the number of single people in the 30–39 range rose 10 percentage points (from 24% to 34%). During the same time period, those groups saw similar shifts in the number of those married, dropping 7 percentage points in the 25–29 range (from 43% to 36%) and 8 percentage points in the 30–39 range (from 65% to 57%). These confirm massive generational shifts among younger Americans toward a broader move to delay marriage.

When it comes to the faithful, there is both difference and likeness. The difference is that practicing Christians and evangelicals are much more likely to be married than the average American. Almost six in 10 practicing Christians (59%) are married (a number that has remained steady since 2000), compared to just over half of the general population (52%).

## Not Alone: Percentage of Singles on the Rise

● 2000  ● 2016      ● 2000  ● 2016

**Married**              **Single**

52%  52%              27%  30%
All adults               All adults

43%  36%              50%  59%
25–29                    25–29

65%  57%              24%  34%
30–39                    30–39

58%  59%              **Ever Divorced**
Practicing Christians    All adults
                         [ 2016 ]  25%

68%  67%              Practicing Christians
Evangelicals             [ 2016 ]  25%

                         Evangelicals
                         [ 2016 ]  25%

This is even more pronounced among evangelicals, 67 percent of whom are married. But the divorce rate (both historically and currently) among practicing Christians and evangelicals equals that of the general adult population, matching 25 percent as of 2016 data. So although those with strong religious convictions are more likely to be married than those without, they are just as likely to have experienced a divorce.

*n=3,059 | January 2000 and October 2000;*
*n=12,677 | January 2015–November 2016*

# Scrolling Steady: A Look at Online Dating

These days, dating is increasingly as much a digital experiment as a relational one. Overall, almost three in 10 American adults (28%) have either tried online dating once or twice (14%), use it regularly (5%), or have used it previously but not anymore (9%). Still, almost three-quarters (72%) haven't tried it at all, and more than half (52%) would never do so. That said, of those who have never tried it, 16 percent are still open to it. Gen X (7%) and Millennials (6%) are the most regular users of online dating, and Gen X are also more likely to have tried it (37%) than any other age group. Interestingly, Millennials, who have come of age in a digital generation, are not much more likely to be users than Boomers (27% vs. 24%). Evangelicals tend to stay away from online dating. They are the group most likely to say they would never use online dating (75%), and only one in 10 have either used it once or twice (9%) or use it regularly (1%).

Among users, the most popular site is Match.com, which is frequented by more than one-third of users (34%). The next most popular sites are OK Cupid (21%) and eHarmony (19%), with Tinder coming in at just over one in 10 users (11%). Match.com is the most popular site or app among each age group except Millennials, who prefer OK Cupid and Tinder. But whatever site or app is used, it seems there's still a deep level of uncertainty about the medium. Among those who have previously used or currently use online dating, a plurality (39%) has had a mixed experience. Almost three in 10 (29%) have had a very positive (13%) or mostly positive (16%) experience, while almost one-third (32%) has had a very (15%) or somewhat negative (17%) experience.

But people are still finding love online. Among users of online dating sites and apps, one in three (29%) says they met their current partner online, and on average, 2.4 of their friends also met their current partner online.

## A Majority Doesn't See Online Dating as an Option

**Have you ever tried online dating?**

- 14% Yes, but only once or twice
- 5% Yes, I use it regularly
- 16% No, but I'm open to trying it
- 56% No, I would never
- 9% Not anymore, but I have

**Overall, how was your experience with online dating?**

- 13% Very positive
- 16% Mostly positive
- 39% Mixed, positive and negative
- 17% Somewhat negative
- 15% Very negative

*n=1,097 | April 7–14, 2016*

# Just Friends?

Can men and women be just friends?

It's a perennial question long debated in romantic comedies, churches, workplaces, and even political offices. While there is no shortage of opinions on the matter, most people do think it's possible, according to Barna data, and they back up that belief in reporting that they have at least one friend of the opposite gender.

The majority of adults has anywhere between two and five close friends (62%), and within that circle are a differing number of friends of the opposite sex. A plurality (25%), however, indicates they have just one close friend of the opposite sex, and the average among all adults is 1.4. Interestingly, almost half of Millennial respondents (46%) say they have no close friends of the opposite sex, more than the percentage of any other generational group (40% to 45%). On the other end of the age spectrum, Elders are the most likely to have two friends of the opposite sex (24%), with the rest of the generations being much less likely (15% to 16%). Small percentages of all adults identify more than one or two dear friends not of their own sex (7% have three friends, 3% have four friends, 2% have five friends).

It appears that the older you get, the more likely you are to have friends of the opposite gender. Perhaps with the assurance of life experience, marriage, career connections, or long-term friendships, having friends of the opposite sex gets less complicated.

Regardless, young people seem optimistic about the possibilities of men and women being friends, despite being the generation least likely to have cultivated these relationships at this point in their lives. In a survey exclusive to Millennials, Barna asked whether men and women can be "just friends" if they are both single. A large majority—more than nine in 10 (92%)—says yes. And what if at least one of them is in a committed relationship? Nothing much should change, according to Millennials: slightly less than nine in 10 (89%) again say yes.

Among the minority who believes it could be difficult for men and women to be "just friends," a number of arguments are presented. One in three (36%) claims that attraction/feelings exist or will develop at some point. Beyond that, another one in four (24%) says the reality of sexual tension and temptation will get in the way. And finally, 17 percent believe it complicates other friendships/relationships. A little more than one-quarter (27%) say they have other reasons in mind.

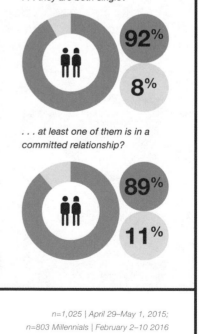

## A Familiar Question

*Do you believe men and women can be "just friends" if . . .*

● Yes    ○ No
*(among Millennials only)*

*. . . they are both single?*

92%
8%

*. . . at least one of them is in a committed relationship?*

89%
11%

*n=1,025 | April 29–May 1, 2015;*
*n=803 Millennials | February 2–10 2016*

# One in Four Senses Coworker Chemistry

The workplace is rife with romantic (or simply sexual) chemistry: one-quarter of all adults (25%) believes a coworker or supervisor has been attracted to them and 16 percent say that coworker or supervisor actually told them about this attraction. Nearly one in five (18%) has been asked out on a date by a coworker, but fewer (6%) have had supervisors do the same.

But that attention is not always appreciated. For instance, 13 percent have had unwanted sexual or romantic attention from a coworker and 4 percent from a supervisor. It may seem like a given that these numbers would increase for single Americans, but that's not the case. Married adults are just as likely to experience unwanted sexual or romantic attention from a coworker (14%, compared to 12% of singles), to have a coworker tell them they are attracted to them (18%, compared to 15% of singles), or to have a supervisor ask them out on a date (7%, compared to 6% of singles). They are also as likely to say a coworker has asked them out (both 19%).

When it comes to watercooler conversation, 44 percent of employed adults have heard men discussing the physical attractiveness of female coworkers and one-third (33%) has heard women discussing the physical attractiveness of male coworkers

Today's world demands that men and women interact at unprecedented levels. They are coworkers, friends, supervisors, partners, and more. The social narrative has often been that men and women cannot be in a relationship without sexual tension getting in the way (see page 96). However, most Americans' lived experiences do not bear that out: the majority says they have never felt unspoken romantic tension with someone of the opposite sex. Of course, there are understandable expectations: younger Americans and those who are single have experienced more sexual tension than their married counterparts and other groups, whether with coworkers, casual acquaintances, close friends, or casual friends. The most likely relationship for anyone to feel such romantic tension: casual friendships (20%), followed by close friends (19%), coworkers (17%), and casual acquaintants (16%).

## Workplace Romance

**Has the following ever happened at a place where you work?**        *(% among all employed adults)*

Heard men discussing the physical attractiveness of female coworkers
**44%**

Heard women discussing the physical attractiveness of male coworkers
**33%**

Thought that a coworker or supervisor was attracted to you
**25%**

Had a coworker ask you out on a date
**18%**

Had a coworker or supervisor tell you they were attracted to you
**16%**

Had unwanted sexual or romantic attention from a coworker
**13%**

Had a supervisor ask you out on a date
**6%**

*n=564 employed adults | February 2014*

# Expectations for Sex Education

Sexual norms and attitudes have changed dramatically in American culture over the years, and today's young people face opportunities and choices their forbears may not have imagined. So how do Americans see their responsibility to educate and equip teens to make choices about sex? A Barna study, conducted in partnership with Ascend, uncovers what adults believe about teen sex and the best approaches to sex education.

## Millennials See Teen Sex Differently

When asked whether they personally believe it's OK for teens to have sex, assuming the sex is consensual and a contraceptive is used, 37 percent of all adults affirm such sexual activity among teens—and males much more so than females (46% and 28%, respectively). Sexual behavior is a topic on which generations predictably disagree, and Millennials really stand apart. Among Millennials, more than half (54%) feel consensual, safe sex among teens is OK.

While seven in 10 adults (71%) believe sex education classes should primarily use practical skills to reinforce waiting for sex, a smaller majority of Millennials (57%) agrees. This compares to 74 percent of Gen X, 75 percent of Boomers, and 85 percent of Elders. The other 43 percent of Millennials believe sex education should communicate that teen sex is OK, so long as young people consent and use contraception. Overall, only 29 percent of adults agree with this approach. Additionally, Millennials (38%) are more likely to say federal funding should be used to support this point of view compared to Boomers (9%) and Elders (6%).

## Family Status Shapes Perspectives

Those with children under 18 (77%) strongly believe sex education should support a message of waiting, while those without minor children still favor this idea but to a lesser degree (68%). Even so, parents who are actively raising children are more likely to say teen sex is OK (48% vs. 31% of those not raising children). Given that Millennials and Gen X are most likely to currently have children under 18, these statistics indicate young parents may struggle for moderation between their broader progressive values and a desire for their own children to be selective.

## Most Americans Hope Teens Are Encouraged to Wait for Sex

*The primary message of sex education should be …*

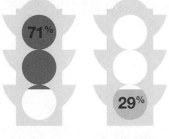

One that reinforces waiting for sex — 71%

One that says teen sex is OK, as long as they use contraception — 29%

*Tax revenue should be allocated for sex ed that reinforces …*

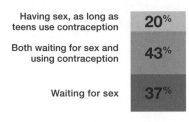

Having sex, as long as teens use contraception — **20%**

Both waiting for sex and using contraception — **43%**

Waiting for sex — **37%**

*n=1,281 | November 4–16, 2016*

Married people (80%) and those who have been divorced (76%) are most likely to say the primary message of sex education should reinforce waiting, in contrast with the 57 percent of those who have never been married and 58 percent of those who have ever cohabited. Nearly all married (91%) and divorced (92%) people also believe it's at least somewhat important that teens be encouraged to avoid sex. Among those who have never been married, three-quarters (73%) agree. It's possible the experience of commitment in marriage fosters a less lenient view of sexuality or that holding stringent perspectives encourages people to pursue marriage.

### Faith Influences Sex Ed Standards

Faith is the single most powerful factor influencing views of teen sex and sex education. When asked what primary message sex education classes should offer, 78 percent of self-identified Christians and 86 percent of practicing Christians agree it should be a message that uses practical skills to reinforce waiting for sex. By comparison, 52 percent of non-Christians agree. The group most enthusiastic about this approach is evangelicals, with 94 percent in agreement. Church activity makes a difference as well. Among weekly church attenders, 84 percent agree that sex education should encourage teens to wait. This presents a marked contrast with those who attend monthly (79%) or less often (63%).

These statistics are in keeping with the personal views of people in different faith segments, who hold varying opinions on the question of whether it's permissible for teens to have sex. Evangelicals stand out, with 96 percent saying teens should be encouraged to abstain. This is a far higher percentage than all other groups, including non-evangelical born again Christians (72%), notional Christians (49%), people of other faiths (57%), and those with no faith (28%). Those who rarely attend church (less often than once a month) are less certain of their views on whether it's all right for teens to have sex, with 14 percent saying they're not sure and the rest evenly split between those who say it's OK (42%) and those who believe teens should be encouraged to wait (44%). Those who attend weekly (69%) or monthly (60%) are more likely to say teens should wait.

Catholics are the most permissive faith group, with 41 percent saying teen sex is acceptable. By contrast, 23 percent of Protestants agree. However, those who consider themselves practicing Catholics (32%) are somewhat less likely to hold this view. Similarly, 22 percent of Catholics (vs. 12% of Protestants) believe most federal funding should focus on supporting programs that tell teens it's fine to be sexually active, but only 13 percent of practicing Catholics say the same.

When considering federal funding for sex education approaches, the highest percentage of Americans (43%) believe the two approaches should receive equal funding: telling teens they're allowed to be sexually active as long as contraception is used and giving teens skills to help them hold off on sex. Among those who endorse one view or the other, 37 percent say most funding should go to the latter approach, while one in five (20%) supports the former. Practicing Christians are more likely to support funding for education that encourages teens to wait, with half (51%) favoring this approach and only 9 percent saying federal funding should support a message that condones safe teen sex. For evangelicals, the preference is very strong, with 80 percent advocating for the approach that encourages teens to refrain from sex. This dramatically outweighs all other groups: non-evangelicals (47%), notional Christians (34%), people of other faiths (34%), and those of no faith (21%).

It seems Christian beliefs—particularly evangelical beliefs—and active involvement in church are major factors in influencing both a sense of certainty and more traditional opinions about both teen sex and sex education.

### Facts About Teens' Habits Change Responses

When questions about sex education are framed within the context of information about teens' habits and concerns about at-risk behavior, people's views become slightly more conservative. For

## Testing Adults on Sex Ed

*Recent research shows that the majority of teens are not sexually active, and that fewer are sexually active today compared with 20 years ago. Is this surprising to you?*   *n=1,281 | November 4–16, 2016*

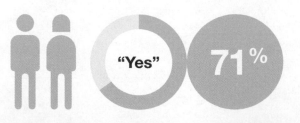

"Yes" 71%

## The Evangelical Approach to Sex Ed

*A majority of evangelicals say ...*

n=1,281 | November 4–16, 2016

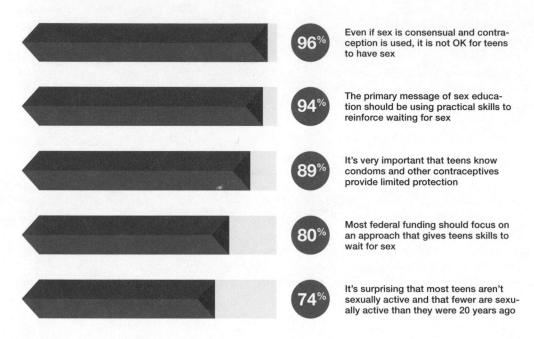

**96%** Even if sex is consensual and contraception is used, it is not OK for teens to have sex

**94%** The primary message of sex education should be using practical skills to reinforce waiting for sex

**89%** It's very important that teens know condoms and other contraceptives provide limited protection

**80%** Most federal funding should focus on an approach that gives teens skills to wait for sex

**74%** It's surprising that most teens aren't sexually active and that fewer are sexually active than they were 20 years ago

example, when informed that the majority of teens is not sexually active and that fewer are sexually active today compared to teens 20 years ago[19]—facts that surprised two-thirds of respondents (65%)—77 percent indicate that a message that reinforces waiting for sex should be the primary approach to sex education. Before they received this information, however, 71 percent held this view. Women are more influenced by this knowledge, going from 72 to 82 percent who advocate for a message of waiting. All generational groups became more favorable of this message, with the biggest difference emerging among Millennials, who moved from 57 percent to 64 percent.

When reminded that the Centers for Disease Control describes teen sex as at-risk behavior, like smoking and drinking alcohol[20], the vast majority (84%) claims it's important to encourage teens to avoid sex. Three percent say they are unsure. When simply asked to give their opinion, without contextualizing teen sex as at-risk behavior, only 53 percent say teens should be encouraged to wait to participate and 11 percent were unsure.

It's possible that many Americans respond instinctively out of a cynical view of teen behavior, a reaction to perceived cultural norms, or a reluctance to make moral judgments. But when given

the opportunity to consider the reality of teens' decisions about sex, some appear to change their thinking on the subject. This demonstrates another need in regard to sex education: equipping adults for a grounded and informed discussion of morality, sexual values, and what's best for teens.

One thing all Americans are well aware of and appear to agree on when it comes to sex education: it's vital to teach teens that condoms offer limited protection against STDs and other contraceptives offer none. Eighty-one percent of adults and a majority of all segments say this is very important.

# Eight in 10 Parents Say Their Job Has Never Been Harder

Recent technological advancements are creating uncharted waters for parents of children who have never known a world without smartphones. In this tech-driven world, almost eight in 10 parents agree strongly (44%) or somewhat (35%) that raising kids today is more complicated than it was when they were a kid, Barna's *The Tech-Wise Family* research shows.

Most parents believe technology and social media (65%) are the major reasons why parenting is more difficult today. One of the biggest challenges when it comes to technology is balancing physical activity with online activity (31%)—it's harder than ever to pull children away from the screen to go outside. Parents not only struggle to limit their children's time with and use of technology (30%), but they also struggle to maintain a sense of control over what their children consume (30%). Because kids have their own devices and increased Wi-Fi access, parents find it increasingly difficult to filter the content their children watch, read, or use—including pornography (18%)—and to know what they are exposed to via friends (30%) or social media (20%). Devices are so ubiquitous that one-quarter of parents (25%) has difficulty even gathering their family together without technology.

Another major challenge to contemporary parenting: more than half of parents (52%) feel the world is more dangerous. This foreboding is interesting considering that rates of violence of any kind have been declining for decades, in the United States and internationally. Technology could again be the culprit. Information overload and sensational headlines in an oversaturated, competitive media space may be responsible for the disconnect between perception and reality.

Parents also claim a lack of common morality (40%) as a key challenge. Less pressing are financial factors (26%) and school-related issues, such as bullying (20%) and academic pressure (16%).

## What Makes Parenting More Difficult Now Than in the Past?

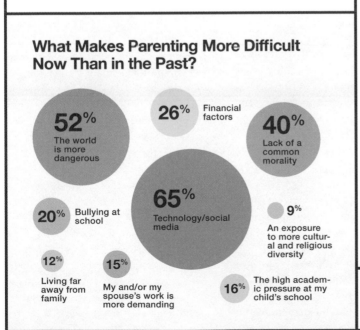

**52%** The world is more dangerous

**26%** Financial factors

**40%** Lack of a common morality

**20%** Bullying at school

**65%** Technology/social media

**9%** An exposure to more cultural and religious diversity

**12%** Living far away from family

**15%** My and/or my spouse's work is more demanding

**16%** The high academic pressure at my child's school

*n=1,021 U.S. parents of children ages 4–17 | January 25–February 4, 2016*

# A Q&A on Managing Technology

## with Andy Crouch

*Crouch is senior communication strategist at John Templeton Foundation and former executive editor of* Christianity Today. *His latest book is* The Tech-Wise Family, *which features original Barna research. This is an adapted Q&A from Barna and Pepperdine University's The State of Pastors 2017 event.*

***How has technology made parenting more difficult today?***
What really makes it hard is we're the first ones to have to deal with it. We can't go to the wisdom of previous generations. There is no inherited cultural tradition. Even in the most expansive definition of technology, we're only 200 years into this story, out of thousands and thousands of years of the human race. In many ways, we're 20 years into the real effect of technology, in all of its ramifications. We're all just figuring this out as we go along.

Young people are really facile with this; they figure it out very quickly. Adults often just aren't motivated to figure it out, or sometimes they're a little slower. So you also have this turning upside down of expertise, where parents used to be the experts on the world. They knew how to operate in the world, and they could teach their children that. [Children] are better technically, but they actually, just like all the generations, are absolutely adrift in how we manage [technology] in a healthy way. None of us know how to do this. We all need help. This is not just a parenting problem or a family problem; it's a human problem.

By the way, when we ask kids, "What do you most wish was different in your relationship with your parents?" their number one answer is, "I wish they would get off their screens and talk to me."

***Share some of the things you've done to help guide parents spiritually, more than just tips and tricks for keeping kids safe from the internet.***
When the kids were very small, we said, "We're going to put all the glowing things, all the glowing rectangles, at the very edges of our house." They are not going to be at the center of our house, and if you come to our home and walk in our first floor to the heart of the home where we spend most of our time as a family, there's almost nothing technological visible, and that's totally intentional. . . . The various screens are kept at the edge, and instead we've filled the center of the home, the space where we spend the most time, with things that actually require embodied engagement.

One of the really scary things we found out in the research is that the great majority of teenagers takes their phones to bed with them. The problem is that to be a healthy, human, embodied creature, you need, especially in your teen years, eight to nine hours of total rest. So one of the things we say in [*The Tech-Wise Family*] is, a rule we have at our house is [that] our devices go to bed before we do and we wake up before they do. . . . The device can keep gathering email. I'm not supposed to do that. I'm supposed to rest from that. And I think you need to help your kids to have that discipline.

# Exploring the Digital Family Dynamic

THE

## TECH-WISE
## FAMILY

Everyday Steps for Putting Technology
in Its Proper Place

MIN    MAX

ANDY CROUCH

AUTHOR OF *CULTURE MAKING*

With new insights and research from **Barna**

## Provides a framework for tough questions such as:

- What are some important family values to embrace in the digital age?
- Does our use of technology move us closer to the values we've embraced?
- Are familial relationships suffering as a result of technology's distractions?
- Has "real life" taken a backseat to virtual life?

Making wise choices about technology in the context of family is more than just setting internet filters and screen-time limits for children. It's about developing wisdom, character, and courage in the way we use digital media rather than accepting technology's promises of ease, instant gratification, and the world's knowledge at our fingertips. And that's true for everyone in the family, not just the kids. Drawing on in-depth original research from Barna, Andy Crouch (leading cultural commentator and the author of *Playing God* and *Culture Making*) shows how the choices we make about technology have consequences we may never have considered. For anyone who has felt their family relationships suffer or their time slip away amid technology's distractions, this book will provide a path forward to reclaiming "real life" in a world of digital devices.

**BakerBooks**
a division of Baker Publishing Group
Grand Rapids, Michigan

Available wherever
books and ebooks
are sold

# Community

How do you connect with the
world next door?

# 3 Trends Among Teen Friends

Conventional wisdom tells us teen friendships are important, and most parents see their adolescent children enter a stage in which peer relationships have tremendous influence (good or bad). But how do today's teens feel about their friends? And in this age of social media, where are they meeting people? A Barna study conducted in partnership with Impact 360 Institute explores these questions with American youth (ages 13–19).

### Teens Still Find Friends at School

Teens are most likely to form friendships at school. Overall, 86 percent indicate they have found friends in their classes. This is more common than school-based extracurricular activities (31%), athletic teams (25%), church or another place of worship (20%), their neighborhood (24%), or anywhere else (18%). Engaged Christians (76%) are less likely to find their friends in class (compared with 88% from other faiths, 86% of those with no faith). They are more likely to form friendships where they worship (66%), compared to teens of other faiths (19%) or no faith (5%).

### Friends Shape (But Don't Always Reflect) Identity

More than three-quarters of teens (76%) agree with the statement "My group of friends is very important to my sense of self." At the same time, young people do not necessarily feel like they are on the same page with everyone around them. Most teens (81%) say they often or occasionally interact with people who do not share or do not understand important parts of their identity. This may be a result of teens presenting limited glimpses of themselves via social media. Additionally, teens' identities are likely very much in flux at this point in their lives. But the survey also indicates another reason for this high likelihood of teens' not seeing themselves reflected in their social circles: a great openness to dissimilar people and beliefs.

### Teens Don't Avoid Differences

Nearly two-thirds of teens (63%) enjoy spending time with people who are different from them. Only 12 percent indicate they do not. A smaller majority (56%) is comfortable in this situation, while one in four (24%) is unsure.

Thirty-one percent say they don't share the same belief system as most of their friends. This is especially true for those of non-Christian faiths (50%, compared to 33% engaged Christians), who follow a minority religion and more likely encounter peers of different beliefs.

Most teens (65%) feel comfortable talking about their views even with those who believe differently. Only 15 percent are not comfortable (20% are unsure). This comfort exists among all faith segments, though engaged Christians (81%) are significantly more comfortable talking about their views than those of other faiths (66%) or no faith (64%), perhaps because these young Christians can feel confident in representing the religious majority in America and are often encouraged to share about their faith.

*n=1,450 teens ages 13–19 | November 2016*

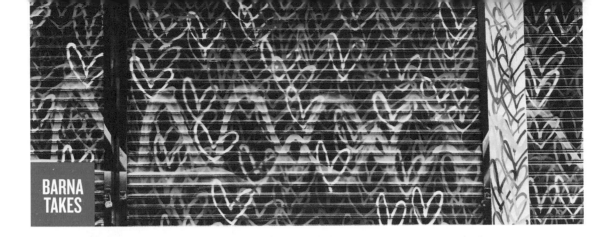

# The Multicultural World of Millennials

Sara Tandon
Barna Group
Research Assistant

As America becomes increasingly diverse, Millennials are trailblazers when it comes to growing up, working, and being in relationships with others who don't look like them. There are more minorities among Millennials than any other adult generation. According to the U.S. Census Bureau, over 40 percent of Millennials identify as an ethnic minority today, equating to twice the proportion of all Americans who identified as a minority just 30 years ago.[21] In a recent Barna study in partnership with Impact 360 Institute, 44 percent of Millennials said they often interact with people who do not share/understand important parts of their identities (compared to 36% Gen X, 26% Boomers, 20% Elders)—and this is good for them. Research of college campuses shows that exposure to diversity improves problem solving, critical-thinking ability, motivation, and intellectual self-confidence, leading to engaged and open-minded classroom discussion.[22]

Millennials aren't content to simply appreciate other cultures' art, food, and traditions; they want to learn how to deal with privilege, bias, and justice in America and collaborate with generations that may not understand their perspective. For example, Millennials are significantly more likely (85%) than other generations to be accepting of a family member marrying outside of their race.

As the child of immigrants, I see myself and my mixed or first-generation peers struggle to know which "circle" we fit in. We are encouraged to embrace our respective cultures—however, doing so can prove isolating. Although many of us grew up in America, know American history as our own, and love our country, our ancestry sets us apart from the majority. At the same time, many of us don't speak the language of our parents' country, follow their major religion, or even know the history of the heritage with which we identify.

A multicultural community is a gift, but it has its tense and lonely moments in a by no means post-racial society. It's easier to stay in our homogenous comfort zones. Indeed, the same Barna study found just 22 percent of Millennials agree strongly with the phrase "I usually enjoy spending time with people who are different from me." But Christ has called his Church to something more.

The Lord is the maker of us all and we are one in Christ, no matter where we come from (Proverbs 22:2; Galatians 3:28). Jesus tells us to love our neighbors, even if they come from a background against which we hold biases (explicit or implicit). The Church should cultivate Millennials' passion for racial reconciliation and dialogue about our mistakes and prejudices, because we know we have been redeemed. It should welcome people as Christ does, no matter their cultural identity. The Church is multicultural and multicolored, and its message transcends boundaries and borders.

# The Gift of Volunteering

According to the Bureau of Labor Statistics' National Time Use survey, roughly 6 percent of adults volunteer on any given day in America.[23] Those who serve usually spend between two and three hours at a stretch doing so.

In partnership with Thrivent Financial, Barna surveyed U.S. interested Christians (self-identified Christians, excluding those who have never been to a worship service and those who disagree that their faith is very important for their lives) and found that Gen X (28%) is the generation most likely to volunteer. Millennials are least likely (19%). When hours of service are accounted for, Boomers and Elders pull ahead of young adults: older Americans volunteer an average of 94 hours annually, more than twice the average of 36 hours among people under 35. This is likely, at least in part, because Elders are often no longer working full-time, giving them greater flexibility with their schedule.

If a person has volunteered their time on behalf of an organization within the past six months, they are more likely to associate volunteering with generosity. The reverse is also true: people who have not volunteered are less likely to think of volunteering as particularly generous.

When people think about serving, they also think beyond organizations. Some interviewees in Barna's qualitative study mentioned taking care of people inside or outside of their household. Other participants mentioned picking up slack at work, singing at funerals, doing housework for extended family members, and meal preparation as ways of volunteering.

Volunteering for an organization, however, is still considered to be more highly generous than volunteering for a person, perhaps because of perceptions of personal cost. For example, volunteering for an organization often requires specialized training, adherence to a set of rules and expectations, and a specific time commitment, compared to helping a friend or family member.

## Volunteers View Volunteering as an Act of Generosity

*(% chose "volunteering for an organization" from a list of options)*

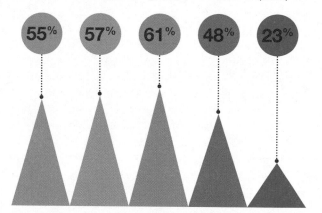

| 55% | 57% | 61% | 48% | 23% |
| Those who volunteered within the past week | Those who volunteered within the past month | Those who volunteered within the past six months | Those who haven't volunteered within the past six months | Those who never volunteer |

*n=1,556 U.S. interested Christians | July 2016*

BARNA
TAKES

# Gender Parity Is a Community Effort

Roxanne Stone
Barna Group
Editor in Chief

In a recent Barna survey (page 73), we found that evangelicals are the group least likely to say they support women in leadership. But one thing I like to point out about this survey is that evangelicals may be the only ones who are being honest—or, at least, self-aware! While most Americans say they are comfortable with women in leadership, the actions of many companies, individuals, conferences, and so on do not reflect such an amenable attitude.

The struggle for women to achieve parity in leadership is still very real—even though, at this point in history, their leadership seems inevitable. Women are more likely to have secondary educations than men, just as likely to have graduate degrees, and nearly as likely to have professional degrees. Younger Americans have grown

up in a time when women in leadership is generally accepted or even expected. Parents are raising their daughters with an expansive idea of their roles in the world. There is great enthusiasm and momentum for women in the workplace and in leadership. Unfortunately, I don't always think that enthusiasm comes with a realistic accounting of the cost—it's a bit naïve, in other words. It has primarily come in the form of women taking on roles men traditionally had, but the reverse has not also happened: men have not taken on the roles that women traditionally had. Neither have political nor economic structures shifted to accommodate that vacuum. Many of the traditional roles of women have been deemed less valuable because they do not have an immediate economic impact (e.g., child-rearing, volunteering, home finances, homemaking). Yet these are important roles for a healthy society, and they should not just be abandoned!

As just one example, Barna data show that women are much more likely than men to volunteer, but we also see that number dropping among employed Millennial women. The volunteer labor force in America—an important, if unpaid, foundation to a healthy society—has traditionally been made up of women. This includes everything from elder care, to after-school clubs, to churches. Many nonprofit organizations rely on unpaid labor and may find it increasingly difficult to secure willing volunteers.

At this point, either (primarily) women are still performing their traditional roles, alongside professional work—and burning out—or women are choosing to drop traditional roles altogether out of necessity or out of a modern value judgment against the significance of those activities. This is evidenced already in the increasing age of childbearing, and even the decision for many women not to get married or have children at all.

Helping women in the context of professional empowerment is one of the most complex undertakings I can think of today. There is no level of society and no institution that goes untouched by the implications of women in the workforce.

Here is where I see a unique, two-fold role for the Church: Not just to empower women in their professional roles of leadership, but also to encourage men's participation in the life of the household and community. Society cannot honestly survive gender parity in the workplace without also striving for a similar gender parity in the emotional labor required for the rest of life.

# It's a Casual Day in the Neighborhood

"Who is my neighbor?" an earnest lawyer asked Jesus in Luke 10:29. It's a question that is uniquely potent today as our densely populated cities, impersonal suburbs, and alienating modern technology make it harder to form and build communities based simply on proximity.

So how well are we connecting with those who share our buildings, street corners, and school districts? How much do we interact with our neighbors? Do we just wave hello and exchange pleasantries, or are we seeking out opportunities to eat with, celebrate with, and care for one another? Recent Barna research on the neighborly habits of American adults hits close to home.

## Most Neighborly Interactions Are Consistent and Casual

Whether they're leaving for work, bringing in the groceries, or mowing the lawn, the interactions Americans have with their neighbors—clarified for participants of this study as "those who live within easy walking distance"—happen either weekly (39%) or daily (28%). Those encounters are usually friendly but consist mostly of a brief greeting with very little interaction otherwise (37%). One in four (25%) has managed to become friends with one

or two of their neighbors. Eleven percent know most of their neighbors' names but would not call them friends. Perhaps the most telling data point is that small talk is the most common activity in which American adults participate with their neighbors (65%). This casual courtesy is cited twice as much as any other activity.

## Millennials Are More Social

The story is a bit more personal for younger generations, particularly Millennials. Not only are their interactions with neighbors more frequent (35% daily, compared to 20% of Boomers), their interactions often go beyond small talk. For example, they are the most likely generational group to say that some of their neighbors are like family (12%, compared to 3% and 5% among Boomers and Elders, respectively). They are also the most likely to take part in activities with their neighbors, including eating dinner together (30%), celebrating birthdays or holidays together (30%), gathering for neighborhood events (26%), and participating in hobbies together (23%). This could be a result of young Americans'

# The World Next Door

*Examining the habits that make a neighborhood*

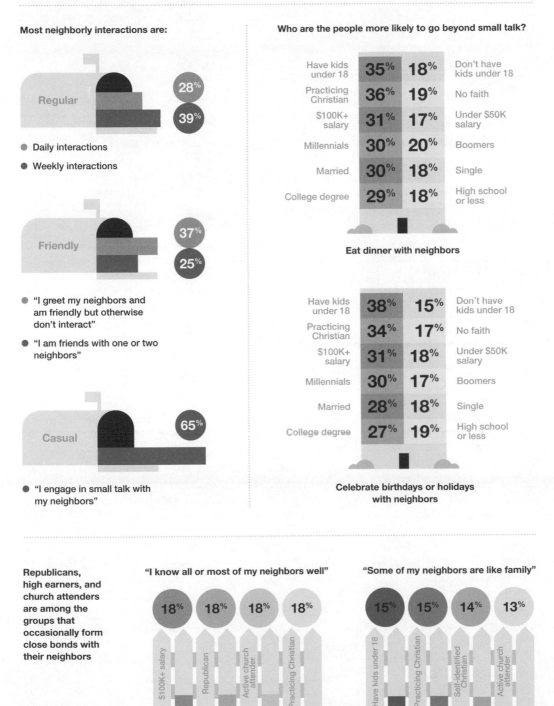

## Most neighborly interactions are:

**Regular** — 28% / 39%

- Daily interactions
- Weekly interactions

**Friendly** — 37% / 25%

- "I greet my neighbors and am friendly but otherwise don't interact"
- "I am friends with one or two neighbors"

**Casual** — 65%

- "I engage in small talk with my neighbors"

## Who are the people more likely to go beyond small talk?

| | | | |
|---|---|---|---|
| Have kids under 18 | 35% | 18% | Don't have kids under 18 |
| Practicing Christian | 36% | 19% | No faith |
| $100K+ salary | 31% | 17% | Under $50K salary |
| Millennials | 30% | 20% | Boomers |
| Married | 30% | 18% | Single |
| College degree | 29% | 18% | High school or less |

**Eat dinner with neighbors**

| | | | |
|---|---|---|---|
| Have kids under 18 | 38% | 15% | Don't have kids under 18 |
| Practicing Christian | 34% | 17% | No faith |
| $100K+ salary | 31% | 18% | Under $50K salary |
| Millennials | 30% | 17% | Boomers |
| Married | 28% | 18% | Single |
| College degree | 27% | 19% | High school or less |

**Celebrate birthdays or holidays with neighbors**

Republicans, high earners, and church attenders are among the groups that occasionally form close bonds with their neighbors

**"I know all or most of my neighbors well"**

- $100K+ salary — 18%
- Republican — 18%
- Active church attender — 18%
- Practicing Christian — 18%

**"Some of my neighbors are like family"**

- Have kids under 18 — 15%
- Practicing Christian — 15%
- Self-identified Christian — 14%
- Active church attender — 13%

*n=1,019 | May 2017*

mindsets—Millennials highly value their friendships and community—or a consequence of their stage of life, which may afford more free time and higher energy levels. Millennials also gravitate toward living in apartments and/or cities, where closer proximity can be conducive to neighborly interaction.

## From Saying Hello to Hanging Out
Celebrations are among the most common activities American adults claim they participate in with their neighbors. For instance, one-quarter says they eat dinner together (24%), celebrate birthdays or holidays together (23%), and gather for neighborhood events (22%). Attending church or a small group is an opportunity to get to know neighbors for 15 percent of respondents. Less rarely, neighbors participate in some kind of hobby together (14%).

## Socioeconomic Situation Affects Interaction
Socioeconomic status makes a significant difference to neighborly engagement. Those who make over $50K annually, have a college degree, or are employed full-time interact more with their neighbors. Greater resources and flexibility also provide occasional opportunities for social rapport. For instance, three in 10 (29%) with a college degree eat dinner with their neighbors compared to only 18 percent of those with only a high school education or less. Similarly, 18 percent of those who make $100K or more per year say they know all or most of their neighbors well, compared to only one in 10 (10%) among those with a salary under $50K.

## Elders Come through in Crises
If you've ever experienced a life-altering event, you know how important it is to be supported with meals, encouragement, and hospitality. And the good news is, people can usually rely on neighbors to have their back. Among all of the interactions that neighbors have, the second most common is helping one another during a crisis, transition, or illness (32%). This willingness to serve seems to increase with age; Elders are more likely to say they've assisted a neighbor during a crisis, transition, or illness (43%, compared to 28% of Millennials). This could be a result of greater empathy or simply a reality of growing older and gaining neighbors, as this age group has likely had more opportunity to live close to those in crisis over the years.

## Faith Drives Community Engagement
Mark 12:31 says, "Love thy neighbour as thyself" (KJV). The faithful are living out this commandment with enthusiasm. People of faith, whether they are born again, a practicing Christian, an active churchgoer, or simply a self-identified Christian, are not only more likely to interact with their neighbors regularly but also more likely to see them as family and know them well. And their interaction goes deeper than eating dinner or celebrating a birthday. For instance, almost four in 10 (38%) practicing Christians and an equal number of evangelicals (37%) say they have helped their neighbor during a crisis, transition, or illness.

## Families Help Form Community
Across the board, American adults who are married and/or have children under the age of 18 are up to two times more likely than those who are single or without children to engage their neighbors. For instance, three in 10 married adults (30%) eat dinner with their neighbors compared to only 18 percent of single adults. The same is true for those who have children under the age of 18; almost four in 10 (38%) say they celebrate birthdays or holidays together, compared to only 15 percent of those without young children at home. As more Millennials are getting married or raising young children, this family factor could reinforce their generally high neighborliness. Having children can certainly open up ample opportunities to engage other families. For example, those who are married (23%, compared to 8% of singles) and/or with children under 18 (32%, compared to 7% who don't) are more likely to interact based on the fact that their children or spouses are friends. In this way, those with families have a head start when it comes to community building.

# A Q&A on Gentrification

## with Dr. John M. Perkins

*Perkins, a noted civil rights leader and speaker, is founder and president emeritus of the John and Vera Mae Perkins Foundation. With his wife, Dr. Vera Mae, he's ministered through Christian community development, multiethnic churches, health centers, leadership development, schools, legal assistance, and more. Perkins is joined in this work by his daughters, now co-presidents of the foundation. He's written 16 books, received 13 honorary doctorates, and served under five U.S. presidents.*

## and Mac Pier

*Pier is the founder and CEO of The New York City Leadership Center, where he seeks to increase the leadership effectiveness of ministry and marketplace leaders. He is also the founder of Concerts of Prayer Greater New York, which serves to build bridges between pastors of various races and denominations across the New York metro area. Pier hopes to see the birth of citywide "gospel movements" that measurably impact a city's most vulnerable citizens.*

***Barna data show that white Millennials are gravitating toward living in urban and metropolitan areas. These areas have an opportunity to be melting pots but often still segregate. At the same time, we know Millennials are concerned about their role in racial reconciliation—particularly in cities, which are often the site of both radical inequality and integration. What does it look like for white residents and community leaders, especially Christian ones, to responsibly build diverse community without centering it around themselves or displacing others?***
**JMP:** Gentrification is one of the nastiest dynamics coming out of the time in which we live. It's a distribution issue, a consumer

issue, and an economic issue. We have been integrating the schools, colleges, and workplaces, but what hasn't been integrated are our social and spiritual lives. The white culture accepts black culture and the black culture accepts white culture only when it's to our best interests. We've got to help people become friends, because when you become friends, you will help one another. If we could lay hold of integration in relationship to the Great Commission, we could see the blessing of

God instead of fear of the other. We've got to hit the problem head-on, and that's usually painful. But it's in that pain that we find a way. We don't run away; we do what God says: fear not.

That's what makes eating together so important: the next thing you know, you've got conversation going. These are some divine signs. If we live more collectively, we can help some of the poor enfranchise themselves. Don't just move around. Limit your living space, live together, share your lives as much as you can together, minimize your costs, conserve more. How can we do these things and live together so we can enjoy the culture?

Don't think that "the program" is going to do it alone. It's got to be multifaceted, it's got to be holistic, it's got to speak to the pain of the people. We put more attention on our programs than we put on the sharing and explaining of this historical incarnation of the gospel message. I think the programs ought to be there, but we need to pray that God's presence is there with us too. We get reconciliation mixed up with today's secular issues, when reconciliation is first to God and then to our fellow man. The local church has a call from God to facilitate this reconciliation.

The mandate now is for the Church to obey the Great Commission. Now is the time for multicultural churches. "Go into all the world and preach the gospel" to the ethnicities that were broken up back in the time of Babel. Unite the Church back to God and back to each other and make us friends. We are at a crucial time, and what I want to do personally with the remainder of my life is to focus on churches that see this need but are culturally gridlocked.

**MP:** I have lived in New York City for 33 years. My neighborhood—Flushing, Queens—represents more than 100 languages. In our local church, First Baptist, over 60 languages are spoken.

Queens has been described as the most linguistically diverse community on the planet. One estimate is that over 90 percent of the active Christians in New York City are minority or immigrant. We have approximately 2,500 Hispanic churches, hundreds of Korean and Chinese churches, hundreds of African churches, and thousands of African American churches. The Church's center of gravity here would be the African American Church in Brooklyn.

Over the past 30 years, my team and I have built a multiracial, multidenominational prayer movement that has brought thousands of churches together and hundreds of thousands of leaders together. Together as the broader body of Christ, we have prayed together and done mission together. That mission has included church planting, humanitarian work, racial reconciliation dialogue, and community building in New York City.

For white Christians to be effective as bridge-builders and contributors in cities, the following things are important:

*Know your city.* You can only love that which you know. It is important to understand the city—its history, its demography, its spiritual story—and the current landscape of influential Christians across the pastoral, mission agency, and marketplace communities.

*Be present to your city.* What makes Christianity is the incarnation. Have a long-term commitment to live in the city and to intentionally live, if possible, in an ethnically diverse community. Take the initiative and plant a community of people who will live together. Remember that proximity to a community and your church, along with continuity, will be your greatest success factors in impacting your city. Be willing to be the "minority" as a white Christian in your context if that is what it takes to build the necessary trust. Trust is the difference-maker. The greatest deficit in any city is never money, space, or programs; it's always a lack of trust.

*Share power.* White Christians often have access to resources and opportunities that some minority leaders do not have. Think creatively about how to empower younger minority leaders by investing in their organizations and in them as leaders.

*Think young.* [I've heard that] most spiritual movements are started by leaders under the age of 28. One of the most impactful ways you can lead in your city is to be vigilant in identifying younger leaders during their high school and university years and in their early careers. If you can find a young leader who has a dream, familiarize yourself with that dream and invest in it.

I couldn't agree more with John Perkins's teaching, including his emphasis on reconciliation, relocation, and redistribution of opportunity from white Christians to the broader community.

# How Well Do You Know Your City?

CITIES

Barna

2017-2018

## Featuring 250+ data points such as:

- Religious affiliation
- Church attendance
- Bible engagement
- Faith habits
- Demographics

In an information-driven, post-Christian culture, you need the most current data to find new ways to partner with and serve your city. Equip yourself with the nation's most powerful database on faith so you can connect with the people in your area more effectively. These individual city reports are a simple and affordable way to access just the information you need. Now featuring 131 cities, regional comparative analysis, and over 76,000 interviews, Barna's Cities reports offer an expanded, new view of your area and help you gain a greater understanding of the people you're trying to serve. Barna's proprietary theolographic® data provide a unique resource for leaders, helping you navigate a changing world.

# The Truth about a Post-Truth Society

## Barna Identifies Five Reasons the World Is No Longer in Agreement about Anything

*The term "post-truth" is now often used to describe the current political climate in the United States, in which talking points, groupthink, and social media furor seem to eclipse the specifics about policy or people. But this phenomenon isn't merely tied to our engagement with the government; it has roots in spiritual, social, and cultural shifts that Barna has observed in multiple studies over several years. This post-truth world might be increasingly puzzling and polarizing, but it's not all that surprising. Over the following pages—Barna Trends 2018's feature story—Barna's editors, along with some experts in research, media, and ministry, identify some themes that help explain how we came to this point.*

## Distrust of Authority

Barna has seen a steady upward creep in America's distrust toward institutions and authority over the past decade. The promises coming from long-esteemed institutions—churches, government, media, universities—have come under scrutiny of late.

Only about one-third of Americans (36%) strongly believes churches "have their best interest at heart," a paltry 6 percent believe the government does, and only a slightly larger 16 percent trust that universities do. Nearly three-quarters of registered voters (72%) believe the United States is headed in the wrong direction. When it comes to the media, Americans' expectations are also low. Of the 2016 election, Americans describe the media's coverage as, at best, inconsistent (38%); just one-quarter believes it was fair and objective while a full 36 percent say it was the opposite: unfair and subjective.

This growing distrust is a result, perhaps, of promises serially broken, of authorities in those institutions falling short of ideals, and of an individualistic mindset that no longer believes these collective institutions have much to offer on a personal level. Whatever the mix of causes, the effect is an erosion of authority.

Instead, Barna sees people turning inward for truth: a majority of Americans (57%) and even 41 percent of practicing Christians say the only truth is "what is right for your life or works best for you." (This climbs to three-quarters among Millennials.) This relative morality is likely both a cause and effect of the erosion of authority. As individuals filter everything through the lens of their own lives and interests, they dismiss any claims counter to that truth. Simultaneously, as institutions disappoint people, they confirm people's experience of being unable to trust anyone outside themselves. Such attitudes ultimately lead to a world in which everyone is looking out primarily for themselves while the common good—or a common vision for a good society—withers.

*n–996 | July–August 2012; n–1,237 | July 2015*
*n=1,023 | September 2016; n=1,021 | February 2017*

# An Erosion of the Sacred

Parallel to the growing distrust of earthly institutions, Americans are increasingly questioning divine authorities as well. Namely, they are less and less likely to seek out guidance or truth from God (or any god) or from God's appointed manifestations: the Church and scripture.

While a majority of Americans still claims a religious faith (only 13% say they are atheists or agnostics), this belief in a higher power seems, for many, to be more theoretical than directly applicable to life. We see this evidenced in a variety of ways: a decreasing number of people who believe the Bible is sacred; an increase in the number who say instead that it is merely a book written by men; a decrease in the belief that the Bible is a source for moral truth; a skepticism toward the role pastors and the Church play in society; a decrease in church attendance; and, finally, a shift in how people view God.

In 1966, a *TIME* magazine cover famously asked, "Is God Dead?" In a tribute to that cover, in 2017, *TIME* released another feature asking, "Is Truth Dead?" The two questions are not unrelated. As

**People are finding it harder to trust authorities:**

*"This institution has my best interest at heart"*

**36%** Churches

**6%** Government

**16%** Universities

**And are instead turning inward for truth:**

*"Whatever is right for your life or works best for you is the only truth you can know"*

**57%** All adults

**74%** Millennials

**41%** Practicing Christians *(agree strongly or somewhat)*

## Scripture *Bible skepticism is on the rise*

- The Bible is considered sacred
- No literature is considered sacred
- The Bible is just another book of teachings written by men that contains stories and advice
- The Bible contains everything a person needs to know to live a meaningful life *(% who disagree)*

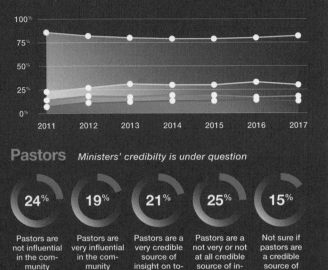

## Pastors *Ministers' credibilty is under question*

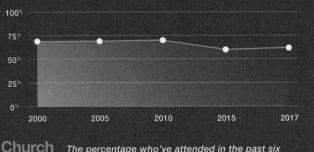

| 24% | 19% | 21% | 25% | 15% |
|---|---|---|---|---|
| Pastors are not influential in the community | Pastors are very influential in the community | Pastors are a very credible source of insight on today's issues | Pastors are a not very or not at all credible source of insight on today's issues | Not sure if pastors are a credible source of insight on today's issues |

## God *How many have an orthodox view of God?*

*"God is the all-knowing, all-powerful, perfect deity who created the universe and still rules it today"*

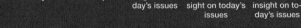

## Church *The percentage who've attended in the past six months has declined*

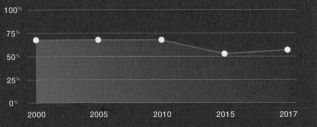

people turn away from both earthly authority and divine authority and as they appoint themselves arbiters of their own truth, the question then becomes, how are they deciding what is true for themselves? It's a question that manifests in the following three truths about a post-truth society.

*n=9,177 | 2009–2016;*
*n=1,025 | April–May 2015*

# 3 A Battle Between Feelings and Facts

One benefit to a skeptical society is the collective acknowledgment that facts can be bent to fit the agenda of the storyteller. For example, it is a fact that medical treatment of depression is on the rise. But is it because more people are depressed or because the stigma of depression has lowered and more people are willing to be treated? Experts have argued for both. And, for many of us, both sides can feel true, depending on our personal experiences. This is the role of feelings in discerning the application of truth. This is the role of emotional intelligence—a critical tool in navigating a post-truth society, because facts do not always equal truth.

This competition between facts is not new, but it is uniquely evidenced today. The old gatekeepers of power are no longer the only ones who publicly interpret facts. Now, through the internet, everyone feels empowered to do so.

This means, though, that consumers can find "facts" being interpreted in contradictory ways on every possible issue: climate change, abortion, racism, the prison system, welfare, immigration, health care. A deluge of information, arguments, and counter-arguments makes discernment of truth incredibly difficult.

So an inevitable battle between the head and the heart begins: can you *know* truth or do you *feel* truth? Is truth based on an objective understanding of the facts, or an internal intuition derived from experience? Is the application of truth about insisting on what is right or about discerning what someone needs in a situation?

When it comes to moral truth, at least, Americans seem divided on their answers: two-thirds of American adults either believe moral truth is relative to circumstances (44%) or have not given it much thought (21%). About one-third, on the other hand, believes moral truth is absolute (35%). Yet, whether or not they believe in moral absolutes, a sizable chunk of the population agrees it's not OK to challenge another person's beliefs (40% agree, 20% are not sure). And a full nine in 10 Americans (89%) say when it comes to people's life choices, criticism is off limits.

Where does this leave us in our pursuit of truth? For Christians, a love of truth must be rooted in a love of God—and scripture admonishes that such a love must be based not just on what we can know with our mind, but also that which we feel and perceive: "You must love the Lord your God with all your heart, all your soul, and all your mind." The second greatest commandment is to love our neighbor as ourselves (Matthew 22:37–38). Discernment, it seems, is a matter of fusing both fact and feeling—both love of truth and love of neighbor.

> ## Is moral truth absolute or relative?

**35%** Absolute

**44%** Relative

**21%** Have never thought about it

n=1,237 | July 2015; n= 1,000 | August 2015; n=1,557 | November 2016

# 4 Unbelievable News

"Fake news" was the major headline of the past year. While Barna has detailed our research on this in depth elsewhere (see page 26), the phenomenon must be included as a significant contributor to a post-truth society. When patently false news spreads like wildfire among those eager to believe it, the value of telling the truth diminishes. Instead, we find, the better storyteller wins. Especially if that storyteller has access to a large audience via social media, email forwards, or questionable news outlets.

In the 2016 election, there were real scandals associated with each presidential candidate (see page 36)—and there were verifiably fake ones that just would not go away (perhaps most notoriously, the "pizzagate" story that insisted the Clintons were running a sex ring through a pizza chain). In the past, such "news" existed alongside sightings of aliens and photoshopped bodies of celebrities doing dubious things in outlets like the *National Enquirer*. Readers knew what they were getting: entertaining stories. Some people believed the stories, but most knew because of the source that it was not verifiable, objective journalism.

Today, such news stories have the power to impact national events, in large part because readers either aren't sure how to verify the news they read—or aren't taking the time to do so before they digest it and spread it to the next person. This coupled with *where* people are receiving their news has created an environment ripe for manipulation.

Consider that when asked what kind of news media people are most likely to share, social media posts tie with traditional reporter-written articles as the top response (25% each). This is the case even though the news people say they are most likely to consume are live broadcasts (54%) and traditional written journalism (44%), compared to 34 percent who primarily consume news via social media. Though a plurality (36%) says they verify reports by comparing to multiple sources, the tendency to share social media posts as news points to a preference for—or at least allows opportunity to perpetuate—more salacious, opinion-forward headlines and reporting.

When it comes to whom people trust as credible sources for news, reporters top the list (39%), but are followed closely by the self: nearly a third (32%) says they trust nobody, only their own instincts. The next response is friends, family members, or peers (27%), again revealing a propensity to turn inward—or to one's tribe—for truth when outside authorities are no longer seen as reliable.

*n=1,021 | February 2017*

# 5 The Rise of Tribalism

While an unrestrained individualism is certainly at the root of the themes explored so far, it is also true that the human species is a social one: individuals never fully exist in isolation. People seek out community, and in a society based on individual self-interest, the community people inevitably seek out is one that looks and believes as they do.

Group solidarity can be a good thing—it can lead to mobilization, to action, to survival. However, in an increasingly pluralistic society, it can also create deep divisions and an "us vs. them" mentality. It leads to echo chambers, ideological stubbornness, and a vulnerability to subjective thinking.

Conversely, Barna has found in many instances, that positive exposure to those outside one's group leads to increased empathy. As one example, a quarter of people who spend time with Muslim friends (24%) strongly disagrees that the majority of terrorism is perpetrated

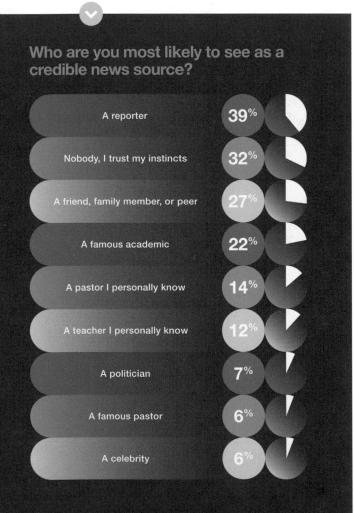

**Who are you most likely to see as a credible news source?**

| | |
|---|---|
| A reporter | 39% |
| Nobody, I trust my instincts | 32% |
| A friend, family member, or peer | 27% |
| A famous academic | 22% |
| A pastor I personally know | 14% |
| A teacher I personally know | 12% |
| A politician | 7% |
| A famous pastor | 6% |
| A celebrity | 6% |

by Muslims (see page 200). This is compared to just 13 percent among those who do not spend time with Muslim friends.

Unfortunately, most Americans do not interact much with those outside their group. In a 2015 Barna study, most people admitted their friends are mostly similar to them in religion, ethnicity, political ideology, socioeconomic group, stage of life, and so on.

How does this tribalism play out in relation to a post-truth society? Primarily, it causes people to believe whatever their group believes, regardless of external evidence or opinion to the contrary. For instance, after the 2016 election, Barna asked Americans about a series of major headlines that came out during the campaigns (see page 37). In every instance,

Republicans are less likely to say their nominee's scandals (Donald Trump) impacted their decision to vote for him and Democrats are less likely to say their nominee's scandals (Hillary Clinton) impacted their decision to vote for her. Conversely, Democrats say stories related to Trump considerably affected their vote while Republicans say stories related to Clinton considerably affected their vote. This unquestioning loyalty to "the group" results in a lack of accountability toward its leaders and an unchecked enmity toward the opposition's leaders.

A group of people searching for or clinging to truth is stronger than an individual doing so. The danger, however, lies in tribal exceptionalism—when every group that isn't your own becomes a threat. In a diverse society, such thinking is increasingly dangerous and divisive. Human history is littered with horrific examples of mob mentality that resulted in great evils justified by so-called "truths" propagated in the name of group unity or survival. Tribalism, then, poses one of the most severe threats in a post-truth society, at the very least keeping groups from welcoming or considering another, let alone learning from them.

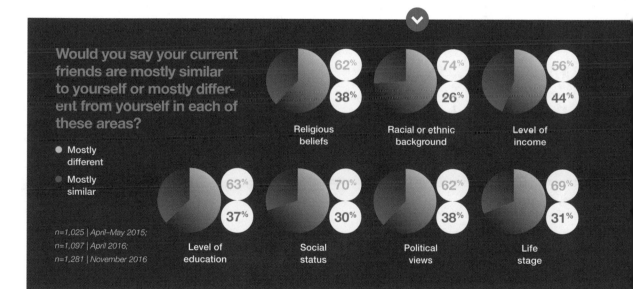

Would you say your current friends are mostly similar to yourself or mostly different from yourself in each of these areas?

● Mostly different
● Mostly similar

n=1,025 | April–May 2015;
n=1,097 | April 2016;
n=1,281 | November 2016

Religious beliefs — 62% / 38%
Racial or ethnic background — 74% / 26%
Level of income — 56% / 44%
Level of education — 63% / 37%
Social status — 70% / 30%
Political views — 62% / 38%
Life stage — 69% / 31%

*If these are the milestones and mindsets that have led to a post-truth culture, what's next? Even now, technological advancements present the possibility of manipulating audio and video in real time—will generations to come be able to believe the things right in front of them? Is it possible to restore trust—or to restore faith—in religion, the press, science, public figures, institutions? These questions have far-reaching implications for the United States, the world, and the Church. The challenge ahead—particularly for leaders—is to steward knowledge and influence with unprecedented care and compassion. It may be the only hope for a society that not only recognizes facts, but believes in truth.*

# What's the Point of Polls?

Brooke Hempell
Barna Group
Senior Vice President
of Research

In July 2016, my family and I traveled to the United Kingdom to visit friends and colleagues for a few weeks. We arrived in Central London, tired from an overnight flight, to be greeted by an enormous protest blocking all routes to our hotel. We would soon find out this was one picture of the response to Brexit. London was largely in shock, as almost no one thought the U.K. would actually vote to exit its collective European neighbors, and few in the most populous city had taken the vote seriously. After all, pollsters had largely failed to predict this turn of events.

Fast-forward six months, and a similar scenario played out in the United States. Americans watched, many incredulously, as Donald Trump was elected president in a vote that seemed to defy nearly all polling predictions. How did so many polls get it so wrong? The answer lies in a combination of social science principles and modern media phenomenon.

First, let's review the constraints of polling. A poll's validity relies on a few things, each of which is fraught with potential missteps that can significantly impact the credibility of a poll.

## 1. The Representativeness of the Sample

First, in our current environment, getting a sample of Americans who actually represent widespread popular opinion can be harder than you would imagine. It used to be that a good poll relied on randomly dialing home phone numbers across a geographically diverse listing. Today, with 90 percent of Americans owning a cell phone,[24] and half of households no longer having a landline,[25] sampling from the "phone book" is no longer representative. Even though polling companies have drastically increased the proportion of cell phones in their polls, this method is still challenging because people's area codes often no longer represent where they currently live, many numbers are unlisted, and many people will not answer a call from an unknown caller.

Also, people in rural areas or over age 65 are significantly more likely to have a landline; Millennials, Hispanics, people in cities, and those in a lower socioeconomic bracket are less likely to have a landline. This is a very important balance to get right for, say, an election poll, as the former group (with higher landline penetration) are more likely to vote Republican and the latter group (with lower landline penetration) are more likely to vote Democrat.

Further challenging polls, the typical response rate (the percentage of people called who will agree to complete a phone survey) has dropped, from one-third of Americans in 1997 to just 9 percent today, according to Pew Research data. More people unwilling to answer a phone poll means more difficulty in ensuring a representative sample via phone.

In many cases, it can be easier to get a representative sample online than via phone, as more households have internet access than a landline. However, people who are older, Hispanic, African American, or live in rural areas are less represented online.

Considering all of the above, getting to an equal starting place—a representative sample of the population—is not that easy!

## 2. Understandable and Unbiased Questions

Next, the validity of questions asked can drastically skew findings. For example, a 2006 *New York Times* poll asked, "Do you favor a gasoline tax?" Just 12 percent of adults answered yes. But when the poll asked, "Do you favor a gasoline tax to reduce U.S. dependence on foreign oil?," 55 percent answered yes. "Do you favor a gasoline tax to reduce global warming?" yielded 63 percent agreement.[26] Political pollsters are notorious for asking biased questions to get responses that will produce evidence of support for lobbying or political agendas. When examining polling results, it's essential to be on the lookout for bias in question wording.

Other items that can bias responses include the order of questions (other questions in a survey may bias later question responses) and simply conducting an interview via phone (a respondent is sometimes compelled to give the more "socially acceptable" answer instead of their real opinion when a live person is on the other end of a call).

## 3. The Reliability of Respondents' Predictions of Their Future Behavior

Finally, and very importantly, predicting future behavior is extremely difficult! In market research, when we aim to predict future uptake of a product or endorsement for a nonprofit, for example, we ask about propensity to do various things and then construct probability models with multitudinous caveats and assumptions built into them. This is because people are very bad at predicting their future behavior, especially around something like choosing a political candidate.

Many factors can influence one's decision up until the last minute, and inevitably the decision will be much more emotional than logical (an idea which gave birth to an entire field of study: behavioral economics).

Furthermore, the action of going to vote is also unpredictable. Again, this is true of any model or research that tries to predict behavior: despite our greatest intentions, "life gets in the way." Over half of eligible voters (61%) actually cast a ballot in November 2016, yet, if polled, presumably more than this would have listed their intended vote. In studies on this topic, people give many reasons why they do not make it to the polls: they couldn't get off work, got stuck in traffic, had a sick kid at home, or simply didn't feel like making the effort on the day. In the 2016 presidential election, for instance, the latter excuse is commonly cited for lower than anticipated Democratic voters.

Additionally, factors such as media coverage, peer influence, a compelling Sunday sermon, or one's own conscience can sway people in the opposite direction as well—to go out and vote when they might not have been so inclined in the past. In sum, predicting *whether* someone will vote at all is probably more difficult than predicting *how* they will vote in an election.

So, with all these risk factors, is there any point in polls?

At Barna, well, perhaps we're showing our own bias, but we believe polls have an important role to play in understanding our current "post-truth" context—at least to the degree that they illuminate and interpret popular public opinion rather than attempt to predict it.

# A Q&A on Teaching Truth

## with Jonathan Morrow

*Morrow (DMin) has worked with students and parents for 15 years. He is currently the director of cultural engagement at Impact 360 Institute and an adjunct professor of apologetics at Biola University. Morrow has written several books including* Welcome to College *and contributed to the* Apologetics Study Bible for Students.

***When it comes to speaking into moral topics and concerns, what will it take for parents, pastors, and the Church as a whole to have influence and credibility with young people moving forward?***

We first need to be authentic. We need to be ourselves and not come across as uncaring or appear to be super spiritual at church and then approach life like the rest of our culture the rest of time. They will sniff hypocrisy a mile away. Nothing builds credibility with a teenager faster than having something thoughtful and careful to say when they ask tough questions. It will make all the difference if you don't just give them a "the-Bible-says-so," spiritually cliché type of answer but instead help them understand and think Christianly about an issue or topic. They need reasons, evidence, and good explanations. Draw them out with questions and press them on their initial answers. If Christianity is true, then all of life is connected. We need to help them connect the dots when it comes to spiritual and moral reality. Students need to understand that just because you believe something doesn't make it true. Sincerity is not enough, because we all know we can be sincerely wrong.

Knowing and understanding the truth is essential for following Christ. Young Christians don't just need to know *what* they believe, as important as that is—they also need to know *why*. Most students who have grown up in Christian homes, youth groups, or homeschool environments can repeat a lot of "right answers." But what they need are reasons for those right answers so they can deepen their faith and be ready to engage others who challenge their core beliefs.

***What can we learn from young people's willingness to embrace "grey" thinking?***

We live in an ever-changing and increasingly complex world. One of the opportunities that we have with the next generation is to see this complexity and understand various competing perspectives. That is the good side to "grey" thinking. Teenagers can help us gain valuable perspective and context because they naturally see things we don't see. At the same time, the kind of "grey" thinking we need to avoid is the kind that says there is no truth in a moral or spiritual claim that might make us uncomfortable or even be difficult to understand or apply. As Christians, complexity should lead us to greater compassion and careful thinking, not relativism. Encouraging people to live in our world as if there is no objective right and wrong is not compassionate. After all, this is God's world, and flourishing as a human being involves cooperating with God's good design.

# A Q&A on Journalism's Future

## with Tom Krattenmaker

*Krattenmaker is a member of* USA Today's *Board of Contributors, an author and columnist specializing in religion in public life, and communications director at Yale Divinity School. His most recent book is* Confessions of a Secular Jesus Follower. *You can follow him on Twitter @tkrattenmaker.*

***Is there such a thing as truly objective journalism? What unique roles do you think both unbiased and biased media can play?***

Even if I write one of my pieces in the most objective manner possible, the very process of choosing what to write about, and how, is shot through with subjectivity. The same is true with media in general. What constitutes news? What is emphasized and deemphasized in a story, and which voices are included and which are not? Subjectivity plays a role in all this.

Objectivity is too high a standard to achieve—but that does not mean we cannot strive for and achieve other important objectives. Like being fair, even-handed, honest, and willing to convey information that is inconvenient not only to our audiences but also to ourselves as conveyors of that information.

***What can be done for media—regardless of its ties or biases—to regain credibility with a wary public?***

Here's a glib answer: The media will have to stop getting major things wrong! It'll take time, effort, and a strong body of work for mainstream media to restore the credibility lost by their whiffing so badly on the 2016 presidential election. Major media will have to do more, too, to make it clear that they serve all citizens, irrespective of their political and cultural affiliations.

But consumers of media also have a role to play in this restoration project. The public must stop dismissing coverage it dislikes as "fake" or "biased." If we reject plainly accurate, verifiable information because it challenges our worldview, who then is truly guilty of being ruled by bias?

***What would you recommend as a "balanced diet" when it comes to the ways in which people receive news?***

The key is to push ourselves to go outside our comfort zone and consume media that we would not naturally consume. For example, I "force" myself to watch Fox News and read the newsfeed of the Christian Broadcasting Network from time to time. It can be a jolt to the system for a northeast liberal (and former Portland, Oregon, resident) like me. It can even be a little bewildering, but that's good. It's good to receive reminders that what I see as obviously true and good can look so different from another perspective.

Generally, I think you're spot-on with the premise of your question. It's all about balance. This means sampling more liberal media if you're a conservative, and vice-versa. It means balance between the formats we engage: quick-hit hard

news coverage balanced with books, social media balanced with old-school newspapers and magazines (on and offline), online interactions balanced with face-to-face conversations in which we can process all that media and make sense of it in the company of conversation partners.

***What are the limits of even the strongest reporting and journalism, in regard to how it can be understood and used by its audience?***
As crucial as they are to the functioning of democracy, facts alone do not change hearts and spur positive social change. Stories are what move people. That said, journalism encompasses a broad range of forms and styles, very much including stories and portraits of human beings and human lives. Some of these can be quite illuminating and even inspiring.

Who knows? Maybe the heart of a dedicated Islamophobe can be changed by a story about a Muslim fellow citizen who loves America unabashedly and is serving her/his community irrespective of their religion, or who is serving bravely in the U.S. military. Who knows? Maybe the most ardent secularist can be touched by the tale of a devout Christian taking principled action at considerable cost to herself or himself to serve vulnerable people. So from that standpoint—forgive

my idealism—there really aren't limits. The main limit I can see is the one we impose on journalism—and ourselves. The journalism you avoid has no ability to touch you and move you.

***What is the "next frontier" when it comes to religion reporting in America? What are the trends you're watching that are affecting your subjects or your industry at large?***
I've been reading numerous articles and a book exploring the nexus between faith and technology. There's so much talk now about things like the singularity, the possibilities of technological immortality or resurrection, life on other planets, and so on. These have huge implications for religion; they could profoundly destabilize traditional religion. It's my sense that religion journalism is only beginning to grapple with these fascinating stories.

However, going back over several years and looking into the future, the trend most striking to me is the religious disaffiliation we hear so much about. Similar to the faith and technology nexus, we are only beginning to see and understand disaffiliation and its ramifications. These ramifications are huge, of course—not just for religious people and institutions but for society as a whole. As religion recedes in the Western world, what will fill that vacuum? That's a big question that hangs over our time, and an important frontier in the religion reporting that's to come.

**BARNA TAKES**

# Speaking Truth in a Post-Truth Society

David Kinnaman
Barna Group
President

I was first introduced to the "propinquity effect" in a college social psychology course. (It's fun to say aloud. *Pro-PING-quity.*) The idea is that we grow to like and to be like people around us. It's essentially an adaptation of the old adage "Birds of a feather flock together." Instead "Birds who flock together start to look alike."

When we hang out on a regular basis with sisters and brothers who prioritize following Christ, we're more likely to do likewise. No wonder the writer of Hebrews was so adamant about regular church gatherings (see 10:23–25); keeping faith with faithful people fosters faithfulness to Christ.

But propinquity has at least two potential downsides. Combined, they make speaking truth in our current cultural climate a challenging proposition.

The first is familiar to anyone who survived junior high: peer pressure. We're likelier to do something if everybody's doing it. (See: fidget spinners.) When people around us believe an idea, we're more likely to believe it—even if "it" is untrue. And in so believing, we increase the likelihood that those close to us will start believing it too.

A recent example comes from new Barna research, conducted in partnership with Impact 360 Institute, that shows a majority of teens (58%) agrees somewhat or strongly that morality changes over time based on society. A similar percentage (53%) feel right and wrong depends on an individual's beliefs. The peer-pressure effect of propinquity is one big reason our society can legitimately be called "post-truth": as more and more people believe those around them, actual truth becomes irrelevant. "Truth" is what people close to me feel is true at any given moment.

The second potential drawback of propinquity is the "echo-chamber effect," which is scientifically tested on social media 24 hours a day. We prefer people like us—making it hard to listen to and understand anyone who is different. In research for my book *Good Faith*, Barna found that evangelicals are more likely than other U.S. adults to say they would find it difficult to have a natural, normal conversation with someone unlike themselves. Nearly nine out of 10 evangelicals would have a hard time chatting with a Muslim (87% vs. 73% all adults) or a person who identifies as LGBT (87% vs. 52% all adults).

Can you see the danger? The more we become like the people already close to us, the crazier everybody else seems to get. At some point, "we" lose the ability to speak truth in a way "they" can understand, because we (and they) live in conversational ghettos full of people who only speak our language and exert enormous pressure on each other—whether we know it or not—to keep it that way.

In stark contrast, Christ's incarnation demonstrates exactly how God intends his people to use the awesome power of propinquity: "The Word became flesh and made his dwelling among us" (John 1:14 NIV).

"We" get close to "them"—not the other way around. Incarnational propinquity is how we earn a chance to speak the truth.

# Trending in ...
# Faith

The final section of *Barna Trends* is anchored in groundbreaking studies of the men and women in the pulpit, as well as the practices of the people attending their services. But it also goes beyond Sunday sermons and church walls to ask questions about the broader landscape of religion and spirituality: What will it take for Generation Z to cultivate an enduring faith? Can someone truly "love Jesus but not the church?" How do Christians in America regard minority religions and their sacred texts? These pages highlight the vulnerabilities of the Church in modern society while also bearing witness to the ways in which it can remain a powerful force for good.

In FAITH, Barna looks at trends such as:
- how people see, study, and value the Bible today
- mindsets of the "spiritual but not religious"
- the Church's present relationship to liturgy
- motivations behind congregants' giving habits
- pastors' well-being, from the time of calling to retirement

**Practices**

**Church**

**Beliefs**

**Leadership**

**Global Religion**

Featuring:

Francis Chan, Inga Dahlstedt, Chuck DeGroat, Mark DeYmaz, Brooke Hempell, Cheryl Bridges Johns, Sharon Ketchum, David Kinnaman, Stanley McChrystal, Gareth Russell, Roxanne Stone

# At a Glance: Faith

# Youth Pastors' Approach to Small Groups

A slight majority of youth pastors (53%) reports that the small groups provided to their ministry are coed rather than gender-specific groups that separate boys and girls (47%). A Barna study in partnership with Impact 360 Institute shows that this seems to be an approach leaders become more comfortable with over time; 54 percent of youth pastors under 45 say these groups are divided between boys and girls, a percentage that drops to 40 among youth leaders over age 45. The shift is similar to the one seen when looking at tenure (54% of those with less than five years vs. 41% of those with more than 10 years). Overall, ministers are much more comfortable splitting students up by age or grade (74%). Almost all of these small groups (86%) meet weekly and more than half (55%) do so outside of the regular youth ministry time. Youth pastors say adult volunteers are often responsible for these meetings with teens (85%), though half of the youth pastors themselves (51%) also lead, and one in four (23%) points to parents of teens as small group guides. A minority of youth pastors (16%) reports peer-led small groups in their ministry.  *n=335 U.S. youth pastors | November 2016–January 2017*

# The Motivations of Expanding Churches

Geographical outreach, mission, and calling are the three primary reasons cited by most churches as motivation to pursue various expansion strategies. Facility constraints or accommodating growth barely register as primary reasons. Even among the secondary reasons for adopting their particular model, these drivers are mentioned by only one-quarter or less of any multisite or church-planting group.

*n=222 multisite or church-plant leaders | March 7–April 6, 2016*

# 29 Percent of Pastors Don't Attend Conferences

In today's conference culture, pastors can attend any number of leadership and ministry gatherings, complete with large venues, high-profile speaking lineups, and big-name sponsors. However, a sizable minority of ministers has not experienced such an event. When Barna asked U.S. Protestant pastors which national or regional ministry conferences they regularly attend, three in 10 (29%) say they go to none.

*n=600 U.S. Protestant pastors | October 27– November 17, 2016*

**53%** of youth pastors keep boys and girls together for small group ministry

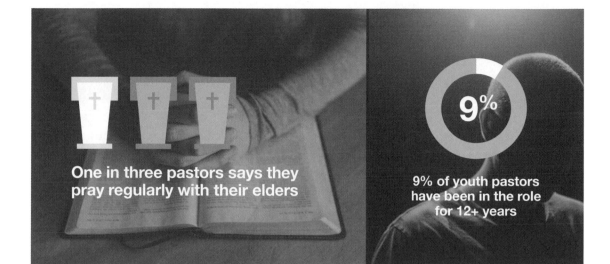

One in three pastors says they pray regularly with their elders

9%

9% of youth pastors have been in the role for 12+ years

## Prayer Is a Rarity Among Church Teams

A significant red flag revealed in Barna's *The State of Pastors* report, produced in partnership with Pepperdine University, is how infrequently pastors and elders pray together. A mere third of U.S. Protestant pastors (34%) says their relationship with their elders could be characterized by frequent prayer together. Given that 81 percent of pastors also identify prayer as essential to spiritual development and pastors are more likely than the general population to feel lonely or isolated, the study poses a follow-up question: How can pastors strengthen the practice of spiritual disciplines in the teams with whom they lead?

*n=297 U.S. Protestant pastors | October 2016*

## The Short Tenure of Youth Ministers

Among youth pastors surveyed by Barna in partnership with Youth Specialties and YouthWorks, a plurality—almost one in five (18%)—has only been in youth ministry at their current church for one year. Thirteen percent have held their current ministry post for three years. Beyond that length of tenure, percentages generally taper off. Just one in 10 (9%) has been pastoring their youth group for 12 or more years.

*n=352 U.S. youth pastors | March 15–June 16, 2016*

The greatest roadblock [that keeps spiritual leaders from finding time to invest in their own spiritual growth], I believe, is a lack of good models. As evangelical leaders, we have inherited a history of activism that goes back more than 200 years. Our great gift is mission: mobilizing believers and leading people to Christ. But this great gift can also be a liability. Spiritually indispensable concepts like silence, slowness, solitude, and being (instead of doing) are difficult for most of us who are heirs to evangelicalism's activist impulse. That is why I'm convinced we must learn from the wider Church tradition—Roman Catholic, Orthodox, and Protestant—and mine the spiritual riches of our shared history."—*Pete Scazzero, founder of New Life Fellowship Church in Queens, New York, in Barna's* The State of Pastors

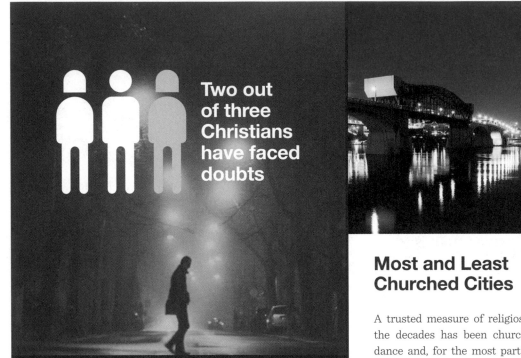

Two out
of three
Christians
have faced
doubts

## Most and Least Churched Cities

A trusted measure of religiosity over the decades has been church attendance and, for the most part, Americans are attending church less. Based on Barna's most recent data, almost four in 10 (38%) Americans are active churchgoers, slightly more (43%) are unchurched, and around one-third (34%) is dechurched.

## What We Do with Doubt

Two-thirds of self-identified Christians or past Christians (66%) admit to experiencing a season of spiritual doubt. More than a quarter (26%) still find themselves doubting, while 40 percent feel they have worked through their faith crisis. More than a third (35%) say they have never faced spiritual doubts. A common response during times of doubt was to quit attending church (46%). Three in 10 stopped reading the Bible (30%) or praying (28%). One in four (24%) ceased discussing spirituality, God, or religion with their friends and families, but such community is also the place they were most likely to turn for help (40%). Twenty-nine percent sought answers in the Bible and one in five looked to church (21%), a spouse (19%), or a pastor or spiritual leader (18%). Some addressed their doubt with spiritual or religious books (16%), online resources (12%), counseling (5%), or conferences and retreats (3%). For the most part, these approaches worked; 52 percent of these Christians say their faith is now stronger or at least unchanged (28%). Just 8 percent say it is weaker, and 12 percent lost their faith entirely.

Topping the list of the most churched cities in America are:
1. Chattanooga, TN: 59%
2. Salt Lake City, UT: 59%
3. Augusta/Aiken, GA: 57%
4. Baton Rouge, LA: 57%
5. Birmingham/Anniston/
   Tuscaloosa, AL: 56%

The top 5 dechurched cities include:
1. San Francisco/Oakland/
   San Jose, CA: 47%
2. Boston/Manchester, MA: 46%
3. Seattle/Tacoma, WA: 45%
4. Portland/Auburn, ME: 45%
5. Springfield/Holyoke, MA: 43%

*n=888 self-identified Christians or past Christians | June 5–9, 2017*

*n=76,505 | 2000–2016*

# Facility Needs of New Congregations

When it comes to building or expanding a church, what are the essential physical needs of a congregation when facing budget restraints? According to a Barna study in partnership with Cornerstone Knowledge Network, church plants most highly prioritize children's ministry spaces, suggesting that many of these communities tend to attract and serve young families. While multisite churches also count children's ministry as their number one priority, audio/visual capabilities and lighting are an important investment for them. Four out of 10 multisite churches overall prioritize these technical aspects, perhaps because they often rely on broadcasts or videos to deliver sermons or other community information.

*n=222 multisite or church-plant leaders| March 7–April 6, 2016*

## 84%

of church planting strategists financially prioritize children's ministry spaces when expanding

Most people say, 'Well, I'm not a racist.' We've really demeaned [the meaning of racism] down to racial slurs. When you support a racist system—when you support a judicial system or an education system that's not for everyone, that doesn't have the marginalized at the heart of what we're doing—then you are creating marginalization, you are creating a system that's not for everyone. You're looking out for one group of people. Those are the things we have to understand: these barriers that separate us. We really have to have the same terminology.

". . . I think as a pastor one of the things that you need to think about first is yourself and really start looking at where those blind spots are. I think we have to improve our cultural intelligence, our culture competency. Especially if you are from the majority culture, you need to start looking to people of color. You need to start listening to people of color who are really experts in this. This is no new issue. . . . You can't learn from yourself when you're bringing your prejudice into the conversation. I think it's really good for pastors to really listen to those voices that are unheard. . . . The work of reconciliation is not easy. It's a difficult work; it's worth it."

—*Latasha Morrison, activist and founder of Be the Bridge, at Barna and Pepperdine University's The State of Pastors 2017 event*

# Practices

How Christians today publicly express
and privately cultivate their faith

# Annual Reports of Bible Engagement

Barna's annual State of the Bible survey, in partnership with American Bible Society, examines behaviors and beliefs about the Bible among U.S. adults. The results show that Americans overwhelmingly believe the Bible is a source of hope and a force for good even as they express growing concern for our nation's morals. These and other snapshots are included in our top findings from 2017.

### Bible Engagement Is Stabilizing
Levels of Bible engagement appear to be stabilizing after the brief dip in the Engaged segment since 2013 and the steady increase in Skeptics in recent years. (Refer to chart for definitions of Bible engagement.) Levels of the Neutral segment have remained somewhat steady since 2011, hovering around the low- to mid-twenties. After a significant drop from 2011 to 2012, the Friendly segment has also remained steady in the high thirties and still represents the largest segment of the American population. In general, women are more likely to be Engaged than men (24%, compared to 17%).

### Engagement Increases with Age
The older you are, the more likely you are to be engaged with the Bible. That is, the average age increases with each Bible engagement segment, from Skeptic to Engaged. The average age among Skeptics is 43, which increases to 45 for Neutral, 47 for Friendly, and 53 for Engaged. Nearly one-quarter of Millennials (24%)

qualifies as Skeptics, compared to 14 percent who are Engaged. Just one in eight Elders (12%) is a Skeptic, compared to 27 percent among this age group who are Engaged.

### Bible Users Increasingly Drawn Beyond Print
The way Americans engage with the Bible is changing. Though most Bible readers (91%) still prefer to use a print version of the Bible when engaging with scripture, an equal number (92%) report using a Bible format other than print in the past year. Use of technology-related formats is on the rise. More than half of users now search for Bible content on the internet (55%) or smartphones (53%), and another 43 percent use an app on their phones. Since 2011, the use of every other Bible format has increased.

### Most Households Own a Bible
The vast majority of households owns at least one Bible (87%), a proportion that has stayed relatively consistent since 2011. Even the majority (62%) of Hostile and Skeptic (67%) households

## Bible Engagement Definitions

**20%**

**Bible Engaged**
- View the Bible as a) the actual or b) the inspired word of God with no errors, or as c) the inspired word of God with some errors
- Read, use, or listen to the Bible four times a week or more

**38%**

**Bible Friendly**
- View the Bible as a) the actual or b) the inspired word of God with no errors
- Read, use, or listen to the Bible fewer than four times per week

**23%**

**Bible Neutral**
- View the Bible as the inspired word of God with some factual or historical errors OR believe that it is not inspired by God but tells how the writers understood the ways and principles of God
- Read, use, or listen to the Bible one time a month or less

**19%**

**Bible Skeptic**
- View the Bible as "just another book of teachings written by men"

**13%**

**Bible Hostile**
- (a subset of Bible skeptics) View the Bible as a book of teachings written by men that's intended to manipulate and control other people

## Motivations for Increased Bible Engagement

Important part of my faith journey

**56%**

Difficult experience, searching for answers

**39%**

Saw how it changed someone else for the better

**30%**

Went to a church where Bible became more accessible

**23%**

Significant life change

**22%**

Someone asked me to read it with them

**20%**

Downloaded onto smartphone

**17%**

Media conversations around religion/spirituality

**11%**

owns a Bible. Ownership of a Bible is universal among Bible Engaged and nearly so among those who are Bible Friendly (93%) compared to Bible Neutrals (86%). Millennials (82%) and Gen X (86%) continue to be the generations least likely to live in a home with a Bible, compared to Boomers (90%) and Elders (93%). Black Americans (95%) are more likely than white (87%) and Hispanic Americans (88%) to own a Bible.

### Most Skeptics Are Hostile toward the Bible

The Skeptic segment accounts for one in five American adults (19%). They do not hold a high view of scripture, believing it to be just another book of teachings written by men that contains stories and advice. In 2017, Barna asked a follow-up question to see if Skeptics hold hostile views toward the Bible—and they do. More than three-quarters of Skeptics (78%) are hostile toward the Bible and believe it "was written to control or manipulate other people."

### Half of Americans Read, Listen to, or Pray with the Bible

Fifty percent of Americans are "Bible users"—that is, they engage with the Bible by reading, listening to, or praying with the Bible

on their own at least three to four times a year. This proportion has remained relatively consistent since 2011. But nearly one-third of adults (32%) says they never read, listen to, or pray with the Bible, up five percentage points over 2016.

### Americans Desire More Bible Use

More than half of all adults (58%) wish they read the Bible more often. This is down slightly from 2016 (61%). Each segment expresses a desire for more Bible reading. In fact, one in five Skeptics (22%) and one in five non-Christians (21%) wishes they read or listened to the Bible more. Also, this desire is particularly high among Friendlies (78%). But despite most Americans wanting to read the Bible more, two-thirds of them (67%) say their level of Bible reading is about the same as it was one year ago.

### Increased Bible Engagement Is Important to Faith Journeys

More than half of those who report an increase in Bible readership (56%) attribute it to their understanding that Bible reading is an important part of their faith journey. Although this number is lower than the previous year (67%), it is on track with 2014 (53%) and 2015 (58%) findings. Many also point to a difficult life experience that led them to search the Bible for direction or answers (39%), an increase of 13 percentage points from the previous year (26%). Seeing how the Bible changed someone they knew for the better was an important motivating factor for 30 percent of adults, as was being asked by someone they know to read the Bible (20%).

*n=2,030 | January 20–February 2, 2017 |*

*American Bible Society*

# Studying the State of Bible Studies

"Bible study" is a term and activity uniquely associated with the Christian community. But what do Bible studies achieve for Christians? Who attends Bible studies and why? How do studies succeed in connecting a person to their beliefs—or to God? Barna partnered with Bible Study Fellowship to survey practicing Christians and learn more about Bible studies in America today, from frequency and format to personal motivation and expectation.

Nearly three in five Christians (58%) participate in a Bible study—meaning, using prepared Bible study materials as part of a group or on their own. A strong majority of participation is found among evangelicals (80%), to a lesser degree among non-evangelicals (58%) and notional Christians (49%). Seven out of 10 Millennials (72%)—the most of any generation—say they engage in regular Bible study. This is likely boosted by Millennials gravitating toward group study for community-building and belonging; more Millennials meet in person for Bible studies than any other age group— nearly four out of 10 (38%)—while two out of 10 Gen X (26%), Boomers (21%), or Elders (22%) do the same. Overall, Elders are the least involved in Bible studies, with just over a third (37%) reporting current participation.

Christians who do not currently participate in a Bible study have three equally strong reasons: a belief that their study of the Bible at church services is sufficient (26%), a lack of interest (25%), and simply not having enough time to give to a group (23%).

Half of all Christians (48%) participate in Bible studies on a weekly basis, and the majority of those (66%) does so in group settings. Over half (57%) attend a Bible study in the evening (vs. afternoon or morning), and the large majority of Bible study groups (76%) is mixed gender. Technological resources typically correlate to church size; Bible study participants in churches with over 100 attendees (12%) are three times more likely to participate in a study via video or audio recording as those in churches of less than 100 (4%).

## Surprising Trends in Participation

Throughout this survey, Barna observed that many of the groups one might traditionally associate with the resources, relationships, or commitment that promote Bible study are actually less likely to participate. For example, one might assume that not having children at home allows for more time to focus on or gather for biblical study, but Christian parents with children under 18 are actually much more likely to make it a priority (68%, compared to 52% of those without kids at home who say they participate in a Bible study).

It may also seem counterintuitive that the number of people engaged in Bible studies in the South—typically a highly religious region—is actually the same as that in the West (63% and 64%, respectively), while the Midwest has significantly less involvement (49%) than either of those regions. This poses questions about shifts in regional culture, as well as the relationship between professed faith and resultant actions.

Interestingly, those attending church in rural areas participate in Bible studies almost as much as those in urban areas (61% and 68%, respectively). Another parallel between rural and urban Bible study participants is the use of online or app-based Bible studies: the frequency of usage is nearly double in urban and rural settings (17% and 14%, respectively) than in small town and suburban areas (8% and 9%, respectively). These results could be explained by the fact that these two ends of the population spectrum—density and scarcity—tend to similarly motivate individuals to dedicate time and effort to specific community groups. Further, a lack of local opportunities in rural surroundings may inspire engagement with digital sources, while the all-things-online lifestyle of urban living likely makes seeking internet and phone-based resources second nature for city dwellers.

However, these findings suggest that the theory of suburban isolationism unfortunately holds true; Christians living in the suburbs are less likely to participate in Bible studies than those

# What Would Be Your Ideal Bible Study Format?

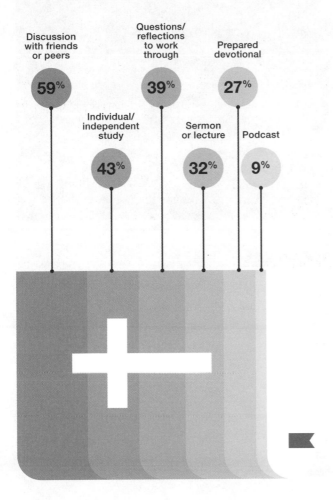

Discussion with friends or peers — **59%**

Questions/ reflections to work through — **39%**

Prepared devotional — **27%**

Individual/ independent study — **43%**

Sermon or lecture — **32%**

Podcast — **9%**

who live in urban areas (52% as compared to 68%) and even rural areas (61%).

Similarly, it may be expected that the larger the church, the more opportunities and resources, and therefore the greatest participation. However, Barna found that those who attend large churches (over 1,000 attendees) have the smallest amount of Bible study participation (52%), while those in moderately sized congregations (churches of 100–500) and small churches (less than 100) are more likely to be Bible study participants (60% and 59%). While this is not a vast margin of difference, it is still notable that churches with at least double the attendees (and often more)

do not draw significantly more people to participate in one of the most common spiritual routines. It's possible that churches with fewer attendees facilitate more effective engagement by virtue of the intimacy and accessibility inherent in smaller church settings.

## Spiritual Growth Drives Scripture Study

"A desire to grow in one's faith" (54%) is the top reason Christians say they joined a Bible study, followed by "wanting to understand the Bible better" (32%). When these ideas are reframed in regard to what individuals hope to achieve if they participate in and complete a Bible study, the numbers are even stronger: nearly seven out of 10 people choose both "significant growth in my faith" (69%) and "gaining a better understanding of the Bible" (70%) as their study goals. More than six out of 10 (63%) also choose "helping me understand how to apply the Bible to my life and the culture I live in" and half (50%) choose "developing fellowship and community with other Christians" as Bible study objectives.

When asked to choose the *most important* goal of a Bible study, four in 10 (39%) remain focused primarily on significant personal growth in their faith. One-fifth (21%) chooses greater understanding of biblical application to life and culture as their top priority, and an equal percentage aim to gain a better understanding of the Bible more than anything else. One in 10 (9%) is motivated to take part in Bible study to build community with other Christians, and five percent pursue Bible study so they can learn more about what it means to be a Christian.

*n=1,807 practicing Christians | October 2016*

# The Church's Modern Relationship to Liturgy

Denominational or generational preferences about worship styles have at times drawn lines between Christian communities, pitting contemporary expressions against liturgical traditions. But in recent years, there have been hints of a surge in interest regarding liturgy, or at least a blending of ancient and modern worship forms and styles.

Barna wondered, do these informal conversations evidence a broader shift toward liturgical churches? Could fusions of various expressions allow for an end to the "worship wars"? Or do individual preferences prompt people to move from one church to another—and in which direction? Here is what Barna learned about American practicing Christians' current commitment to a particular style of service or spiritual expression.

### No Large Trend toward Liturgy

Despite seemingly renewed public attention, particularly from young people, a survey of practicing Christians reveals no significant trend toward liturgical worship. While some (14%) have moved in this direction, Christians are in fact more likely to say

they have made a move in the opposite direction, with 30 percent indicating they have left a liturgical church for a non-liturgical church.

Millennials are the most transient generation of practicing Christians, most likely to make a shift from a non-liturgical church to a liturgical one—and to make the opposite move as well. More than one in five (22%) have moved to a liturgical tradition (compared to 16% of Gen X, 11% of Boomers, and 12% of Elders), while 44 percent have shifted away from it. Gen X (40%) are close behind in leaving liturgical churches, followed by Boomers (23%) and Elders (14%).

Older practicing Christians are less likely to shift, and they are most likely to attend a liturgical church. More than half of Elders (53%) say their church follows a liturgical calendar very closely throughout the year. This percentage is significantly higher than Boomers and Gen X (both at 41%) and Millennials (34%).

Older practicing Christians are also more likely to say a liturgical style of worship is an important part of their culture and tradition, with 43 percent of Elders

# Spiritual Disciplines, by Denomination

*% practicing Christians who participated or engaged with this practice in the past month or more frequently*

● all   ● Catholic   ● Protestant Mainline   ● Protestant Non-Mainline

*n=1,020 U.S. practicing Christians | April 2017*

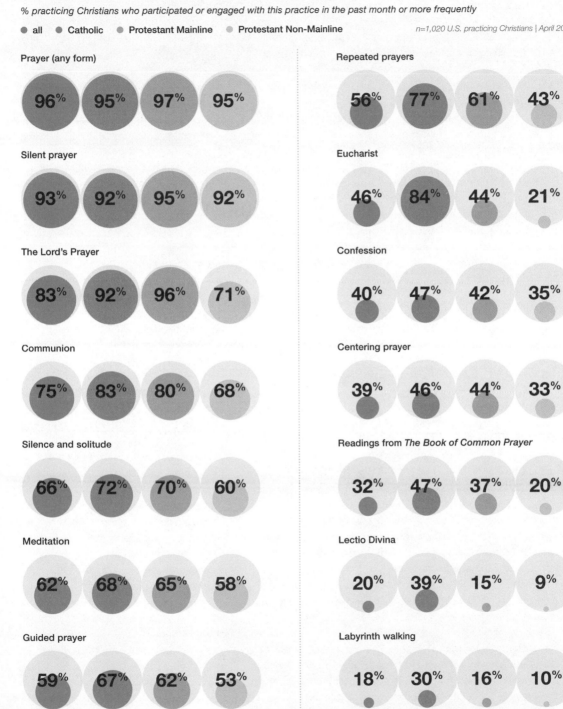

**Prayer (any form)**
96%   95%   97%   95%

**Silent prayer**
93%   92%   95%   92%

**The Lord's Prayer**
83%   92%   96%   71%

**Communion**
75%   83%   80%   68%

**Silence and solitude**
66%   72%   70%   60%

**Meditation**
62%   68%   65%   58%

**Guided prayer**
59%   67%   62%   53%

**Repeated prayers**
56%   77%   61%   43%

**Eucharist**
46%   84%   44%   21%

**Confession**
40%   47%   42%   35%

**Centering prayer**
39%   46%   44%   33%

**Readings from *The Book of Common Prayer***
32%   47%   37%   20%

**Lectio Divina**
20%   39%   15%   9%

**Labyrinth walking**
18%   30%   16%   10%

and 39 percent of Boomers affirming this statement (compared to 27% of Gen X and 29% of Millennials). When asked about their personal experiences with liturgical worship, Elders (39%) and Boomers (34%) are more likely than Gen X (24%) and Millennials (26%) to say it helps them feel connected to Church history. Compared to Boomers (5%) and Elders (1%), Millennials (14%) and Gen X (11%) are more likely to find this style of worship outdated, although the majority of them do not.

When practicing Christians shift *toward* a liturgical tradition, their reasons for doing so are more often about relationships than style. While one in four says they wanted a deeper connection to Church history (27%) or to experience God more deeply in the liturgies (24%), similar proportions say their new church is more welcoming (29%), they like the priest or pastor (29%), or they had friends who attended the church (25%).

When practicing Christians move *away* from a liturgical church, style and theology matter a bit more. The plurality (32%) says they experience God more at their new church. Many also say they were drawn to the worship music (24%), their new church is more welcoming (23%), they no longer connected with the style of their former church (21%), or they align more closely with the theology of worship in their new church (21%).

## Generations and Spiritual Practices

With Elder practicing Christians being most likely to attend liturgical churches, this generation is most engaged in weekly corporate practices, such as communion (49%), praying the Lord's Prayer (65%), reciting a historical creed (50%), and following a service from a worship or prayer book (44%). Millennials are the generation least likely to have these weekly experiences in their churches (34%, 28%, 20%, and 24%). Older generations are also more engaged in daily prayer, with Elders and Boomers (both at 81%) outpacing Gen X (65%) and Millennials (60%). They are also more likely to engage in daily silent prayer or solitude.

However, younger practicing Christians are more engaged in other spiritual practices that are less familiar to older adults. For example, many Millennials (22%) and Gen X (21%) participate in a daily centering prayer, while Boomers (12%) and Elders (6%) are less involved. In fact, Elders (41%) and Boomers (38%) are far more likely to say they have never heard of this discipline (compared to 27% of Gen X and 13% of Millennials). Younger adults are also more involved in contemplative exercises, such as Lectio Divina, guided prayer, labyrinth walking, confession, and reading from *The Book of Common Prayer*. With the exception of confession, older practicing Christians are significantly more likely to say they are unfamiliar with these practices.

At the same time, when asked how familiar they are with the concept of Christian liturgy, Elders (63%) and Boomers (56%) show similar levels of familiarity as Gen X and Millennials (both at 67%). It seems the differences between generations are not in their understanding of the concept, but in their familiarity with, and participation in, specific practices. And while older practicing Christians participate more frequently in more well-known practices, often within the context of a church service, younger ones seem more likely to explore less common or mystical disciplines. It's also possible they engage in these practices on their own rather than during church services or corporate gatherings.

## Evangelicals Are Least Liturgical

Among practicing Christians, evangelicals are least likely to be aware of, and involved in, many liturgical forms of worship. Exceptions to this include silent prayer (74% of evangelicals and 61% of non-evangelicals practice this on a daily basis) and prayer in general (90% of evangelicals and 69% of non-evangelicals say they pray daily).

Not surprisingly, practicing Catholics (86%) are more likely than their mainline Protestant (64%) and non-mainline Protestant (44%) counterparts to be at least somewhat familiar with the concept of Christian liturgy. Compared to the other two groups, non-mainline Protestants are less familiar with specific spiritual practices and less likely to engage in them. Again, prayer in any form is a striking exception, as both individual and corporate prayer are heavily emphasized in the evangelical tradition.

*n=1,020 U.S. practicing Christians | April 2017*

# A Q&A on Worship Traditions

## with Cheryl Bridges Johns

*Bridges Johns (PhD) is the Robert E. Fisher Professor of Spiritual Formation and Christian Formation at the Pentecostal Theological Seminary. She is past president of the Society for Pentecostal Studies and the author of* Finding Eternal Treasures *and* Pentecostal Formation: A Pedagogy among the Oppressed. *She is married to Jackie David Johns, with whom she copastored for over 27 years. They have two daughters and five grandchildren.*

*When it comes to preference for worship style, Barna has found that Millennials are the most transient generation—as in, they are most likely to make a shift from a non-liturgical church to a liturgical one, or vice versa. Millennials are also more familiar than their older peers with some contemplative practices, such as daily centering prayer, Lectio Divina, labyrinth walking, etc. What do you think contributes to this curiosity in religious Millennials?*

I think Millennials, being more fluid regarding boundaries in all things, can more easily move back and forth between "liturgical" and "non-liturgical." However, I do know of many Millennials so disenchanted with what they call "the liturgy of the rock concert," they refuse to worship in evangelical churches and are even adverse to evangelical forms of praise and worship.

> "The dialectical tension of order and freedom is powerful. I hope this integration will be the worship of the future."

Perhaps Millennials finding spiritual depth in ancient practices such as Lectio Divina represents a deeply felt need to be "centered." Imagine growing up in a world filled with social media, 24/7 news, and entertainment noise. I think this frenetic environment creates a deep hunger for stillness, centering, and solitude.

*Rather than pitting ancient and modern styles against each other, what might a healthy both/and approach look like? What do both spontaneity and structure uniquely reveal about the character of God, worship, or spiritual formation?*

I love this question. I am one of those people who desires both liturgical and charismatic/Pentecostal worship. It is very hard to manage, and usually one (in my case, the liturgical) wins out over the other. But the dialectical tension of order and freedom is powerful. I hope this integration will be the worship of the future.

# THE MYTH OF THE LAZY TEEN

There might not be too much to the stereotype of self-absorbed or "slacktivist" teens. Barna, in partnership with Youth Specialties and YouthWorks, found today's youth are actively engaged in service and volunteer projects—and youth ministry is a primary channel through which they serve. Here are a few themes of the altruistic habits of teens, as reported by their parents.

## TEENS ARE ACTIVE VOLUNTEERS

According to their parents, a majority of teens (65%) is fairly active when it comes to volunteering at least once every few months.

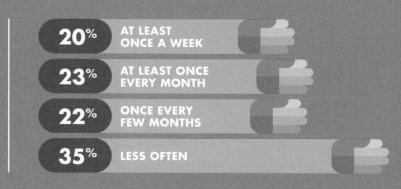

| 20% | AT LEAST ONCE A WEEK |
| 23% | AT LEAST ONCE EVERY MONTH |
| 22% | ONCE EVERY FEW MONTHS |
| 35% | LESS OFTEN |

## TEEN VOLUNTEERING FOCUSES ON CHURCH SERVICE & POVERTY ALLEVIATION

The most common forms of service for teens are those associated with their church or youth group. But there are some other key areas in which teens express compassion and give of their time.

| 38% | 34% | 31% | 26% | 23% | 13% | 13% | 9% |
| Church/ ministry | Feeding the hungry/helping the homeless | Educational | Environmental/ cleanup | Animals | Service trips | Social or political advocacy | Medical or health care |

# THE CHURCH IS CENTRAL TO TEEN VOLUNTEERING EFFORTS

When parents of teens who regularly attend youth group are asked specifically whether their teen has participated in a service project with a church, six in 10 (58%) say yes.

## THE PRIMARY WAYS TEENS ENGAGE IN SERVICE THROUGH THEIR CHURCH

**55%** DAYS OF SERVICE AT CHURCH

**49%** DAYS OF SERVICE IN THEIR TOWN

**44%** A SERVICE COMMITMENT ON A REGULAR BASIS

**35%** SERVICE AT A DESTINATION THAT COULD BE REACHED IN A DAY'S DRIVE

**19%** SERVICE AT A DESTINATION IN THE U.S. THAT IS FARTHER THAN A DAY'S DRIVE

**10%** A MISSION TRIP OUTSIDE THE U.S.

## THE GOALS OF SERVICE ARE TO LOVE AND SERVE OTHERS

**73%** **56%**

THREE-QUARTERS OF YOUTH PASTORS SAY LOVING AND SERVING OTHERS ARE THE PRIMARY GOALS OF YOUTH MISSION TRIPS. MORE THAN HALF OF PARENTS AGREE.

## OTHER GOALS OF MISSION TRIPS

● Youth pastors  ● Parents

| Goal | Youth pastors | Parents |
|---|---|---|
| Loving and serving others | 73% | 56% |
| Being the hands and feet of Jesus | 56% | 35% |
| Discipleship for youth on trip | 41% | 12% |
| Outreach/evangelism to people you are serving | 36% | 18% |
| Teaching and modeling compassion | 30% | 31% |
| Providing for the poor | 15% | 32% |
| Responses to systemic injustice | 15% | 15% |
| Opportunity for the youth to "see the world" | 12% | 25% |
| Outreach/evangelism to the youth | 11% | 19% |
| Other | 1% | 0% |

*n=606 parents of teenagers ages 13–19 (295 parents of teenagers who attend youth group regularly) | n=352 youth pastors | February 2016*

# The Prayer Patterns of Americans

Over the past five years, Americans' overall prayer habits stayed relatively stable. In 2012, nearly three-quarters (73%) prayed to God at least once per week. In 2014, the highest point in the five-year period, 78 percent of Americans prayed weekly. And 2015 returned to the 2013 level (75%), with little change in 2016 (73%) and 2017 (74%). In other words, Americans are a praying people.

In 2017, as in the previous five years, women (79%) are more likely than men (68%) to pray weekly. Marital status makes a difference as well, with married people (79%) praying at higher rates than single people (69%).

Looking at ethnicity, black Americans are the group most likely to pray weekly (82%), compared to white (72%) and Hispanic (77%) Americans.

Midwesterners (78%) and Southerners (76%) practice weekly prayer more than those in the Northeast (68%) and the West (71%). While prayer remained mostly consistent in each of the demographic regions, this represents some change from 2012, when the South (82%) prayed at higher rates than the Midwest (73%), the Northeast (70%), and the West (64%). This particular shift could be influenced by an influx of non-Southerners into some Southern cities.

Evangelicals (99%) and non-evangelical born again Christians (97%) are far more engaged in regular prayer than those in other faith segments. At the same time, notional Christians (80%) and people of other faiths (62%) still pray in high numbers. Surprisingly, more than one in five (22%) of those who claim no faith has prayed within the last week, double the percentage in 2012 (11%).

Protestants (92%) outpace Catholics (85%) in prayer, with non-mainline Protestants leading at 95 percent. When it comes to practicing Protestants (100%) and practicing Catholics (97%), however, the gap virtually disappears, indicating prayerful Christians are those also consistent in other areas of their faith. For example, church attendance makes a difference: 97 percent of those attending church in the past week prayed in that same period. Those who have attended in the past month aren't far behind at 93 percent. Among less-frequent attenders, who have been to church in the last six months, 71 percent have prayed in the last week. Half (51%) of unchurched people have done the same.

*n=2,002 | February 24–March 21, 2012; n=2,027 | January 20–February 2, 2017*

# A Generous Understanding

How do Christians view living and giving generously—and how does this compare to the beliefs and teachings of church leaders? In partnership with Thrivent Financial, Barna conducted a study among Protestant pastors and interested Christians (self-identified Christians, excluding those who have never been to a worship service and those who disagree that their faith is very important for their lives). Here's a summary of how Christians and pastors have similar, but not identical, ideas about what qualifies as generosity.

## What Makes an Act Generous?

In general, most people agree that generosity comes from an unselfish, sincere spirit—not a sense of obligation or self-interest. Compared with Christians, a larger percentage of pastors agree that generosity is "a response to Christ's love" (66% vs. 47% of all Christian adults). Church leaders are also more likely to believe generosity is both an inward attitude and an outward discipline and are less likely than Christians generally to say it has to do with either spontaneity or a sense of duty.

However, Christians are more likely than pastors to say generosity is spur-of-the-moment and a result of compassion—beliefs that may indicate some romanticism attached to the notion of generosity. They are also more likely to say it is not "sacrificial" (16% vs. 5% of pastors).

Younger Christians are more likely than older adults to perceive generosity to be a spontaneous response to the circumstances of the moment. In contrast to Boomers (28% "always" + "often") and Elders (15%), more Gen X (37%) and Millennials (45%) say spontaneity is a core feature of generosity. Pastors, in contrast, are least likely among the groups surveyed to say so: just one in five says generosity is spur-of-the-moment (20%).

The notion that generosity is best expressed in the moment indicates a different set of expectations among younger Christians that may lead to fundraising headwinds for churches and organizations that depend on systematic giving and volunteering.

Elders appear to have more cerebral, less circumstantial ideals for generosity, especially compared to Millennials. For example, Elders are more likely to say generosity is a discipline (62% vs.

51% of Millennials) and is planned (43% vs. 31%). These differences might signal a cultural transition (from thinking to feeling) in how people process their ideas and impulses related to generosity, or simply a shift in mindsets about money and institutions as people age.

## How Pastors Talk about Giving

The gap is immense between pastors and Christians on whether it is acceptable for a church member to substitute volunteering for financial giving. Pastors disagree that these two forms of generosity are interchangeable. More than eight out of 10 disagree strongly (67%) or somewhat (18%) that "it is OK for a member who volunteers extensively not to give

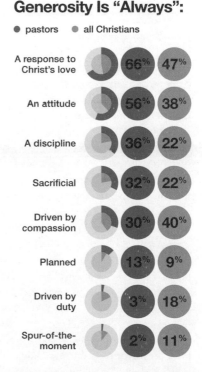

## Generosity Is "Always":

● pastors   ● all Christians

| | pastors | all Christians |
|---|---|---|
| A response to Christ's love | 66% | 47% |
| An attitude | 56% | 38% |
| A discipline | 36% | 22% |
| Sacrificial | 32% | 22% |
| Driven by compassion | 30% | 40% |
| Planned | 13% | 9% |
| Driven by duty | 3% | 18% |
| Spur-of-the-moment | 2% | 11% |

*n=606 U.S. Protestant senior pastors | June 2016;*
*n=1,556 U.S. interested Christians | July 2016*

## The Last Time People Volunteered, by Reported Annual Giving

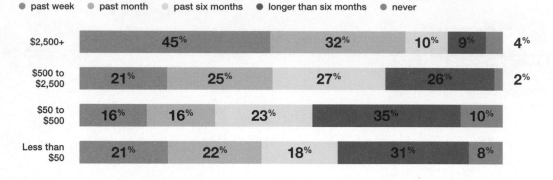

● past week    ● past month    ● past six months    ● longer than six months    ● never

**$2,500+**: 45% | 32% | 10% | 9% | 4%

**$500 to $2,500**: 21% | 25% | 27% | 26% | 2%

**$50 to $500**: 16% | 16% | 23% | 35% | 10%

**Less than $50**: 21% | 22% | 18% | 31% | 8%

financially." But just one in five Christians (10% "strongly" + 11% "somewhat" disagree) is on the same page with pastors.

Ironically, some parishioners' confusion on this question may come from pastors themselves. Only 39 percent of pastors say they or other leaders speak from the pulpit about tithing or giving to the church at least once a month (17% once per month, 22% multiple times per month). But more than six in 10 say they or other leaders speak from the pulpit at least once a month on the topic of volunteering (35% once, 27% multiple times). So, by their own estimates, pastors talk about volunteering more than they talk about financial giving—thus, it's no surprise that some of their congregants believe serving is an acceptable substitute for tithing.

### Connecting Giving and Serving

Before church leaders cut back on the amount of time they spend talking about volunteerism, however, it's important to note that serving and financial giving appear to go hand in hand. As the chart shows, Christians who give most are also most likely to say they have volunteered within the past week or month.

Those who give more are most likely to spend time serving others—but they are also more likely to say generosity is a frequent topic of conversation in their homes. Two-thirds of Christians who consider generosity to be extremely important say they talked with their spouses (67%) or children (64%) about generosity within the past week, compared to fewer than half of all others. It appears that generosity is developed at home—good news for churches structured to support families.

### Personal Appeals Prompt Giving

Barna asked Christians how likely they are to give when petitioned individually or as part of a larger group. Across the board,

more people say they are likelier to give when asked one-on-one. But only one-third of all pastors (32%) says they make a personal, one-on-one appeal twice a month or more often. Those who lead large and growing churches, however, appear to be more comfortable with a personal "ask." Pastors of churches with 250 or more in weekend attendance (34%) are more likely to invite someone to give at least twice a month compared to those with 100 or fewer in attendance (27%). And those who pastor growing churches are more likely than leaders of declining churches to do so (35% vs. 22%).

This is not to say that willingness to ask individuals is causal of church size or growth—it's not clear from this study which factors combine to grow attendance. But statistical correlation exists between church size/growth and more frequent face-to-face invitations to give. It's worth asking, then, if church leaders should branch out from their "offering ask" of the whole congregation to a combination of group and personal appeals.

n=606 U.S. Protestant senior pastors | June 2016;

n=1,556 U.S. interested Christians | July 2016

# How Do People Express Generosity?

**Barna**

## THE GENEROSITY GAP

How Christians' Perceptions and Practices of Giving Are Changing—
and What It Means for the Church

A Barna Report Produced in Partnership with Thrivent Financial

## The research explores:

- Views on how people ought to express generosity

- Generational differences in how people think about and practice generosity

- How financial goals and motivations impact giving habits

- Methods and invitations that strengthen giving

There are both practical and spiritual reasons for churches and Christian organizations to encourage generosity in Christians. The needs of churches and Christian nonprofits are real and ongoing, and most can be met only with dollars donated by consistent Christian givers. Most U.S. Christians today tend to think of themselves as at least somewhat generous—however, few give as much as they would like. Pastors and organizational leaders need both accurate information and wisdom if the groups they lead are to survive and adapt to a changing religious and economic landscape. The data contained in *The Generosity Gap* will help you strategize for the future and devise fresh tactical ideas for how to connect Christians' hearts, minds, and souls with their potential giving strength.

Order at
**barna.com
/generosity**

# Church

Getting to know the people
who are in the pews

# OUTREACH
## AND ITS OUTCOMES

How often, and how well, are churches engaging in service and evangelism to their communities?

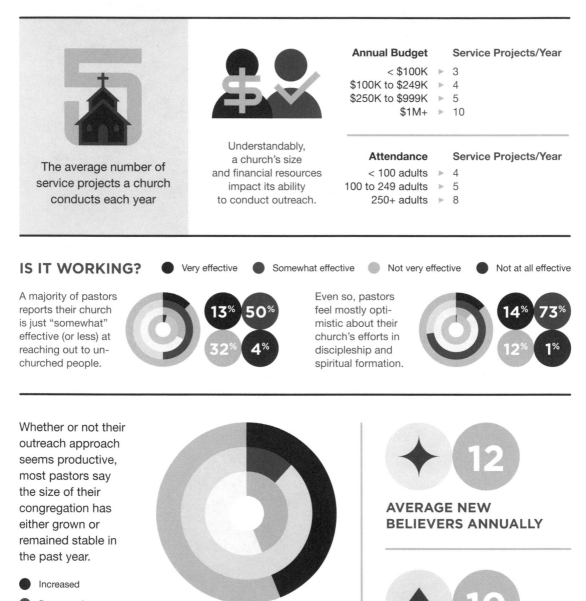

**5**

The average number of service projects a church conducts each year

Understandably, a church's size and financial resources impact its ability to conduct outreach.

| Annual Budget | Service Projects/Year |
|---|---|
| < $100K | 3 |
| $100K to $249K | 4 |
| $250K to $999K | 5 |
| $1M+ | 10 |

| Attendance | Service Projects/Year |
|---|---|
| < 100 adults | 4 |
| 100 to 249 adults | 5 |
| 250+ adults | 8 |

## IS IT WORKING?

● Very effective ● Somewhat effective ○ Not very effective ● Not at all effective

A majority of pastors reports their church is just "somewhat" effective (or less) at reaching out to un-churched people.

13% 50%
32% 4%

Even so, pastors feel mostly optimistic about their church's efforts in discipleship and spiritual formation.

14% 73%
12% 1%

Whether or not their outreach approach seems productive, most pastors say the size of their congregation has either grown or remained stable in the past year.

● Increased
● Decreased
● Stayed the same

44% 12% 44%

**12**

AVERAGE NEW BELIEVERS ANNUALLY

**10**

AVERAGE BAPTISMS ANNUALLY

# Reaching Out or Falling Flat?

For many churches, particularly those that consider themselves evangelical, outreach is central to the idea of "cultural leadership." After all, making disciples was the risen Christ's Great Commission to his followers—a commission that, if wholly fulfilled, would undeniably transform culture. So how do pastors think their churches are doing when it comes to outreach and growing disciples? Barna research conducted in partnership with Pepperdine University offers some answers.

Most pastors are apt to think their church is more effective at discipleship than at evangelism and outreach. Nearly nine out of 10 rate their church's discipleship or spiritual formation efforts as "very" (14%) or "somewhat effective" (73%), compared to two-thirds who say so about their church "reaching out to unchurched people" (13% very, 50% somewhat effective).

Note that, on both counts, the percentage that rates their congregation as very effective is comparatively small. However, black pastors tend to rate their congregations better than the national norm on outreach (25%). And one in five pastors of growing churches says their congregation is very effective at both outreach (21%) and discipleship (22%), compared to just 4 percent of pastors who helm churches experiencing declines in attendance.

When it comes to the effectiveness of their discipleship ministry, leaders of large churches are in the same statistical ballpark as those who lead small and midsize congregations but are far more likely to say they are very effective at outreach to the unchurched (20% large, 14% small, 9% midsize).

There is also a fairly stark split between mainline and non-mainline churches when it comes to outreach effectiveness. Less than half of mainline pastors say their church is effective at reaching out to unchurched people (9% very, 37% somewhat), compared to seven in 10 non-mainline leaders (15% very, 55% somewhat).

On a personal level, just 10 percent of pastors give themselves an "excellent" rating when it comes to the task of evangelizing and sharing the gospel. Similarly, when it comes to identifying their top personal frustrations with their job, "how to do effective outreach" concerns only 11 percent of pastors.

## Service Projects

Most congregations do a handful of service projects each year that are designed to serve people outside their church body. The average (median) number of projects completed in the last 12 months is five. There is, of course, a wide range of variation: 3 percent of pastors say their church did more than 50 service initiatives in the past year, while 5 percent report no such events.

Not surprisingly, church size and budget are factors here. One in nine churches with fewer than 100 adult attenders and 17 percent of churches with an annual budget of less than $100,000 did not complete any service projects in the last 12 months. However, large churches and congregations with a budget of $1 million or more completed an average of eight and 10 events last year, respectively, and none of them report having done none at all.

Regardless of church size, there is broad consensus that the main goals of community service are "loving/serving others as Jesus taught," "being the hands and feet of Jesus," and "outreach/evangelism to the people we serve." The last of these is more of a priority among non-mainline pastors than mainline, but "embodying the kingdom of God" is a greater concern for mainline pastors than non-mainline.

There are also a few notable differences between younger and older pastors. Leaders under 50 are more prone to prioritize outreach and evangelism and blessing their neighborhood, while leaders 50 and older are especially keen to help their congregation act as "the hands and feet of Jesus."

(Learn more about how youth ministries specifically perceive and conduct outreach on page 144.)

*n=900 U.S. Protestant senior pastors | April–December 2015*

# Built to Grow

*n=222 leaders of multisite and church-planting ministries | March 7–April 6, 2016*

## The physical dimensions of adding a congregation

In a study among expanding churches, conducted in partnership with Cornerstone Knowledge Network, Barna examined church leaders' views on building and investing in ministry facilities. Here's a look at priorities and strategies of church growth.

More than half of all actively expanding churches are most concerned with the location or functional design of their building

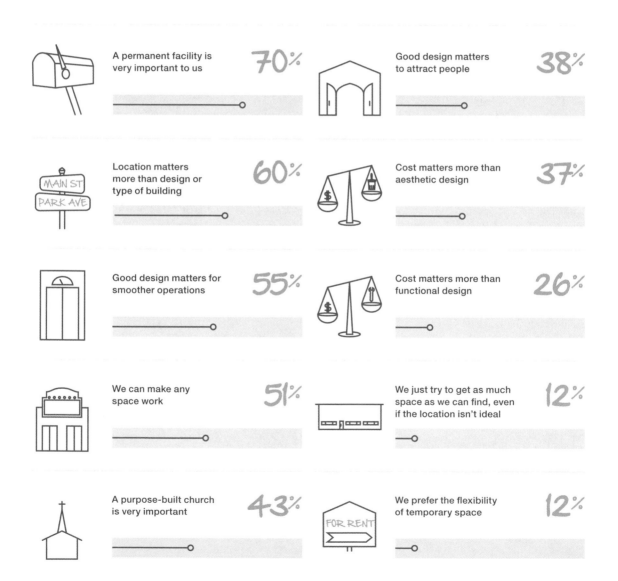

A permanent facility is very important to us — **70%**

Good design matters to attract people — **38%**

Location matters more than design or type of building — **60%**

Cost matters more than aesthetic design — **37%**

Good design matters for smoother operations — **55%**

Cost matters more than functional design — **26%**

We can make any space work — **51%**

We just try to get as much space as we can find, even if the location isn't ideal — **12%**

A purpose-built church is very important — **43%**

We prefer the flexibility of temporary space — **12%**

## A Fixed Spot

Permanency is seen as vital, no matter what a church's philosophy of facilities may be.

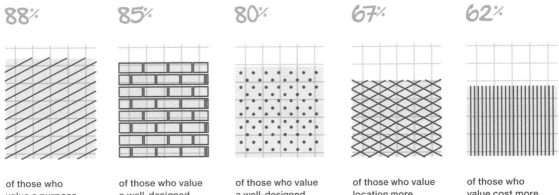

**88%** of those who value a purpose-built church

**85%** of those who value a well-designed building to attract people

**80%** of those who value a well-designed building to make operations smoother

**67%** of those who value location more than design

**62%** of those who value cost more than aesthetics

## Facilities with a Mission

How does a church's ministry strategy affect their building decisions? Churches that are expanding to better reach a community to which they feel called typically place greater emphasis on having a well-designed building. Meanwhile, ministries that are fulfilling a specific strategy are more cost-conscious in their building efforts.

● Churches reproducing to be more effective in reaching their city/region

● Churches reproducing to fulfill their mission/strategic plan

## Even if it costs more, a well-designed building is important because . . .

it attracts people to the church

47%　31%

it makes operations smoother

65%　53%

## Cost matters more than . . .

aesthetic design

51%　31%

functional design

36%　18%

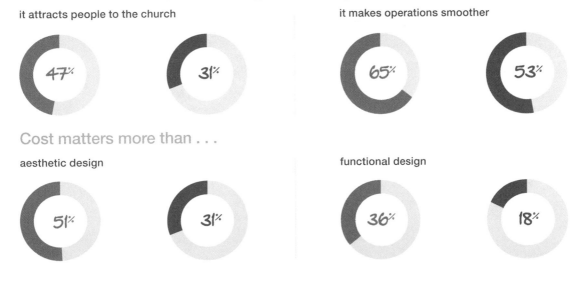

# Today's Best Practices for Church Expansion

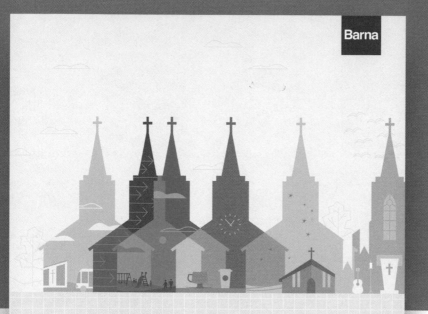

Barna

## More Than Multisite
Inside Today's Methods and Models for Launching New Congregations

A Barna Report Produced in Partnership
with Cornerstone Knowledge Network

## This book includes an in-depth look at the following:

- Profiles of five major models of church expansion

- Statistics about pastors in actively reproducing churches

- The logistics of church extension

- Analysis of the motivations, processes, and impact of adding congregations

The recent advent of multisite and church-planting strategies has introduced unprecedented opportunity for the Church. Today, entire networks of proliferating churches exist, with their own structures, terminologies, and metrics for growth. Faith leaders who contemplate moving their churches beyond a single campus face a variety of daunting questions—*More Than Multisite* can help. On whatever scale it occurs, healthy church expansion requires strategy—not merely for the growth of a congregation or the construction of a building, but ultimately for the spread of the gospel. *More Than Multisite* will equip you to make informed decisions about intentional ministry design, helping you to stay on mission as you lead.

Order at
**barna.com
/multisite**

**BARNA TAKES**

# The Church Needs to Consider Special Needs

Brooke Hempell
Barna Group
Senior Vice President
of Research

With growing public awareness of special needs and public programs to accommodate them, many churches have followed suit to extend assistance to people with special needs or their families. In a study of U.S. Protestant pastors, more than two-thirds (68%) say that providing specific programming for people with special needs and their families was important to them—a sentiment relatively equivalent across different denominations and church sizes, locations, budgets, and other demographic segments.

The vast majority of churches (88%) says they offer some type of special needs programming, often relatively basic assistance for the hearing or visually impaired. Adaptive facilities are the most commonly offered service, present in 68 percent of churches. These mainly consist of Americans with Disabilities Act (ADA) compliant facilities, such as ramps. Not surprisingly, larger churches are more likely to offer special needs programming than smaller churches, as they often have both more needs to meet and more resources. Inclusion programs and special needs events are offered by one-third of churches (38% and 35%, respectively). Just one in seven churches (14%) has dedicated special needs staff.

My own brother-in-law and his family have benefitted tremendously from special needs programming at churches. Their 14-year-old son has autism and a number of related psychological and behavioral challenges. While my nephew is precious and sweet at times, caring for him feels a bit like living in a war zone, not knowing when something might set off an outburst and when their day will come to a crashing halt as they try to stabilize his emotions and behavior. Every aspect of their lives is dictated by the premise of avoiding a breakdown.

Not surprisingly, they desperately need the support of the local church. Not only do they have logistical and physical needs, but spiritually, they need God every day to sustain them through what feels like a lifelong battle. They rely on the incredible special needs staff and volunteers at their church to care for their son while they attend the worship service and get the encouragement and refreshment they crave. Then the body of the church surrounds them throughout the week with physical support and emotional encouragement.

Sadly, one in 10 churches still doesn't offer programming for those with special needs, including 7 percent who say they don't feel a need for such programming and 4 percent who don't have programs in place even though they recognize the need. I hope they have the opportunity to listen to the stories of those like my brother-in-law's family, who chose their church largely because of the special needs services offered. Without these, they could not attend a worship service uninterrupted or become part of the church community. This is life-giving work and a beautiful picture of the church fulfilling its mission.

*n=600 U.S. Protestant senior pastors | October 27–November 17, 2016*

# Youth Group Staffing

Most churches have one youth ministry staff member, according to a Barna study commissioned by Youth Specialties and YouthWorks. More than half have one paid staff member dedicated to youth (55%) and 17 percent have two or more. The number of paid staff is weakly correlated with youth group size, with the largest groups having an average of two paid staff members.

What is the general profile of today's youth pastors?

- **Young.** Most youth pastors are under the age of 40. The largest age group represented is 30–39 years old (49%), followed by the 26–29 (18%) and 40–49 (16%) age groups.

- **Educated.** Nearly half are college graduates (47%). One-third attended seminary (34%), and 7 percent have "some" seminary training. This reflects the high regard senior pastors have for specific youth ministry training; the majority says this kind of education is important (24% "extremely," 43% "very").
- **Married.** Youth pastors are typically married (84%); just 16 percent have either never been or are no longer married.
- **Male.** The majority of youth pastors—four out of five—is male (81%). In non-mainline churches, an overwhelming 90 percent of youth pastors are men, while a smaller gender gap exists in mainline churches (42% female). Larger churches have a higher proportion of male youth ministers.

Of course, volunteers also play a significant role in youth groups. Overall, groups have an average of 12 adult volunteers on a regular basis, with an average of seven who are not parents of students. The average number of volunteers is correlated with both youth group size and church size. Of parents whose teens attend a youth group consistently, most volunteer regularly (42%) or occasionally (33%).

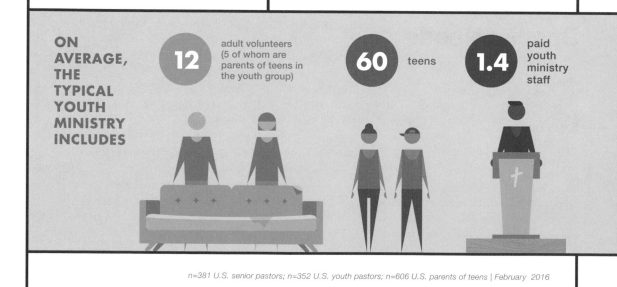

ON AVERAGE, THE TYPICAL YOUTH MINISTRY INCLUDES

**12** adult volunteers (5 of whom are parents of teens in the youth group)

**60** teens

**1.4** paid youth ministry staff

n=381 U.S. senior pastors; n=352 U.S. youth pastors; n=606 U.S. parents of teens | February 2016

# Youth Group Activities

In Barna's study with Youth Specialties and YouthWorks, more than eight in 10 pastors (87% senior pastors, 84% youth pastors) mention that youth attendance in the main worship service is an activity regularly offered by their youth ministry.

Social activities are a common aspect as well (85% youth pastors, 84% senior pastors). When the social and spiritual overlap, the result often takes the form of small discipleship or Bible study groups (80% all pastors). Small groups designated specifically for prayer aren't quite as common.

Youth pastors are more likely than senior pastors to mention offering activities such as large group teaching (71% vs. 49%) and large group

worship (48% vs. 30%). However, more than half of all pastors (56% youth pastors, 54% senior pastors) say their church takes teens to youth conferences.

Valuable one-on-one time with adults is a rarer option. One-quarter of pastors (25% senior pastors, 23% youth pastors) says they offer adult-teen mentoring programs. Urban churches seem to favor intimacy; their senior pastors are more likely than suburban and rural pastors to say they offer small prayer groups and adult-teen mentoring programs and less likely to list youth attendance in the main service or large group teaching as regular activities.

Seven in 10 report (71%) building their curriculum in-house, and about the same percentage (70%) say they purchase teaching tools from outside the church—meaning a sizable number (46%) use both approaches. The more paid staff, the more likely a church is able to develop custom resources.

When it comes to operational budgets, according to senior pastors, a majority of churches allocates 10 percent or less to youth ministry, with an average of 8 percent. Youth pastors report their churches spend an average of 3 percent of the overall budget on youth ministry, excluding the salaries for paid staff positions.

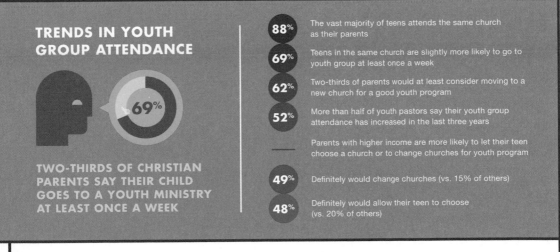

## TRENDS IN YOUTH GROUP ATTENDANCE

69%

**TWO-THIRDS OF CHRISTIAN PARENTS SAY THEIR CHILD GOES TO A YOUTH MINISTRY AT LEAST ONCE A WEEK**

**88%** The vast majority of teens attends the same church as their parents

**69%** Teens in the same church are slightly more likely to go to youth group at least once a week

**62%** Two-thirds of parents would at least consider moving to a new church for a good youth program

**52%** More than half of youth pastors say their youth group attendance has increased in the last three years

Parents with higher income are more likely to let their teen choose a church or to change churches for youth program

**49%** Definitely would change churches (vs. 15% of others)

**48%** Definitely would allow their teen to choose (vs. 20% of others)

*n=381 U.S. senior pastors; n=352 U.S. youth pastors | February 2016*

# A Q&A on Understanding Youth

## with Sharon Galgay Ketcham

*Ketcham is associate professor of theology and Christian ministries at Gordon College in Massachusetts and holds a PhD in theology and education from Boston College. Her two decades of experience include serving in full-time ministry, researching, writing, teaching, and mentoring.*

*Barna findings indicate that social issues, safe spaces, and healthy friendships are of great concern to the parents of teens in youth ministry. Why do you think these feel so urgent for parents of teens today?*

There is a well-known narrative shaping our perception of teenagers. The narrative is as old as the socially created category "teenager" that emerged in the 1900s. We hear it daily in the media, in helicopter parenting, and even in our approaches to youth ministry: the idea that teenagers are broken, deficient, and in need of help. We problematize teenagers and use significant resources to try to fix them.

This narrative evokes fear and, in loving response, parents are desperate to keep them safe. I am not saying we live in a danger-free world; of course there are real dangers. What I am saying is that teenagers are more than problems to solve—they have potential as human beings, and surely God sees their potential in Jesus Christ through the work of the Spirit.

Helping teenagers imagine how they might contribute to God's redemptive movement in the world will unveil their potential. When parents, youth pastors, and church leaders train their eyes to look beyond the dominant problem narrative, to recognize teenage potential, and provide a place in the [local] church for teenagers to practice using their gifts, teenagers will find a meaningful purpose in the church. The busyness of teenagers is connected to the longing of adults to help problematized teenagers make it into adulthood. Imagine if we saw teenagers as Christ does: full of potential to join God's purpose.

*How can a church body better acknowledge and understand the presence of youth in their congregation?*

Mission statements for youth ministries often describe fostering a teenager's relationship with Jesus Christ (with varying theological nuance) but rarely include a focus on a teenager's relationship with the church. This relationship becomes ancillary. A theological question arises: How should we understand a teenager's relationship with the church? Perhaps we do not believe this to be a vital relationship, and if this is so, we should not be surprised when teenagers leave the church after high school. Leaders might connect them to Jesus, but what happened to connecting them to the church? Pastors, youth pastors, and parents need to reflect theologically on whether fostering a teenager's relationship with the church is vital. If it is, sermons will include relevant illustrations for teenagers, teenagers will contribute in main worship, and programming for teenagers will cease to occur simultaneously with the adult service.

# What's Going On in Youth Group?

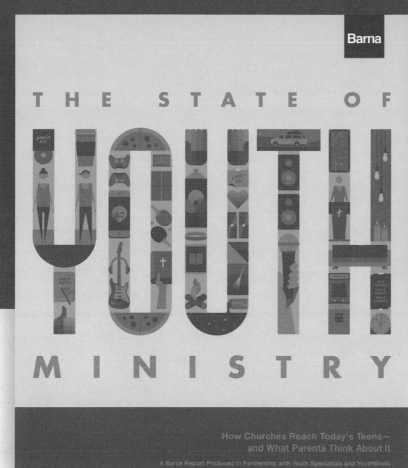

## This research uncovers the following:

- What parents are looking for in church youth programs
- How pastors define the purpose and priorities of youth ministry
- Specific activities, events, and opportunities that churches offer to teens
- The biggest challenges facing effective youth ministry today

From one church to the next, youth programs are anything but standard. Every leader has their own goals, priorities, skills, and strategies, and it's not always clear what works and what doesn't. What, exactly, is youth ministry *for,* and how do churches and parents of teens measure success?

This report offers in-depth analysis and expert commentary that will spark conversations and lead to more effective student ministries, healthier youth workers, and, ultimately, stronger churches and sturdier teen faith. Most of all, you will gain an overwhelming sense that you are not alone in your ministry to teenagers.

Order at
**barna.com**
**/youthministry**

# Serving God—with Money

The U.S. Bureau of Economic Analysis reports the average American has $39,424 in annual disposable income (that is, the amount that remains after taxes are paid).[27] According to analysis of data Barna gathered on U.S. adults between 2013 and 2016, practicing Christians report giving an average (median) of $1,400 a year to their church—thus, between 3 and 4 percent of the median disposable income.

Yet the $1,400 "per person" is not evenly spread across the Christian population. According to a Barna study conducted in partnership with Thrivent Financial, some are giving much more and some much less. More than half of all interested Christians (self-identified Christians, excluding those who have never been to a worship service and those who disagree that their faith is very important for their lives) say they gave less than $500 last year; 15 percent did not donate at all.

Aside from any specific theology about tithing, most leaders will agree that $1,400 a year is modest compared to the economic capacity of the average person of faith. An examination of

## The Ultimate Financial Goal for Life, by Generation

*Goal by ranking among all Christians*
*n=1,556 U.S. interested Christians | July 2016*

| | all Christians | Millennials | Gen X | Boomers | Elders |
|---|---|---|---|---|---|
| Provide for my family | 22% | 31% | 18% | 18% | 13% |
| Support the lifestyle I want | 15% | 14% | 17% | 13% | 7% |
| Meet my obligations and needs | 13% | 8% | 15% | 15% | 16% |
| Be content | 13% | 11% | 14% | 13% | 14% |
| Give charitably | 11% | 8% | 11% | 15% | 18% |
| Serve God with my money | 10% | 10% | 9% | 11% | 19% |
| Establish a financial legacy | 7% | 7% | 8% | 6% | 6% |
| Be debt-free | 6% | 6% | 5% | 6% | 4% |
| Show my talent/hard work | 2% | 4% | 1% | 1% | 0% |
| Other | 2% | 1% | 2% | 2% | 4% |

Christians' priorities for money reveals one reason why: of 10 possible answers to the question, "What would you consider to be the ultimate financial goal in life?" the option "to serve God with my money" ranks at number six, with just one in 10 Christians choosing that answer. Serving God with one's money is, for most people, not as urgent as other priorities—though Elders are twice as likely as other generations to say it is, which makes serving God the number-one financial goal among senior Christians. The percentage of Elders whose goal is "to have enough money to give charitably" is also higher than average (18% vs. 11% of all Christians).

"Providing for my family" tops the list among all Christians (22%), and Millennials are more likely than the norm to select this option (31%). Since many young adults are starting their family (or at least contemplating it), it makes sense that this financial obligation would be on their minds. It's less clear whether this is a true generational difference or if Millennials' goals will change with their stage of life over time.

These differences show that a Christian audience—especially one that is intergenerational—will hear teaching and other messaging about money through a variety of personal filters. For all but the small percentage of Christians who already view money primarily as an opportunity to serve God, teaching on biblical generosity will have to start with why to give, not how to give.

## Givers and Keepers

To find out if Christians' ultimate financial goal correlates with behaviors and attitudes related to generosity, Barna analysts created two groups:

- *Givers* are motivated by "others-focused" goals: to provide for their family (43% of Givers), to give charitably (23%), to serve God with their money (20%), or to leave a legacy for others (14%). Fifty percent of Christians are Givers.
- *Keepers* are motivated by "self-focused" goals: to support the lifestyle they want (42% of Keepers), to be content (37%), to be debt-free (16%), or to earn enough to show how hard they work (5%). Thirty-five percent of Christians are Keepers.

Fifteen percent of Christians don't fall into either category because they are primarily motivated to meet their financial obligations, a goal considered "indeterminate" by researchers. For the other 85 percent who are either Givers or Keepers, ultimate financial goals make a significant difference in both generous habits and perspectives on generosity. Christians with giving goals give a lot, and Christians with keeping goals give less or not at all. The challenge for leaders is not to coax Keepers to give more, but to

help them become sincere Givers from the inside out.

In short, motivations matter.

One in three Givers (33%) says they donated $500 or more last year to their church or other nonprofits, compared to about one in five Keepers (22%); they are nearly twice as likely to report donating $2,500 or more (14% vs. 8%). Plus, they are more likely to report setting their own giving at 10 percent or more of their income (25% vs. 13%).

These findings dovetail with ongoing research Barna has conducted since 2011 with American Bible Society on U.S. adults' level of engagement with the Bible: those with a higher level of engagement tend to give more. Specifically, the Bible Engaged have a "high" view of the scriptures and read the Bible four or more times per week. Compared to those who read the Bible less often or hold "lower" views of the scriptures, Bible Engaged Americans are far more likely to report donating $2,000 or more to their church or a charity last year (49% vs. 17% of Bible Friendly, 18% of Bible Neutral, and 13% of Bible Skeptics). (See the Glossary on page 13 for complete definitions of Bible engagement.)

Not surprisingly, Givers are more apt to say generosity is extremely important to them (33% vs. 24% of Keepers). They are also more convinced Christians should financially support their home church: 42 percent strongly agree that "every member should give some amount," versus 30 percent of Keepers. Additionally, they are more likely to specify that Christians should give their church 10 percent or more of their income (30% vs. 22%).

*n=1,556 U.S. interested Christians | July 2016*

# A Q&A on the Multicultural Church

## with Mark DeYmaz

*DeYmaz is founding pastor of Mosaic Church of Central Arkansas, cofounder and executive director of Mosaix Global Network, and author of* Building a Healthy Multi-Ethnic Church *and* Ethnic Blends. *This is an adapted Q&A from Barna and Pepperdine University's The State of Pastors 2017 event.*

***On multiculturalism as a gospel mandate, not just a trend in modern ministry:***

Christ taught us to pray, "Thy kingdom come. Thy will be done." Where? "On earth, as it is in heaven." This is biblical, it's right, it's the hope of the gospel. In fact, every church in the New Testament outside of Jerusalem was what we would call today a multiethnic church—with Jews and Gentiles, men and women, rich and poor—walking, working, and worshiping God together as one. Christ envisioned it on the night before he died, [we read in] John 17. Luke described it in action at the Church of Antioch, the greatest church of the New Testament, in Acts 11 and 13. Ultimately, Paul prescribes it throughout his writings in Romans, Galatians, but particularly in the book of Ephesians. This is a New Testament issue. It's sound exegetically; we're not "reading into" scripture. You've got to wrap your head and heart particularly around the theology of the New Testament on this new issue.

One other thing pushing it forward is, in our country today, there's such a compartmentalization between issues of the gospel or justice, or even economic reform. It's long past time for us to recognize that lament, corporate repentance, reconciliation, justice are not peripheral to the gospel; they're intrinsic to the gospel.

***On the difference between assimilation and accommodation in multicultural ministry:***

When people say, "We welcome anyone at our church," what they typically mean is, "As long as they—whoever they are—like the way we do things." They want *assimilation*, which essentially means, "Check your culture at the door." The flip side of that is *accommodation*. We change our structures, our forms, our practices in the elder room, with the deacons, in the pulpit. We're sharing authority and responsibility for the church, modeling what Antioch did in Acts 13:1 with five diverse leaders. Two from Africa, one from the Middle East, one from the Mediterranean, and one from Asia Minor. We have to empower diverse leadership at the top. It's not just about diversity in the pews. Hey, that's a great step, but we've got to keep going on.

We preach and teach individual sanctification; it's long past time we think about *corporate* sanctification. Revelation 7:9 says every nation, tribe, people, and tongue will be in the same room walking, working, worshiping God together as one. If it's going on up there, it ought to be going on down here.

We preach a message of God's love for all people, but it's otherwise undermined in an increasingly diverse society that's not buying it due to the systemic segregation of our churches.

# The Dechurched: America's Greatest Mission Field

Roxanne Stone
Barna Group
Editor in Chief

When I lived in New York City, I once heard a pastor bemoan the lack of new converts to Christianity at his church. His concern was that our church was merely acquiring Christians rather than leading "lost" people to Christ.

I understood his concern: no church wants to be in the business of "stealing" Christians from other churches. We want more people to know the love of Jesus—people who never have before. But, as I looked around the congregation and thought of the stories of my friends who attended there, I wondered: *Would some of these people even be attending church if it weren't for this one?* Surely, the discipleship of these Christians—their continued faith in Jesus—mattered as much as new conversions.

New York City is filled with stories of Christians who did not stay Christians—the city has a secularizing effect. The Christians in the pews around me were an exception to this rule. I believed my church was playing an important role.

While New York City may be an extreme example, every city in America is filled with the dechurched: people who once attended church but no longer do. In fact, the majority of the unchurched in America (79%) are dechurched. This, coupled with the reality that most people in America still claim to be Christian, means that if you run into someone who does not attend church, it's most likely not because they don't believe in Jesus. It's because they don't like church—or got hurt by it, or lost interest in it, or got too busy, or started hanging out with people who don't go to church, or . . .

The reasons for declining church attendance among Christians are myriad and well-documented in Barna's research. But, regardless of their reasons, the truth remains: an increasing number of Christians no longer see church as a vital or essential part of their faith. Unfortunately, we also know through our research, that maintaining a vibrant faith outside of church is difficult. Christians who don't attend church are less likely to read the Bible, less likely to have spiritual conversations, and less likely to volunteer or give charitably.

The dechurched represent an important and growing avenue of ministry for churches. The critical message that this group needs to hear is a reason for churches to exist at all. What is it that the local church can offer their faith that they can't get on their own? Churches need to be able to say to these people—and know for themselves—that there is a unique way you can find God only in church. And that faith does not survive or thrive in solitude.

In New York City, I saw my church answering these questions for my friends—many of whom had stopped going to church previously. Through unique community, a shared countercultural vision, a weekly partaking of the eucharist, and intelligent sermons, we had found a church home in a city surrounded by those who hadn't. I hope we can reach more Christians with this good news: the Church is still here for you, and we yearn for you to come back.

# Beliefs

Doubts, doctrines, and other
contemporary spiritual points of view

# Views of the Bible: It's Sacred, but Is It Special?

Barna and American Bible Society have long tracked Americans' Bible practices and perspectives. While the number of Americans who read the Bible weekly or even daily has remained steady over the last seven years, nearly a third now says they never read, listen to, or pray with the Bible on their own, up from a quarter in 2011. This suggests perspectives on the Bible are changing at the spiritual margins of society and the Church rather than at the spiritual center of American Christianity.

Further, perceptions of the sacredness of the Bible have diminished in relative stature to other texts. In 2017, a majority of Americans (82%) identify the Bible as sacred or holy literature, only a 4 percent drop from 2011. In addition, 21 percent of Americans identify the Koran as sacred, doubling from 10 percent in 2011. One in five (20%) sees the Torah and one in 10 (11%) sees the Book of Mormon as sacred or holy, both an increase from 4 percent in 2011. The rate of change increases among younger generations. Millennials are just as likely as the national population to identify the Bible as holy (81%), but more likely to consider the Koran (28%), Torah (24%), and Book of Mormon (18%) sacred too.

The most pressing question relevant to the role of the Bible in Americans' lives seems to be why the Bible and its message are unique among other religious texts. When asked whether the Bible, the Koran, and the Book of Mormon are different expressions of the same spiritual truths, more than half (56%) agree, including nearly two-thirds of Millennials (64%). Practicing Catholics are more likely (33%) than practicing Protestants (10%) to strongly agree, as well as non-practicing Christians (16%) or people of other or no faith (19%).

Given this sense of ambiguity about religious texts, one in four Millennials who have heard/read the Bible (25%) felt confused the last time they read the Bible, compared to 16 percent of Gen X, 5 percent of Boomers, and 6 percent of Elders. Millennials are also more likely to say they felt overwhelmed (19%, compared to 12% Gen X, 6% Boomers, 4% Elders). Even so, among all generations, a sense of confusion or overwhelm is much more common than doubt.

n=1,011 | March 31–April 8, 2011;
n=2,030 | January 20–February 2, 2017

## What Books, if Any, Do You Consider Sacred Literature or Holy Books?

● 2011   ● 2017

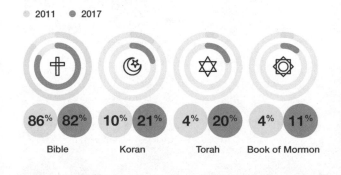

| Bible | Koran | Torah | Book of Mormon |
|---|---|---|---|
| 86%  82% | 10%  21% | 4%  20% | 4%  11% |

# Religion Required, Particulars Optional

There's an ongoing debate about whether America is a Christian nation, and the makeup of American religion today is certainly dominated by those who self-identify as Christian (49%) or specifically Catholic (23%). But Christian or not, Americans are clearly a religious bunch. In fact, more than three-quarters of U.S. adults (76%) identify with one of the major organized religions, with small minorities identifying as Jewish (2%), Muslim (1%), or Buddhist (1%). One percent belongs to some other faith. The non-religious contingent is made up of those who are not affiliated with any religion (12%) or are either agnostic (6%) or atheist (5%).

With such high levels of religious affiliation, it's no surprise that an equally large number of Americans holds favorable views toward religion. Three-quarters (73%) disagree either strongly or somewhat that religion is mostly harmful. And as one might expect, the more religious a person is, the more favorable their views toward it. For instance, almost all evangelicals (98%) and a vast majority of practicing Christians (85%) disagree that religion is mostly harmful. But even among those who claim no faith at all (unaffiliated, agnostic, and atheist), at least half (51%) disagree that religion is mostly harmful. Favorability also increases with age; Elders are significantly more likely to disagree that religion is mostly harmful (85%) compared to Millennials (64%), with both groups in the middle gradually increasing (from Gen X at 70% to Boomers at 81%).

Though Americans feel warmly toward religion in general, they are much more divided on the *distinctiveness* of each faith tradition. Americans are evenly split when it comes to believing that all religions basically teach the same thing (49% agree, 51% disagree). Those who claim no faith (42% disagree) and notional Christians (40% disagree) are least likely to see boundary markers. Beyond basically all evangelicals (99% disagree), those who are more actively engaged with their faith—such as practicing Christians (68% disagree) and regular church attenders (64% disagree)—aren't quite as vigilant about the unique claims of their own faith.

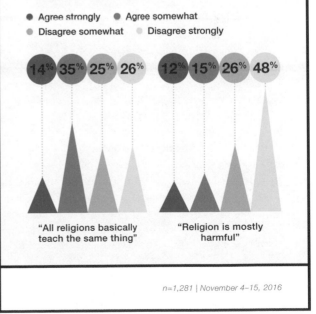

## The Value and Distinctiveness of Faith in America

● Agree strongly    ● Agree somewhat
● Disagree somewhat    ● Disagree strongly

14%  35%  25%  26%        12%  15%  26%  48%

"All religions basically teach the same thing"        "Religion is mostly harmful"

*n=1,281 | November 4–15, 2016*

# Meet the "Spiritual but Not Religious"

"I'm spiritual but not religious." You've heard it—maybe even said it—before. But what does that actually mean? Once synonymous, "religious" and "spiritual" have now come to describe seemingly distinct (but sometimes overlapping) domains of human activity. The twin cultural trends of deinstitutionalization and individualism have, for many, moved spiritual practice away from the public rituals of institutional Christianity to the private experience of God within. To get at a sense of spirituality outside the context of institutional religion, Barna created two key groups that fit the "spiritual but not religious" (SBNR) description.

The first group (SBNR #1) are those who consider themselves "spiritual" but say their religious faith is not very important in their lives. Though some may self-identify as members of a religious faith (22% Christian, 15% Catholic, 2% Jewish, 2% Buddhist, 1% other faith), they are in many ways irreligious—particularly when we take a closer look at their religious practices. For instance, 88 percent haven't been to a religious service in the past six months. This definition accounts for the unreliability of affiliation as a measure of religiosity.

A sizable majority of the SBNR #1 group does not identify with a religious faith at all (6% are atheist, 20% agnostic, 33% unaffiliated). To get a better sense of whether or not a faith affiliation (even if one is irreligious) might affect people's views and practices, Barna created a second group (SBNR #2) that focuses on only those who do not claim any faith at all. This group still says they are "spiritual," but they identify as either atheist (14%), agnostic (28%), or unaffiliated (58%). For perspective, of all those who claim "no faith," around one-third (34%) says they are "spiritual." This is a stricter definition of the "spiritual but not religious," but both groups share key qualities and reflect similar trends despite representing two different kinds of American adults—one more religiously literate than the other. In other words, even if you still affiliate with a religion, if you have discarded it as a central tenet of your life, it seems to hold little sway over your spiritual practices.

## Demographic Trends: Southwestern and Liberal

These two groups equally make up around 8 percent of the population (combined, they make up 11 percent of the population, as there is some overlap between the two). In terms of demographics, the groups include more women than men. They are more likely to be Boomers (41%), though the SBNR #1 group is slightly older and because fewer young people tend to affiliate with a religion, the SBNR #2 group is slightly younger.

Both groups identify as liberal (50% and 54%) or moderate (33% or 35%), with only a fraction identifying as conservative (17% and 11%). It may be that left-leaning spiritual seekers feel they are without a spiritual home in the Church, a place they likely view as hostile to their political attitudes.

## Redefining "God"

Both SBNR groups hold unorthodox views about God or diverge from traditional viewpoints. For instance, they are just as likely to believe God represents a state of higher consciousness that a person may reach (32% SBNR #1 and 22% SBNR #2) than an all-powerful, all-knowing, perfect creator of the universe who rules the world today (20% and 30%). For context, only one in 10 American adults (12%) believes the former, and almost six out of 10 (57%) believe the latter. So these views are certainly out of the norm. The trend continues: they are just as likely to be polytheistic (51% and 52%) as monotheistic (both groups: 48% each), and significantly fewer agree that God is everywhere (41% and 42%) compared to either practicing Christians (92%) or evangelicals (98%). What counts as "God" for the SBNR is contested among them—and that's probably just the way they like it.

## Ambivalent Views of Religion

By definition, the SBNR are religiously disinclined, and the data bear this out. First, both groups are somewhat torn

## Practices of the Spiritual but Not Religious Groups

*n=1,281 | November 4–15, 2016*

● SBNR #1    ● SBNR #2    ● Practicing Christians    ● Evangelicals

| SBNR #1 | SBNR #2 | Practicing Christians | Evangelicals | |
|---|---|---|---|---|
| 40% | 51% | 24% | 13% | Spending time in nature for reflection |
| 26% | 34% | 18% | 5% | Meditation |
| 26% | 32% | 15% | 9% | Practicing silence and/or solitude |
| 21% | 22% | 83% | 98% | Prayer |
| 16% | 22% | 17% | 16% | Journaling or writing your thoughts |
| 15% | 22% | 7% | 1% | Yoga |
| 10% | 13% | 36% | 35% | Reading books on spiritual topics |
| 4% | 10% | 56% | 82% | Scripture reading |
| 3% | 2% | 24% | 31% | Attending groups or retreats |
| 41% | 36% | 6% | 0% | None of these |

about whether religion is harmful, holding ambivalent views (54% and 46% disagree, 45% and 53% agree), especially compared to religious groups (i.e., 85% of practicing Christians disagree, 98% of evangelicals disagree). Seeking autonomy from oppressive religious authority seems to be the central task of the SBNR groups and is very likely the reason for their religious suspicion.

Second, as functional outsiders, their view of religious distinctiveness is much looser than their religious counterparts. A majority of both groups (65% and 73%) is convinced that all religions basically teach the same thing, striking numbers compared to evangelicals (1%) and practicing Christians (32%). For the SBNR, no single religion has a monopoly on truth and reality.

### Spirituality That Looks Within

To be religious is to be institutional and to practice one's spirituality in accordance with an external authority. But to be spiritual

*but not religious* is to possess a deeply personal and private spirituality. Religions point *outside* oneself to a higher power for wisdom and guidance, while a spirituality divorced from religion looks *within*. Only a fraction of the SBNR groups (9% and 7%) talks often with their friends about spiritual matters. Almost half (48% each) rarely do so, and they are 12 (24%) and eight times more likely (17%) to never talk with their friends about spiritual matters than practicing Christians and evangelicals (2% each).

### Spiritually Nourished on Their Own and Outdoors

The SBNR live out their spirituality in the absence of the institutional church. But they still take part in a set of spiritual practices, albeit a mish-mash of them. Somewhat unsurprisingly, they are very unlikely to take part in the most religious practices, such as scripture reading (4% and 10%), prayer (21% and 22%), and even groups or retreats (3% and 2%). Their spiritual nourishment is found in more informal practices, such as yoga (15% and 22%), meditation (26% and 34%), and silence and/or solitude (26% and 32%). But their most common spiritual practice is spending time in nature for reflection (40% and 51%).

The people in this group, who make sense of their lives and the world outside formal religious categories, "display an uncommon inclination to think beyond the material and to experience the transcendent," Roxanne Stone, Barna's editor in chief, says. "Such a desire can open the door to deep, spiritual conversations and, in time, perhaps a willingness to hear about Christian spirituality."

# 20 Years in America's Theology

Barna has been tracking beliefs about God among the American public for decades, and in the past 20 years, certain traditional beliefs are becoming less common. For instance, Americans are slightly less inclined to believe Satan is real and much less likely to believe the Bible is accurate in all it teaches or that God is omnipotent and omniscient. These trends parallel America's broader move toward secularization, which Barna has also been tracking. However, Americans are more likely to believe that Jesus was without sin and are increasingly assured that salvation is dependent on grace, not good deeds.

- "God is the all-powerful, all-knowing, perfect creator of the universe who rules the world today." *(% who selected this option)*

- "The Bible is totally accurate in all of its teachings." *(% who strongly agree)*

- "The Devil, or Satan, is not a living being but is a symbol of evil." *(% who strongly disagree)*

- "When He lived on earth, Jesus Christ was human and committed sins, like other people." *(% who strongly disagree)*

"If a person is generally good or does enough good things for others during their life, they will earn a place in heaven." *(% who strongly disagree)*

30%
29%
27%
42%
40%
37%
28%
27%
39%
34%

22%
24%
24%
25%
42%
46%
45%
38%
26%
70%
69%
66%
62%
32%
56%

1997
2002
2007
2012
2017

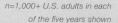

*n=1,000+ U.S. adults in each of the five years shown*

# Faith and the Military

Scripture is replete with military analogies and stories of great battles, and many Christians faithfully serve in America's military. Yet plenty of those in the armed forces do not regularly read the Bible, as Barna and American Bible Society (ABS) observed in a survey among Bible Friendly and Bible Neutral members of the military (see Glossary on page 13 for Bible engagement definitions). These two groups include respondents who are serving or have served in the Army, Marine Corps, Navy, or Air Force. Here are some of their views of the Bible, America, and self-identity.

## Christians in the Military

Three in five of the respondents (60%) say they know someone in the military who they would consider a faithful Christian. One-third (33%) says no and 8 percent are unsure. This might have something to do with how open they are about their faith, as eight in 10 (81%) have engaged in a conversation about their beliefs in God or Jesus. But these Christians have maintained a great reputation: the vast majority of respondents says they have a very positive (55%) or somewhat positive (30%) perception of the faithful Christians they know and believes they represent the Bible's ideals well (26% "very", 46% "somewhat").

## The Bible's Role in America

As Barna has reported, American values and morality have been changing significantly over the last few decades. And military members are concerned: the majority of service men and women who are Bible Friendly or Bible Neutral believes the values and morals of America are declining (86%). This view is strongest among those who have retired or have been discharged (91%) from the military, as well as those who are born again (92%). However, the same group believes scripture could make a big difference in the decline of values and morals in America. Almost half (46%) say the Bible has too little influence in U.S. society today, compared to less than a quarter (22%) who say it has too much influence. Exactly one-third (33%) says the amount of influence the Bible has is just right.

## Non–Bible Readers Are Open to Reading the Bible for Comfort

Turning to the scriptures isn't just a prescription for American society; it's something non–Bible readers are also open to. Service men and women who read the

# Foundations of Identity in the Military

*What is very important to my sense of self?*

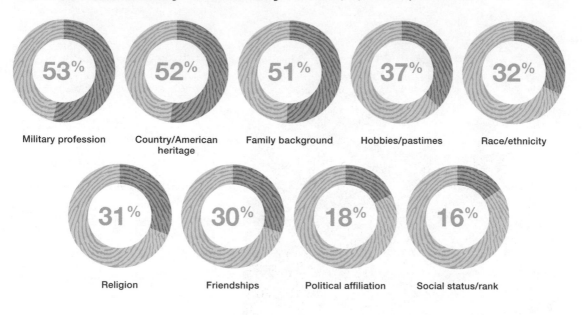

| 53% | 52% | 51% | 37% | 32% |
|:---:|:---:|:---:|:---:|:---:|
| Military profession | Country/American heritage | Family background | Hobbies/pastimes | Race/ethnicity |

| 31% | 30% | 18% | 16% |
|:---:|:---:|:---:|:---:|
| Religion | Friendships | Political affiliation | Social status/rank |

Bible infrequently or not at all say they might read the Bible for many reasons, but the most common is for comfort (37%), and understandably so, given the peace or security its pages may bring to those taking great risks for their fellow Americans. It also comes as no surprise that turning to the scriptures during a deployment is next on the list (30%). Seventeen percent say they might look to the Bible when separated from family, an unfortunate reality service members face when deployed. Others mention turning to scripture if they have a problem they need to solve or desire direction (30%) or simply to be closer to God (28%). Few approach scripture out of obligation (14%). These responses are all more common among Bible Friendlies compared to Bible Neutrals.

Looking back at the entire group as a whole, a plurality hold an orthodox view of the Bible, meaning they believe the Bible is the inspired word of God and has no errors, although some verses are meant to be symbolic rather than literal (35%). A smaller percentage (14%) believe the Bible is the actual word of God and should be taken literally, word for word. Two-thirds (66%) agree at least somewhat that the Bible contains everything a person needs to know to live a meaningful life.

## Military Service Shapes Identity

What most influences the self-image of military members? The bonds formed in battle or training and other life-changing experiences of men and women in the military are so profound that the profession becomes central to their sense of self. Most respondents say their military profession is the most important foundation of their identity (53%). Next on the list is their country/American heritage (52%), followed by their family background (51%). These three are the most common choices, but respondents also say their hobbies/pastimes (37%) help form their sense of self. Race/ethnicity (32%) and religion (31%) rank lower on the scale of self-identifiers, alongside friendships (30%). Political affiliation (18%) and social status/rank (16%), though seemingly difficult to separate from the dynamic and mission of the military, are at the bottom of the list.

*n=500 Bible Friendly/Bible Neutral military members |*

*February 21–March 27, 2017*

# Finding Generation Z's Moral Compass

By this time, the public is armed with plenty of research about, experiences with, and even stereotypes of Millennial morality. But Barna, in partnership with Impact 360 Institute, recently shifted its sights to study the belief systems of the next generation—Gen Z. This survey of teens ages 13 to 19 reveals that, at least for the time being, young people have a pretty flexible sense of right and wrong.

Almost half (48%) agree at least somewhat that religious or moral questions cannot be answered with as much certainty as scientific ones. Nearly six in 10 (58%) agree to some extent that morality is not a fixed concept but something that changes over time based on society. More than half (53%) agree that morality is up to the individual—though a majority of teens (66%) acknowledges a clear line between truth and falsehood and say that people can be wrong even about sincerely held beliefs.

While teens can still be persuaded of the wrongness of some ideas, it's unlikely they would openly express such a feeling. Forty-four percent say that it is not OK to challenge someone else's beliefs; one-third (33%) disagrees. Young people are conflict-averse in this respect, though accepting of the reality that sound beliefs may still make people uncomfortable; nearly two-thirds (63%) disagree that if a belief is offensive, it is also probably wrong. This perhaps contributes to teens' openness toward dialogue with people who hold different beliefs; two-thirds (65%) agree at least somewhat that they would be comfortable discussing their views in this context.

Interestingly, though they are less willing to claim a firm moral or religious guideline, young people do regard God as a present, provable entity in their lives. A majority (63%) trusts that people can know, not just believe, that God exists, 43 percent of whom are very convinced of this. Most are confident (58% "somewhat" and "very") they could even make a sound argument for God's existence with their friends.

It is clear that parents and peers have a key role to play in continuing to shape the values of Gen Z. When asked to point out who they consider to be a trusted source on moral issues, the top response is a parent (45%), followed by a relative (38%) or friend (37%).

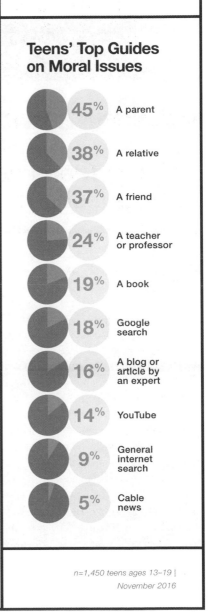

## Teens' Top Guides on Moral Issues

45%  A parent

38%  A relative

37%  A friend

24%  A teacher or professor

19%  A book

18%  Google search

16%  A blog or article by an expert

14%  YouTube

9%  General internet search

5%  Cable news

*n=1,450 teens ages 13–19 |*
*November 2016*

# Helping Teens Ask the Hard Questions

Inga Dahlstedt
Barna Group
Research Associate

In Timothy Keller's book *The Reason for God*, he states, "A faith without some doubts is like a human body without any antibodies in it."[28]

For a Christian, doubt can stem from many areas—an intense one being the relationship between science and the Bible, particularly the origins and reliability of scripture. This topic has become highly scrutinized, debated publicly by the likes of Bill Nye and Ken Ham and privately by teenagers who can easily Google "Where did humans come from?"

When Barna, in partnership with Impact 360 Institute, asked teens how they see science and the Bible, nearly one-third (31%) calls it a relationship of independence (meaning, each refers to a different aspect of reality) and more than one quarter (28%) say it's complementary (as in, each can be used to support the other). Almost half of teens (46%) say they need factual evidence to support their beliefs. Another one in five (21%) disagrees strongly with the idea that if you have enough faith, you don't need evidence. Grounding faith in facts is important to many teens, and it can be difficult when the evidence stands against what they grew up believing

I first started to examine the beliefs of my upbringing when I was in a public university, immersed in classes and textbooks implying that Christianity was "wrong." *If I can't take Genesis literally, why should any of the Bible be interpreted as literal?* I wondered. I discovered that my faith, up to that point, was largely connected to my demographics and culture rather than what I actually believed. I remember distinctly feeling fear—first, that Christianity might be a farce; then, that if it wasn't, God would judge me for my doubts.

Since then, I've navigated my own questions with help from research from all sides, books from influential Christians who have faced doubts, online boards with peers wrestling with these subjects, and discussions with others—Christians and non-Christians—who are important to me.

Even if it is uncomfortable and challenging, it is crucial that Christians ask themselves the hard questions and truly examine what they believe. Secrecy creates shame or fear, but being open with these feelings leaves room for deeper, more learned faith. Teenagers already seem to be open to topics often considered taboo for many older Christians; almost all youth pastors report that their teens are comfortable broaching these topics and expressing doubt. As young people refine their opinions and discover their identities, they can only benefit from adults and leaders who allow for open dialogue.

We need to change the stigma of doubt and allow Christians of all ages to inspect and strengthen their faith. As Keller notes, "Believers should acknowledge and wrestle with doubts—not only their own but their friends' and neighbors'."[28]

# Meet the Next,
# Next Generation

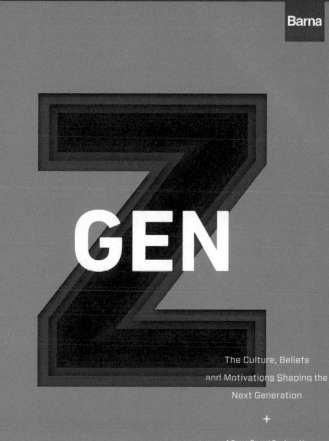

Barna

**GEN Z**

The Culture, Beliefs and Motivations Shaping the Next Generation

+

A Barna Report Produced in Partnership with Impact 360 Institute

National ministries, local churches, and Barna Group have been talking for years about generational differences, especially when it comes to young adults born between 1984 and 2002: the Millennials. But now a new generation is becoming a cultural force in their own right. *Gen Z: The Culture, Beliefs, and Motivations Shaping the Next Generation* is Barna's first major research study investigating the perceptions, experiences, and motivations of teens in Generation Z. In partnership with Impact 360, the study is our best thinking thus far on the values, assumptions, and allegiances of teens in the next, next generation. This definitive report is a must-read for pastors and parents as they help tomorrow's Christian leaders grow.

# Leadership

The obstacles and opportunities
of life behind the pulpit

# Calling: Where Ministry Begins

A majority of pastors (53%) says they felt their calls to ministry between the ages of 14 and 21—but do they still feel it? How confident are church leaders in their calling from God to shepherd his people?

Very confident, in large measure. In a Barna study conducted in partnership with Pepperdine University, three in 10 senior pastors (31%) report they are "just as confident" today as when they first entered pastoral ministry, and two-thirds (66%) say they are even "more confident" now than they were then. Just 3 percent admit they are "less confident," and these leaders tend to be younger, part of a mainline denomination, or, most often, leading a church with declining attendance.

A pastor's confidence in their calling is correlated to how satisfied they are with their work and current church ministry. Pastors who are very satisfied in one or both areas are apt to express increased assurance, while those who are less satisfied also tend to be less confident.

While confidence in pastoral calling remains robust overall, roughly six in 10 pastors (58%) say they have felt "inadequate for [their] ministry or calling" during the past three months, either frequently (12%) or sometimes (45%). Leaders of churches with declining attendance feel this inadequacy most acutely.

Researchers examined the relationship of confidence in one's calling with feelings of ministry inadequacy and of being "energized by ministry work." As one might expect, the small percentage of pastors who feel less confident in their calling today than when they started their ministry do not feel energized by ministry work as often as those who are more confident. Similarly, leaders who are less confident today in their call to ministry feel inadequate for their calling much more frequently than those who are just as or more confident than when they began.

These data suggest the importance of regular reflection on one's motivation for engaging in ministry. As Christian ministries professor Terry Linhart tells Barna, "Calling is not rooted in a desire to be involved in 'religious work,' but rather in a personal response to a personal God."

# THE AGE OF CALLING

More than half of all U.S. pastors sense a call to ministry between the ages of 14 and 21. Here's a timing breakdown of this pivotal experience.

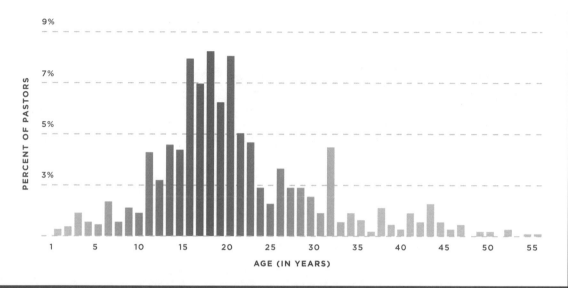

PERCENT OF PASTORS

AGE (IN YEARS)

# PATTERNS OF CALLING

Each pastor's call to vocational ministry is unique, yet there seem to be some common experiences that make answering God's call more likely.

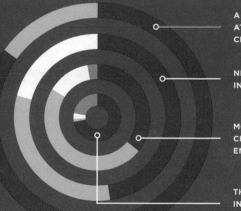

**A LARGE MAJORITY ATTENDED CHURCH AS CHILDREN**

- Yes 85%
- No 15%

**NEARLY HALF GREW UP IN A SMALL CHURCH**

- Small <200 48%
- Medium 200 to 500 32%
- Large 500+ 21%

**MOST CONSIDER THEIR CHILDHOOD CHURCH ENVIRONMENT HEALTHY**

- Very healthy 36%
- Somewhat healthy 48%
- Somewhat unhealthy 13%
- Very unhealthy 3%

**THREE-QUARTERS WERE INVOLVED IN YOUTH MINISTRY AS A TEEN**

- Church youth group 72%
- Parachurch youth ministry 2%
- Church + parachurch groups 4%
- None 22%

*n=900 U.S. Protestant senior pastors | April–December 2015*

# IDENTITY
## WHO ARE TODAY'S PASTORS?

In 1992, George Barna conducted a landmark study of U.S. Protestant senior pastors.[29] Barna, in partnership with Pepperdine University, asked, *What's changed since?*

**Pastors are getting older.**
In 25 years, the median age of a senior pastor has increased from 44 to 54.

**More pastors are women.**
More than 97 percent of pastors in 1992 were men, but today one in 11 are women.

**Nearly all pastors are married.**
This trend is unchanged, actually. But while marriage rates are plummeting among Americans overall, it's worth noting the percentage of married pastors is holding steady.

**Fewer pastors have children.**
The percentage of pastors with children under 18 living at home has dropped by nearly half in 25 years. This is due in part to the significant increase in pastors' age.

**Pastors are staying put.**
Average church tenure in 1992 was just four years, and then pastors moved on to a new congregation. Today the average is more than a decade.

**Pastors make a livable wage.** (Most of them, anyway.)
The annual salary of pastors in 1992 was slightly below U.S. median income. Today the average tops the national norm by a small margin.

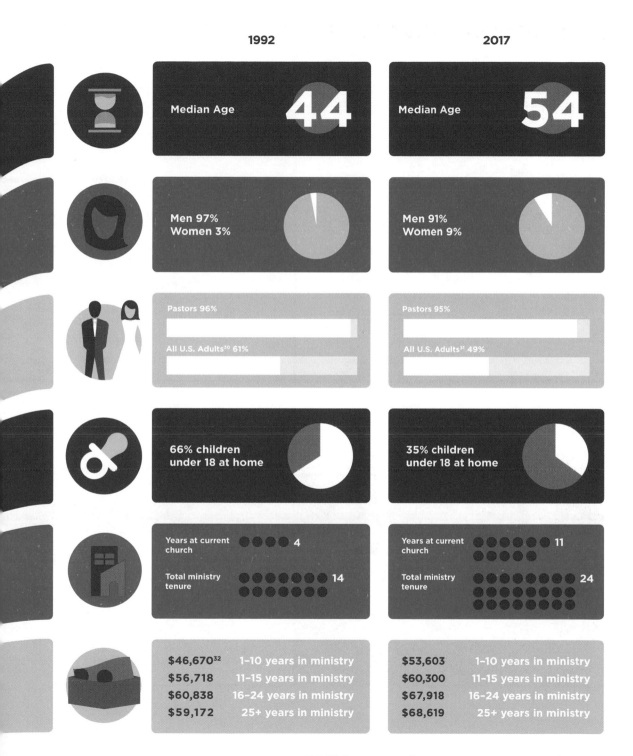

**1992**

**2017**

Median Age **44**

Median Age **54**

Men 97%
Women 3%

Men 91%
Women 9%

Pastors 96%

Pastors 95%

All U.S. Adults[30] 61%

All U.S. Adults[31] 49%

66% children
under 18 at home

35% children
under 18 at home

Years at current church **4**

Years at current church **11**

Total ministry tenure **14**

Total ministry tenure **24**

| | |
|---|---|
| $46,670[32] | 1–10 years in ministry |
| $56,718 | 11–15 years in ministry |
| $60,838 | 16–24 years in ministry |
| $59,172 | 25+ years in ministry |

| | |
|---|---|
| $53,603 | 1–10 years in ministry |
| $60,300 | 11–15 years in ministry |
| $67,918 | 16–24 years in ministry |
| $68,619 | 25+ years in ministry |

*n=1,033 U.S. Protestant pastors | 1992; n=5,067 U.S. Protestant pastors | 2011–2016*

# The Pastor's Family Portrait

How do the pressures of leading a church weigh on a pastor and, inevitably, their family? According to Barna research conducted in partnership with Pepperdine University, there's very good news. Most pastors—96 percent of whom are married—are satisfied with their relationships with their spouses. Seven out of 10 (70%) say their relationships are excellent, and one-quarter (26%) considers them good. By comparison, less than half of all married U.S. adults (46%) rate their marriages as excellent, and one-third (35%) say their marriages are good. Pastors also divorce at lower rates: about 10 percent of Protestant pastors have ever been divorced, compared to one-quarter of all U.S. adults (27%).

Financial constraints can be a relational burden, yet pastors with leaner resources—perhaps paradoxically—tend to report a stronger connection with their spouses. Eighty-three percent of those earning less than $40,000 a year rate their marital satisfaction as excellent.

Pastors with children under 18 (35% of all pastors) are also enthusiastic about their relationships with their kids. Three out of five (60%) view them as excellent, and one-third (36%) reports them as good. Pastors once again rate their relational satisfaction higher than the national average: among all U.S. parents, less than half (46%) say their relationships with their children are excellent, and one in three (32%) says they're good.

Strains of ministry life do surface in the findings. Roughly one-quarter of today's pastors has faced significant marital problems (26%) or parenting problems (27%) during their ministry tenure. Pastors 50 and older are more inclined to report such problems, likely by virtue of their comparatively longer marriages and the fact that many are weathering or have lately survived their kids' teen and young adult years. When asked whether their current church tenures have been difficult on their families, about half of pastors (48%) say it's somewhat or completely true.

Pastors who rate higher on Barna's risk metrics (see page 217 for a summary of Barna's risk metric) are more prone to say their marriages are average or below average, as well as eight times more likely than the norm to say their relationships with their children are average.

n=900 U.S. Protestant senior pastors (175 with children under 18 at home, 490 married) | April–December 2015; n=1,025 (496 with children under 18 at home, 601 married) | April 29–May 1, 2015

# Spiritual Disciplines of Spiritual Leaders

In partnership with Pepperdine University, Barna asked pastors how they feel spiritually and emotionally. Most pastors say they are doing pretty well. Nine in 10 (91%), compared to only six in 10 U.S. adults (62%), are overall satisfied with their quality of life. Pastors rate their emotional health (85% "excellent" + "good") and spiritual health (88%) better than the general population (63% and 60%, respectively).

But Barna did find two critical areas where pastors struggle more than the rest of the population: they are more likely to experience feelings of inadequacy around their work (58% of pastors feel this way frequently or sometimes vs. just 30% of employed U.S. adults) and are more likely to express emotional or mental exhaustion (75% vs. 55% of employed U.S. adults). Nearly half of all pastors (46%) admit having struggled with depression. A similar amount (47%) has difficulty finding time to invest in their own spiritual health.

Yet this investment seems to make a huge difference in overall pastoral health. The consistency of one's spiritual practice correlates to satisfaction and low-risk metrics (see page 217 for a description of Barna's risk metric). Pastors who are very satisfied with

their vocation (75%) and their current ministry (73%), or who rate low on spiritual (81%) or burnout (74%) risk, are most likely to report practicing their top essential discipline (usually prayer) every day or more often. By contrast, those at high spiritual risk (54%) are less prone to practice every day and more inclined to do so only a few times a month or less often (17% high spiritual risk, 15% high burnout risk vs. 5% of all pastors).

If pastors and those who support them should take anything away from these findings, it's that consistent spiritual practices matter—to vocational satisfaction and contentedness with one's own ministry, as well as to emotional, spiritual, and relational well-being.

## Pastors and Soul Care

*About half of pastors find it difficult to invest in their own spiritual health; this is especially true among newer pastors.*

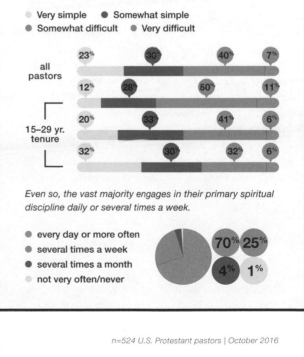

● Very simple   ● Somewhat simple
● Somewhat difficult   ● Very difficult

*Even so, the vast majority engages in their primary spiritual discipline daily or several times a week.*

● every day or more often
● several times a week
● several times a month
● not very often/never

70%   25%
4%   1%

*n=524 U.S. Protestant pastors | October 2016*

# A Q&A on Pastoral Care

## with Chuck DeGroat

*DeGroat has spent the last 20 years in pastoral ministry, seminary teaching, and clinical counseling. Currently, he is professor of counseling and pastoral care at Western Theological Seminary in Holland, Michigan. Formerly, he was a teaching pastor at City Church San Francisco, where he co-founded Newbigin House of Studies, an urban and missional training center. DeGroat is the author of the books* Leaving Egypt, The Toughest People to Love, *and* Wholeheartedness.

***Nearly half of all pastors have struggled with depression at some point during their tenure. In your experience counseling pastors and working with them, what are some of the unique factors in pastoral life that contribute to depression? Do you see depression as having a particular stigma or shame attached to it for pastors?***

I've seen attitudes toward depression change in the 20+ years I've been pastoring. I went on Zoloft myself in the late 90s and didn't share that, apart from a few trusted friends. Today, pastors more freely share basic struggles with anxiety or depression or exhaustion. One major exception I see is in rural pastoral contexts where certain images of the "put-together" pastor still reign.

What contributes to depression is manifold, but at the core (and beyond the necessary caveats about biology and predisposition) is a failure to take suffering and grief seriously. I often call depression unprocessed grief; it's when grief gets stuck. At this point, pastors often feel powerless to change what they're experiencing. The courageous pastor will reach out to a therapist or trusted friend to begin processing what's stuck inside, but I'm afraid too many either stuff it or medicate it. Alcohol dependency,

pornography use, avoidant behavior, and more result. The shame of being broken or damaged keeps the cycle of stuffing and medicating alive, which sometimes results in tragic falls or premature exits from ministry.

***It seems that newer or less tenured pastors are most susceptible to depression or even burnout. As you prepare seminary students for pastoral work, how do you also prepare them for the pressures and stressors that might contribute to depression or burnout (especially in their early career, when there are likely other factors affecting them as well, like young children, financial stress, learning curves, proving themselves to parishioners/elders/etc.)?***

At Western Theological Seminary in Holland, Michigan, where I teach, we have a strong commitment to forming the whole person for mission. This begins with a thorough psychological assessment for each first-year student. That assessment leads to particular recommendations

for care and counseling, and we help pay for their therapy. In addition, I teach two core courses: The Pastor as Person and Pastor Care and Counseling. The first is designed to look at family-of-origin dynamics, shame, addiction, vocational identity, and more. What's also helpful is a one-week Enneagram retreat where first-year students are thoroughly immersed in a process of self-awareness within community, leading to great conversations and growing humility. Beyond this, students are in peer groups each week where they employ the tools of non-violent communication to foster deeper connections to their needs and to the needs of others. Finally, at the mid-program point for each student, two faculty members and one formation staff person sit down with each student to look at all of this together, asking key questions about health and wholeness, vocational identity, and readiness for ministry. Altogether, I think this is very helpful.

***"Counseling others/solving people problems" is the top thing pastors wish seminary*** ***had better prepared them for (tied with "administrative burdens"). In what ways are you seeking to better prepare pastors for this part of their role?***

My own dissertation looked at seminary education and pastoral preparation, so I've heard from many pastors in my research about their desires for a more robust seminary education. Of course, seminary can't do everything. I sense that the desire for counseling coursework is not so much about techniques as much as it is about forming the person to be an attuned, empathetic presence. A pastor who grows in wholeness herself is a pastor who can meet someone in his brokenness, even if she doesn't have a mastery of technique. For some time, there was a kind of prevailing wisdom that taught that new pastors should learn to refer to the real experts: therapists. Now, I'm both a pastor and a therapist, so I'm convinced of the importance of therapeutic insight, but we need pastors who will show up, who are present, who can read the subtle "subtexts" of people's lives (see Craig Barnes's *The Pastor as Minor Poet*). So, I help students become aware of their relational patterns and ways of coping, so that as they move toward both insight and health, they become women and men who can walk others into similar conversations.

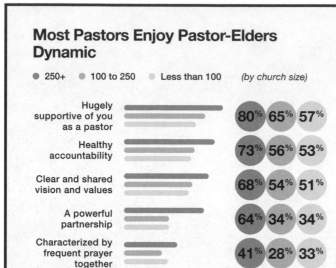

## Most Pastors Enjoy Pastor-Elders Dynamic

● 250+    ● 100 to 250    ● Less than 100    *(by church size)*

| | 250+ | 100 to 250 | Less than 100 |
|---|---|---|---|
| Hugely supportive of you as a pastor | 80% | 65% | 57% |
| Healthy accountability | 73% | 56% | 53% |
| Clear and shared vision and values | 68% | 54% | 51% |
| A powerful partnership | 64% | 34% | 34% |
| Characterized by frequent prayer together | 41% | 28% | 33% |

# What Works on Church Teams

Barna, in partnership with Pepperdine University, delved into the leadership ties that can make or break a congregation: governance. Most pastors are primarily responsible for setting the vision and direction of the church (60%) or are part of a team that does so together (35%). A majority (80%) reports to a board of elders or similar group of laypeople (such as deacons, etc.).

Pastors hold a range of attitudes toward this governing body. Most positively, a majority of pastors says their board is "hugely supportive" of them as a pastor (67%), describe the relationship as generating "healthy accountability" (60%), and indicate they have "clear and shared vision and values" (57%). However, there are signs of possible weakness between pastors and elders. Pastors less commonly categorize their relationships as "powerful" partnerships (44%) or say they engage in "frequent prayer together" (34%). Pastors of larger or growing congregations are more likely than leaders in smaller or shrinking congregations to say their relationships with elders are powerful partnerships.

Pastors who are satisfied with their current church ministry tend to report a more positive relationship with their governing board than those who are less satisfied. Conversely, discontented leaders are more apt than the norm to describe their relationships in negative terms. There are "unclear areas of decision-making authority" (42% vs. 18% all pastors) and "power struggles" (39% vs. 12%). They "feel under-appreciated by the board" (36% vs. 11%). One in five would go so far as to say the pastor-elders dynamic is "one of the worst parts of ministry" (19% vs. 4%).

A parallel trend is at work among pastors who are at high risk of burnout (see page 217 for a summary of Barna's risk metric), suggesting connections between a healthy leadership team, a healthy pastor, and a growing church. Brooke Hempell, Barna's senior vice president of research, says, "Our hope is that denominational support networks as well as church lay leaders will take these findings to heart and inquire about and invest in their pastors' relational support."

*n=499 U.S. Protestant senior pastors |*

*April–December 2015*

# Pastoring in an Age of Complexity

# A Q&A on Team Leadership

## with General Stanley McChrystal

*A retired four-star general, McChrystal developed a comprehensive counterinsurgency strategy in Afghanistan and a counterterrorism organization that revolutionized interagency operating culture. He's founder of The McChrystal Group and author of* Team of Teams. *This is an adapted Q&A from Barna and Pepperdine University's The State of Pastors 2017 event.*

### On getting various organizations to work together:

Give people a chance to interact across [the mission]. Think about the people you don't trust: they're typically people you don't know. And then the first time you know someone from another religion or from another city or from another economic status or race and you're forced [to be] with them for a while, you go, "Wow! You know, you're not so bad. Is everybody else from your tribe like you?" Suddenly, you start to change.

We thought mass communications and social media were going to bridge [us], but we've segmented ourselves by our income level, by our religion, by our political leanings, by you name it. Instead of the information technology actually creating shared consciousness, we tend to watch the news we agree with. We tend to go to the websites and to interact more with those people who are more like us. As a consequence, what we lack is that interaction that's so critical in creating a team of teams.

### On leaders as gardeners:

I'd say a gardener doesn't grow anything; only plants grow things. If the plants are allowed to do that in an effective way, they can do it simultaneously, so you can have this ability to be fast and do it at scale. The leader's role has changed. I think the leader now is like a gardener in the sense that they're an enabler. They create the garden, they create the environment. It's not easy work. . . . In fact, it's more energy-intensive. It's more difficult because the gardener has to constantly be shaping, adjusting. They've got to know when

to water, when to weed, when to do all the things that keep the garden healthy.

### On the difference between education and training:

There are skills you have to develop, [like] the ability to read and write. Those are things I think you train. You develop those skills that give you the ability to do things, and if your skills are very well-trained, then you have this foundation to operate from. Education is really how to think about things, how to use those skills. And the reason they have to go hand in hand is, if you have to spend a lot of time thinking about how to do the basics, you don't have much time left to think about the bigger issue—what you're actually doing. Education comes into values. It comes into our ability to reason, our ability to do the kinds of intellectual exercises we have to do that allow us to really get at a right answer or a right approach or to get our mind around a problem. You can't train that; that, I think, has to be educated into people.

# The Graying of American Clergy

David Kinnaman
Barna Group
President

A recent Barna study conducted in partnership with Pepperdine University reveals that there are now more full-time senior pastors ages 65 and older than under the age of 40. While the data do not reveal exactly why this shift has occurred, possible contributors include factors such as increased life expectancy; the rise of bivocational and second-career pastors; financial pressure facing pastors, including the economic downturn of 2008; the allure of entrepreneurship among young adults; the lack of leadership development among Millennials and Gen X; and a lack of succession planning among Boomers.

All these factors and more contribute to what we're referring to as the "graying" of America's clergy—a phenomenon with more cons than pros. It's surely an upside that older pastors often have wisdom that comes only with much experience, and the Church is in desperate need of such wisdom in this era of unparalleled complexity. Yet God's people also need younger leaders who are being prepared today for an uncertain future. Older pastors are uniquely situated (and called) to raise up, train, and release godly, capable, and resilient young pastors. The problem arises when today's pastors do not represent a healthy mix of young, middle-age, and older leaders.

The bare facts of the matter are that even the wisest of older pastors is not here indefinitely, and their wisdom will be lost to the community of faith unless it is invested with the next generation. (For more data on pastoral succession, see page 192). Even more urgent, however, is the prospect of a massive leadership shortage in the coming decades. In the best-case scenario, Bible-literate, Spirit-filled, missional lay leaders will rise up in the place of a shrinking professional clergy, living as the "holy priesthood" (1 Peter 2:5, NIV) on a scale rarely seen before. This is certainly a possibility, but is it the most likely outcome?

It is urgent that denominations, networks, and independent churches determine how to best motivate, mobilize, resource, and deploy more young pastors. Some solutions to the crisis include creating and demonstrating better cross-generational and cross-functional teams; developing and implementing better succession efforts; challenging more younger leaders to sign on to be spiritual leaders and more established pastors to make space for younger leaders; creating a broader vision for pastoring that includes a renewed vision of the priesthood of all believers; and improving the educational and developmental process to unleash more pastors.

For the Christian community to be at its best, it needs intergenerational leaders to move it forward.

# Four Priorities of Pastoral Succession

At some point, a pastor must pass the pulpit to a new church leader. The motivations that guide such a pivotal transition for a minister and a church are many—and, as a Barna study conducted in partnership with Brotherhood Mutual points out, are very important to the outcomes of pastoral succession.

The study focused on how different Protestant American churches structure the process of transition in context of their denomination, church governance, location, and size (among other factors). The main audience for the study included a national sample of churchgoing Protestant congregation members. The study also surveyed incoming senior pastors, church staff, and outgoing pastors who left the senior role. All audiences were required to have experienced senior pastoral transition in the last five to seven years.

In examining the differences between types of pastoral succession, the leadership's priorities for the church during transition played a key role in the overall impact of the transition. Congregation members were asked to identify the highest priority of the church during the succession process. Most congregation members report that the church emphasized maintaining church unity (42%) or sustaining vision (32%) during the transition. However, a minority of churches feels financial stability (7%) or fresh growth (9%) were the leadership's top priority—and these smaller groups experienced very different pastoral transitions. Specifically, the data reveal that a succession process driven by a concern for finances much more negatively impacts relationships between the congregation and the leadership, as well as the leadership's emotional burdens.

Where finances were seen as the church's top priority, just more than one-third of congregation members (36%) say the transition went extremely smoothly. By comparison, where the leadership prioritized sustained vision (57%) or church unity (52%), more than half say there were few difficulties. Forty-six percent in churches that prioritized fresh growth also experienced an extremely smooth transition. Additionally, according to congregation members, financial priorities contributed to major obstacles (18%), while just 7 percent of those in churches with other transition priorities report such challenges.

Perhaps one of the major obstacles for these churches was their varying success in communicating about the transition to their congregation members. Full knowledge of a church's financial concerns is often limited to the leadership, but a specific vision for the church or a desire for continued unity can be more easily discussed and encouraged among the congregation. In fact, among congregation members, 62 percent of those whose leadership prioritized sustained vision and 52 percent of those whose leadership prioritized church unity report that the church communicated "very well" about the reasons for the pastoral succession. In contrast, only 46 percent of congregants who felt leadership prioritized fresh growth and 36 percent of congregants who felt leadership prioritized financial stability highly rate their leadership's communication about the reasons for transition.

Communication also impacts the congregation's perception of their relationship with the leadership. Just 12 percent of those whose leadership emphasized sustained vision or church unity and 14 percent of those whose leadership prioritized fresh growth say their relationship with the church leadership was weak during that time. However, for congregation members who witnessed pastoral successions driven by financial concerns, nearly one third (31%) describes the transitional relationship with leadership as somewhat weak or very weak.

Pressures of prioritizing financial stability during church succession also affect the emotional experiences among incoming pastors. Six out of ten incoming pastors in an environment focused on financial stability (61%) experienced worry as a primary emotion during the transition, compared to only 28 percent of incoming pastors who emphasized church unity, a quarter (25%) of those who pursued fresh growth, and only 17 percent of those who sought to sustain vision. Doubt (39%), regret (33%), nostalgia (33%), and confusion (28%) were also much more prevalent among incoming pastors who experienced a finance-focused succession. Such emotions could be compounded by tension among other church leaders during transition. When monetary concerns took priority, four in 10 (39%) incoming pastors called the unity within the elder board somewhat weak or very weak. Meanwhile, just one in four incoming pastors who prioritized fresh growth (24%), 18 percent who prioritized church unity, and 7 percent who prioritized sustained vision observed such weakness among the elders.

When a church is focused on finances during pastoral succession, the experience is more emotionally draining and discouraging for the incoming pastor. Further, more tensions are felt by the staff and lay leadership. In the pews, there is a threat to the congregation's trust in leadership and, not uncommonly, division: 15 percent of congregants who underwent a financially fraught transition saw the unity within the congregation as very weak, while fewer than 5 percent in other types of transitions sensed such negativity.

What is happening in these instances? Often, the focus on financial priorities indicates broader challenges and conflicts in the church. There may have been another situation that led to the financial crisis. For example, discontent with an outgoing pastor before their transition may have led to the departure of members—and with them, their tithes. In the midst of transition, lack of trust may cause remaining members to suspend their giving until the situation is righted. These dynamics extend beyond finances and reveal the need for general healthy leadership and relationships.

## Primary Negative Emotions During Transition *(by leadership priority)*

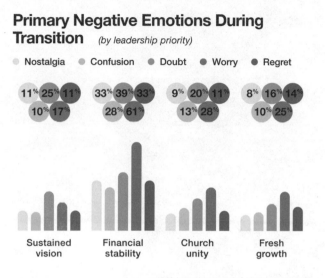

n=249 incoming pastors | March–April 2017

## Unity within the Congregation During Transition *(by leadership priority)*

n=1,517 congregation members | March 2017

n=1,517 practicing Christians | March 2017;

n=129 church staff senior pastors | March–April 2017

(All respondents experienced a senior pastor transition within the last five to seven years.)

# Pastoral Change Doesn't Have to Be a Crisis

Barna

A Barna Report Produced in Partnership with Brotherhood Mutual

## LEADERSHIP TRANSITIONS
How Churches Navigate Pastoral Change—and Stay Healthy

# More than Clever Sermons

Francis Chan
Author, Pastor

*Barna premiered its study of pastors' well-being at The State of Pastors 2017 event, hosted by research partner Pepperdine University. The following is adapted from Francis Chan's closing remarks.*

I've been praying this passage over myself. It's in Ephesians, and I just encourage you to pray this for yourself [too]. Paul writes specifically to the saints: "I do not cease to give thanks for you, remembering you in my prayers, that the God of our Lord Jesus Christ, the Father of glory, may give you the Spirit of wisdom and of revelation in the knowledge of him, having the eyes of your heart enlightened, that you may know what is the hope to which he has called you, what are the riches of his glorious inheritance in the saints, and what is the immeasurable

greatness of his power toward us who believe, according to the working of his great might" (1:16–19, ESV).

As a pastor, I can't just be trying to preach more clever sermons. Something internal, miraculous has to happen through the Spirit of God where the eyes of my heart are enlightened. Do I still know the hope of dying and coming into the presence of God? The hope of dwelling with God and walking with him? Is that hope so real in me that nothing gets me down?

I'm a terrible hoper. I'm one of those people who almost plans and expects the worst so that I won't get let down—and yet God wants me to know this hope of my future, and that's what keeps me going.

Paul talks about our inheritance earlier in the chapter, but then he switches: "What are the riches of *his* glorious inheritance in the saints" (emphasis added). God is looking forward to his inheritance in us. To know that and to internalize that . . . the security that would give us as pastors!

I've got garbage like you too. I've got that baggage of feeling like I had a dad who never wanted me. I'm still human. I still have these insecurities, thinking, *I better do this right. I better grow this. Am I failing him?* rather than looking at the accomplished work of Christ and really believing Jesus did something so beautiful in me. God the Father looks at me and says, "I can't wait to inherit Francis. I can't wait to see him."

The world's constantly changing. It's getting more hostile. But if the spirit of revelation and wisdom enlightens my heart to really see these things, then I'll be unstoppable.

You have a group of people who know the hope to which they've been called and are sure of the riches of his glory, the inheritance in the saints, and really know there's an immeasurable greatness of power toward us who believe.

That's an unstoppable group. And that's what we as pastors need to become.

# Global Religion

Studies focused on the state of the
Christian faith in other countries

# U.K. Christians on Mission

A plurality of active Christians living in the United Kingdom (45%) defines mission work as a balance of social justice and evangelism. How are churches in the U.K.—often considered a highly secular region—carrying out this holy mission on a global scale? In partnership with World Vision UK, Barna surveyed active Christians in the U.K. to learn what that might look like.

It's important to get an idea of the projects and outreaches that come to mind when a U.K. believer considers the concept of "global mission." A large majority (79%) believes it starts with prioritizing the financial support of organizations on the ground. Two-thirds (66%) say it's paramount to educate the congregation about issues pertinent to global mission. Six in 10 (61%) see regular prayer as important. Other responses chosen by substantial minorities include advocating for those in other countries (45%), encouraging involvement outside the church (38%), and supporting an individual/group to serve full-time (36%). Short-term trips, whether organized by a church (24%) or charity (15%), are less of a priority.

Two-thirds (65%) believe local and global mission are not competing endeavors but should be given equal attention. One in three (31%) says the church should focus locally, while just 2 percent say so of global mission. The older the individual, the more likely they stress that local and global mission should be equal concerns; three of four adults 65 and older (74%) affirm this view, compared to two-thirds of those ages 45–64 (67%) and 55 percent of those ages 18–44. Those in Scotland are also likely to place similar value on local and global work (74%).

How effective do these Christians think their church is in global mission work? Most offer lukewarm responses (50% "fairly" effective, 33% "not very" effective). Few have more extreme reviews(6% "very" effective, 7% "not at all" effective). Ethnic minorities are more likely than white adults to rate their church as very effective in mission work (14% vs. 5%).

## Prioritizing Global Justice and Evangelism

*"Local and global mission should be given equal attention."*

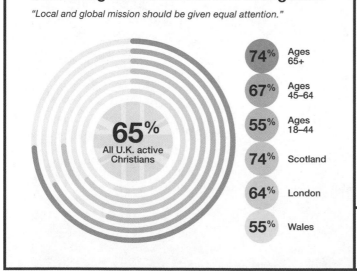

65%
All U.K. active Christians

74% Ages 65+

67% Ages 45–64

55% Ages 18–44

74% Scotland

64% London

55% Wales

*n=1,159 U.K. active Christians | April 2017*

**BARNA TAKES**

# Security Beyond Policy

Gareth Russell
Barna Global
Vice President for the U.K. and Europe

I'm Scottish. I'm also British. And for the time being, I'm European. I'm proud of my background; it has formed a major part of my identity and my outlook. But a seismic shift in global politics over the last few years sometimes complicates that feeling of pride.

There has been a lot of effort to explain what seems to be an international movement toward political rhetoric rooted in self-preservation and an inflamed sense of patriotism. This is not just a British issue either; the same can be said in America and in countries like France, Germany, and the Netherlands that are all experiencing unique political disruption and in many cases the increasing influence of extreme nationalistic ideologies. You see this reflected in proclamations that suggest a return to "the good ol' days." The days when we had control. The days when we were truly American, or British, or Scottish, or [insert nationality here].

Barna data show that almost half of American adults (47%) do feel that other cultures enrich the nation, yet one in four (23%) strongly agrees the country allows too many immigrants. Three in 10 (31%) strongly agree the United States should welcome refugees in a crisis—more than twice the percentage among evangeli-

cals (16%). And, though I don't have stats for Britain, there is currently much fear here caused by terrorism, particularly the randomized form it has taken in recent years and in the work of ISIS. Many of us have walked the streets, crossed the bridges, and traveled through the tube stations where attacks have occurred; in fact, 15 minutes before the March 2017 Westminster Bridge attack, I was in the Houses of Parliament only a few hundred yards away. These threats to life and to our freedom are in the back of our minds as we go about our day-to-day routines. This has led to fear of the unknown—as well as of the other, the foreigner, those who dress or believe differently.

But I don't read anywhere in the Bible that God is a separatist God. He is not tribal, selective, and exclusive. He is open, welcoming, gracious, and merciful. And he calls us to be the same. What if true security lies not in control, but surrender? What if rather than being insulated, we instead chose generous and selfless living?

If we are filled with the Spirit of God, 2 Timothy 1:7 (NIV) tells us, it "does not make us timid, but gives us power, love, and self-discipline." As Christians, no matter where we live or the national legislation, we are called to a higher purpose. We are called to be welcoming, we are called to put others before our own agenda, and we are called ultimately to love—even, as Jesus says, those we perceive to be our enemies.

Our identity and security is ultimately in Christ, who "made himself nothing by taking the very nature of a servant" (Philippians 2:7, NIV). Kingdom citizenship calls us to humility, rather than bluster. To peace, rather than fear. To prioritize what we can sacrifice, rather than store up what we can secure. What might that look like?

# American Ideas about Islam

While a majority of Americans still identifies as Christian, they recognize the religious landscape is shifting. Most now believe they live in a globalized and religiously plural nation. Many of these religions have been in America for centuries, but immigration, increased visibility via social media and news coverage, and a decrease in the number of observant American Christians have all led to a sense that the religious climate is different. Perhaps nowhere has this awareness been more pronounced than in a national ambivalence toward the presence of Islam in America.

In a recent study, Barna gauged American adults' attitudes toward and perceptions of Islam. Americans' responses to these questions highlight the ideological and religious divides that challenge a peaceful coexistence.

### Islam Seen as Conflicting with Christianity and American Values

Though the country is fairly split on the issue, a plurality of adults (41%) disagrees that Muslims and Christians worship the same God. A little more than one-third (34%) agree that Muslims and Christians worship the same God and one-quarter (25%) is not sure. As might be expected, Christians are much less likely than the general population to agree that the God they worship is the same God of Islam (86% of evangelicals and 44% of practicing Christians strongly disagree). When it comes to the compatibility of American values and Islam, Americans are more evenly split on whether the nation's values are inconsistent with teachings of the Islamic faith. Around four in 10 adults (38%) agree teachings of Islam do not align with American values, compared with an equal amount (38%) who disagrees. Just shy of one-quarter of American adults (24%) is not sure.

### Evangelicals Reluctant to Support Religious Freedom for Muslims

Concerns over religious freedom have increased in the last few years, and though evangelicals have often been in the spotlight over this issue, matters of religious freedom impact a number of other faith communities, including Muslims. The majority of American adults is sympathetic to those struggles: almost three in four (72%) are in support of Muslims openly practicing their religion. Only 15 percent disagree and 13 percent are unsure. Despite their concerns over religious liberty, evangelicals are much less likely to support such freedom for Muslims as other groups: just over one-quarter of evangelicals (27%) strongly agree that Muslims should be able to practice their religion openly. Practicing Christians are in step with evangelicals in holding this view (30%). However, Muslims have a strong ally in those who claim no faith: more than half of atheists or agnostics (52%) strongly agree that Muslims should be able to practice their religion openly.

### Americans See Muslims as Peaceful

Despite the increasing number of terror attacks both stateside and abroad, Americans, for the most part, distinguish Muslims from the extremists of ISIS. Most Americans (54%) either strongly or somewhat agree that Muslims are peaceful people. However, more than one-quarter (27%) either strongly or somewhat disagree. Almost two in 10 (19%) are not sure what they believe.

### Very Few Americans Have Muslim Friends

One important way to build bridges across religious divides is to foster friendships. However, the vast majority of American adults does not have a Muslim friend. When asked how often they spend time with friends who are Muslim, almost seven in 10 Americans (68%) report not having any Muslim friends at all. Very few spend time with a Muslim friend often (3%) or very often (1%), though a little more do so sometimes (8%) or seldom (13%). Younger, liberal, non-white, more educated, and less religious Americans are more likely to have Muslim friends than their older, conservative, white, less educated, and more religious counterparts. The difference is small though; it would seem that no individual non-Muslim group is very good at making Muslim friends.

Those who do spend time with Muslim friends, however, are more likely to believe Muslims are peaceful people (35%, compared to 13% who strongly agree) and that they worship the same God as Christians (27%, compared to 14% who strongly agree), less likely to believe teachings of Islam are inconsistent with American values (12%, compared to 22% who strongly agree), and more supportive of Muslims' right to practice religion openly (56%, compared to 37% who strongly agree). It's clear that friendships with Muslims are key to overcoming negative perceptions.

### Americans Divided on Islam

On every question in the survey, the divides within age groups, ideology, education levels, religiosity, and racial groups are significant. Millennials, liberals, college-educated, non-white, and non-religious groups are all less likely to see tension between Christian or American values and Islam and are more likely to support religious freedom for Muslims, to have more Muslim friends, and to believe Islam is a peaceful religion. However, Elders, political conservatives, those with a high school education or less, white Americans, and Christian groups like evangelicals and practicing Christians are much more likely to see tension between their values and Islam and are less likely to support religious freedom for Muslims, to have fewer Muslim friends, and to believe Islam is a peaceful religion.

## Friendships with Muslims Influence Perceptions of Islam

● Strongly agree ● Strongly disagree

**"Muslims and Christians worship the same God"**

**14%** People without Muslim friends

**27%** People who spend time with Muslims

**"Muslims are peaceful people"**

**13%** People without Muslim friends

**35%** People who spend time with Muslims

**"Teachings of the Islamic faith are inconsistent with American values"**

**16%** People without Muslim friends

**29%** People who spend time with Muslims

**"Muslims should be able to practice their religion openly"**

**37%** People without Muslim friends

**56%** People who spend time with Muslims

## Jewish Americans Overwhelmingly Agree Anti-Semitism Exists in the U.S.

● Strongly agree     ● Somewhat agree     ● Somewhat disagree
● Strongly disagree     ● I'm not sure

**Millennials**

44%  41%  6%

3%  5%

**Gen X**

47%  38%  6%

4%  5%

**Boomers**

56%  37%  2%

1%  4%

**Elders**

55%  37%  2%

0%  6%

# The Impact of Anti-Semitism in the U.S.

In 2017, the Anti-Defamation League reported an alarming number of acts of prejudice against Jews in the United States.[33] Indeed, Barna research, conducted in partnership with Jews for Jesus, found that, unsurprisingly, American Jews overwhelmingly affirm the presence of anti-Semitism in the U.S. While the study was completed prior to 2017 incidents (as well as the 2016 election, to which many link a surge in hostility), it highlights the lasting impact of a personal encounter with anti-Semitism.

Nearly all Jews in America (88%) agree anti-Semitism is a domestic issue, and half (50%) do so strongly. Boomers and Elders are more likely to recognize this problem of prejudice (55% of each strongly agree). While a majority of Millennials still says it exists, less than half (44%)—the lowest percentage of all age groups—are in strong agreement. When it comes to international anti-Semitism, Elders again express the strongest emotions on the subject (67% find it "extremely unsettling"), and Gen X are least concerned, though a majority (51%) is still significantly distressed by it.

While the majority of Jewish Millennials has witnessed some form of anti-Semitism, they are the least likely generation to report a personal experience. From there, the percentage climbs with each age segment (13% Millennials, 19% Gen X, 26% Boomers, 32% Elders say "yes, definitely").

However, reports of experiencing anti-Semitism ("definitely" + "sort of") are higher among Jewish Millennials who have been to Israel (73% vs. 52% of those who have not been), those who view their Jewish identity as very important (69% vs. 49% of those who do not see it as important), and those interested in faith and spirituality (61% vs. 49% of those who are not interested).

When American Jewish adults were asked if an experience with anti-Semitism strengthened their perspective toward their Jewish identity, seven in 10 say yes (39% "absolutely," 30% "slightly"). Though Millennials acknowledge facing anti-Semitism less often than their elders, when they are victims of prejudice, they are actually the most likely generation to say the experience had a profound effect on their Jewish identity (44% "absolutely," 35% "slightly").

n=1,503 U.S. adults who identify as Jewish and have at least one Jewish parent | March 2016

# Examining Jewish Millennial Identity

Barna

# JEWISH MILLENNIALS

THE BELIEFS AND BEHAVIORS
SHAPING YOUNG JEWS IN AMERICA

## The research explores the following:

- New data on American Jews' connection to Jewish heritage and tradition
- An examination of the religious beliefs and practices of young Jews
- Insights from scholars of Judaism and Jewish identity
- Comparisons to Barna's existing research on Millennials' faith and lifestyle

Barna has spent much time studying how Millennial spirituality is changing in the United States, pointing to dramatic shifts in worldview and toward secularization. Some of the trends we've observed hold true broadly across religions and generations in the U.S.—and, in the case of this study, for Millennial Jews. Conducted in partnership with Jews for Jesus, this report looks closely at how young Jews in America are experiencing and engaging the faith of their ancestors in the rapidly changing context of the twenty-first century. The goal of *Jewish Millennials* is to explore the mindsets of Millennial Jews and deepen our collective understanding of the future of religion in America.

Order at
**barna.com
/jewishmillennials**

# Christianity in the Australian Workplace

According to a Barna survey conducted in partnership with Reventure, a majority of Australian Christians (80%) believe their faith helps them face the issues and challenges of work. This study of Australian employed adults compares adults who self-identify as church-attending Christians with the general population to gain insight into the way faith plays out at work in Australia.

The experience of work seems much richer for Christians in Australia, compared to the general population. A majority senses their work serves a higher purpose (68%) and believes their church helps them understand how to live out their faith on the job (69%). They are more likely to feel their contributions at work are valued (69% vs. 59%) and have excellent or very good mental health (59% vs. 48%). They also seem much more satisfied with their current job (51% vs. 44%) and are more likely to enjoy going to work each day (63% vs. 53%). Their level of satisfaction with their work-life balance is higher (36% vs. 22%) and includes a greater level of satisfaction with the amount of sleep they're getting (69% vs. 60%).

But even though one's faith is a crucial ingredient in a productive, healthy, and stable workplace in Australia, it is more of a private motivator.

Three-fifths (60%) claim faith and work are two separate parts of their lives. This plays out in numerous ways. For example, even though many feel comfortable speaking about their faith at work (37% very comfortable, 45% somewhat comfortable), they rarely do so (43% do not speak about faith at all). One-third feels it is an inappropriate topic for the workplace (32%) or say they do not normally discuss religion with anyone (31%). Even though six in 10 (60%) feel confident to speak honestly at work, only one in five (22%) feels confident to share the gospel. Australian adults are clearly bringing their faith to work; it just tends to stay at their own desk.

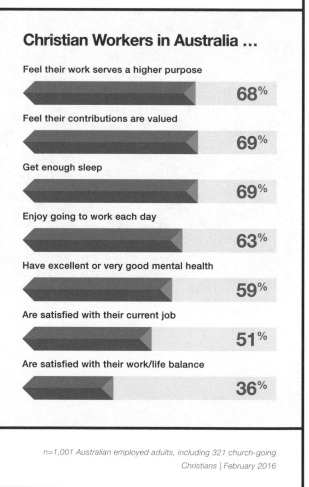

## Christian Workers in Australia ...

**Feel their work serves a higher purpose**

68%

**Feel their contributions are valued**

69%

**Get enough sleep**

69%

**Enjoy going to work each day**

63%

**Have excellent or very good mental health**

59%

**Are satisfied with their current job**

51%

**Are satisfied with their work/life balance**

36%

*n=1,001 Australian employed adults, including 321 church-going Christians | February 2016*

# The Shifting Spiritual Identity of Young People in Ireland

The Republic of Ireland emerged during the 20th Century as one of the most Catholic countries in Western Europe. Most Irish youth (70%) consequently think of themselves as Christians. Of those, 86 percent are Catholics, making Catholicism the majority religious identity (60%). But a Barna study, conducted in partnership with Christ in Youth, shows that developing a deep and lasting faith is not an easy task, even in a culture long associated with the Church.

## Affiliation and Practice

Although it may seem that the pervasiveness of Christian identity lays a foundation for faithfulness, young people seem to be drifting away from an active, embodied religion. A foundational sign of this drift is the significant percentage of young people who do not affiliate with religion. One-quarter of young people in Ireland (25%) is non-religious, and the older a young person is, the less likely he or she is to be Christian.

More young adults (48% ages 19–25) than teenagers (40% ages 14–18) say they are less spiritual today than at age 12. Young adult Christians are less likely than teenagers to agree with the statement: "It's important to me that the way I live reflects my relationship with God." Nearly half say this is not at all true of them (48%, compared to 35% of teens).

Young adults also confirm that their church attendance is declining over time; two-thirds (67%) say they are less active in church than when they were children. Meanwhile, half of teenagers (51%), only newly out of their childhood years, report they are less active in church today than at age 12.

Even if Irish youth don't abandon the label of religion, they may discard its key tenets or spiritual postures. A majority (63%) qualifies as nominal Christians—in other words, many Irish youths identify with a religion whose content and claims they disagree with. Overall, less than half (47%) feel their religious faith is very important, and just one in five (19%) affirms the idea of salvation through grace.

The pressure to continue with this in-name-only version of faith is strong; consider how many desirable schools require baptism for students to attend, which some speculate may support high levels of baptism. In the summer of 2017, the Irish government again stated its intention to no longer permit religious criteria for school admission, a change which, if implemented, may reveal how much of an incentive Catholic schooling was for baptism.[34] Still, other incentives to "be Catholic" remain, like required chapel attendance in some schools or the prospect of having a church wedding.

## Theological Beliefs

The overall religious apathy of most Irish youth who identify as Christian becomes clear when they're asked about their commitments to core teachings of the faith, such as those presented in the Apostles' Creed. Only about half of Christian youth in Ireland agree with any of the ideas in the Apostles' Creed included in the survey. The assumption Barna often heard from youth workers—that young people's grasp of Christian theology is quite poor—is fairly close to the mark.

Self-identified Christians have a broad range of orthodox and unorthodox ideas about God, with confusion over equality within the Trinity, God's power, and the doctrine of hell. For example, four in 10 (41%) believe that Jesus is equal to God the Father. Among practicing Christians, the proportion is higher (50%), but still smaller than youth workers would hope.

It's likely, of course, that some young people simply disagree with traditional Christian theology. One youth worker says this has to do with a "postmodern pluralist mindset. . . . 'Yes, God is good, but I like the idea of reincarnation, too.'" On that point, the same percentages of Catholic and non-Christian youth (10% each) believe that "when you die, you will become another being, such as an animal."

General Christian theology differs between Catholics and non-Catholic Christians, and tends to show Catholic youth to be less convinced of certain Christian teachings. More than one-quarter of Catholics say they do not know whether hell is a real place (29%), whether Jesus was physically raised from the dead (26%) and whether God is the Trinity (24%). Meanwhile, two-thirds of non-Catholic Christians believe in Jesus's resurrection (67% vs. 44% Catholics) and the Trinity (65% vs. 49% Catholics), and more than half (53% vs. 36% Catholics) agree hell is real.

Perhaps most telling: Regardless of their theological ideas, few young Christians seem to believe God understands them. Only one-third of young Christians (32%) trusts that Jesus can understand what their lives are like today. One in four (24%) says Jesus has transformed their life; even among practicing Christians, the number is low (39%). Instead, the young Irish view of Christianity puts more emphasis on rule-following over a relationship with a loving and gracious God. Six in 10 (60%) agree that "if a person is generally good, or does enough good things for others during their life, they will earn a place in heaven." Similarly, 43 percent of Christians believe that Jesus is mostly "concerned about people doing good things and morality in general."

## Faith Transitions

Teenage years are a developmental stage in which individuals form their own opinions. As a result, Irish Christian teenagers often go through a process of questioning and claiming their faith. Some emerge with a more mature understanding of their faith; between early childhood and the end of secondary school, some teenagers (13%) develop a private prayer and devotional life. One in four Irish youth (25%) is currently going through a crisis of faith, however, and four in 10 (40%) have already done so. Fewer practicing Christians (16%) are now experiencing this, but nearly half (49%) have questioned their faith in the past. People who go to church are no more or less likely to have a spiritual crisis than those who no longer go to church (67% of each group are experiencing/ have experienced doubt), suggesting that the process of questioning faith alone does not lead young people to leave the Church. While they might be going through the motions, this willingness to retain a faith identity or remain in a faith community leaves opportunity for youth workers and leaders to help individuals address questions and translate their presence into practice.

*n=790 young people (ages 14–25) in the Republic of Ireland*

*| January–February 2017*

# Inside the Minds of Irish Youth

**Barna**

## FINDING FAITH IN IRELAND

THE SHIFTING SPIRITUAL LANDSCAPE OF IRISH TEENS & YOUNG ADULTS

A Barna Report Produced In Partnership with Christ In Youth

## This report covers:

- New data about the beliefs, concerns, and ambitions of Irish youth
- How young Irish people see and relate to the Church
- In-depth interviews with Irish teens and young adults
- Insights and commentary from youth workers

It can be difficult to develop a deep and lasting faith, even in cultures and regions long associated with the Church. This unique study, conducted in partnership with Christ in Youth, focuses on the Republic of Ireland, where the majority religion is becoming a nominal expression and pluralism and secularization are increasingly influential. In the midst of these changes is a young generation that is anxious and searching. As Irish youth wrestle with the values of popular culture, societal expectations for success, and the nation's transforming spiritual identity, they need guidance from mature believers. *Finding Faith in Ireland* closely examines Irish teenagers and young adults, with a specific emphasis on their faith, worries, and perceptions of Christianity.

Order at
**barna.com
/ireland**

# Uncertain Leaders in the Global Poverty Fight

As of 2015, World Bank reports that global poverty may affect up to 700 million people worldwide, nearly 10 percent of the global population.[35] Such devastating poverty rates are connected to and complicated by crises of health care, education, human rights, water, and the environment. Yet the Bible states that God "secures justice for the poor and upholds the cause of the needy" (Psalm 140:12 NIV). Further, it calls on Christians to speak up for and be generous to the poor when it is in their power to act (see Proverbs 3:27; 31:8).

Pastors are uniquely positioned to help the Church fulfill the spiritual mandate to lift up those in poverty. Yet, as a Barna study conducted in partnership with Compassion International reveals, many American pastors—though stirred by this calling—may also feel overwhelmed when broaching the issue of poverty on a broader, global scale.

When asked about global poverty, a majority of pastors shows great concern (61% "mostly" + "extremely" concerned), more so than the general population (53% "mostly" + "extremely" concerned), though practicing Christians are more likely to express the highest level of concern (34% of practicing Christians are "extremely" concerned, compared to 21% of pastors). Though a plurality of pastors says humanitarian organizations should assume the bulk of the responsibility for the world's poor (30%), more than a quarter (26%) firmly feel that addressing global poverty is the role of the Church (compared to 10% of practicing Christians and 3% of the general population). As such, they are less likely to look to a nation's government to deal with it (19%, compared to 33% of practicing Christians and 39% of the general population).

Given the nature of their work and study, pastors are familiar with scripture's remarks about the poor, including that Christians should help children living in poverty (67%) and that this act helps believers understand the heart of Christ more deeply (65%). More than four in 10 pastors (43%) affirm that, at its root, poverty is a consequence of a "fallen world," one that will remain until Christ returns. Most pastors, however, don't feel that helping the poor is a litmus test for being an authentic person of faith; just one in five (20%) says that Christians who don't help the vulnerable are not true Christians. Practicing Christians (27%) and the general

## Pastors Trust Nonprofits, Churches to Address Global Poverty

*Overall, who do you think should have the primary responsibility for dealing with poverty overseas?*

- Their country's government
- Churches/places of worship
- Individual citizens in that country
- Businesses in that country
- International humanitarian and non-profit organizations
- Local humanitarian and nonprofit organizations
- Individuals like you by donating through non-profit organizations

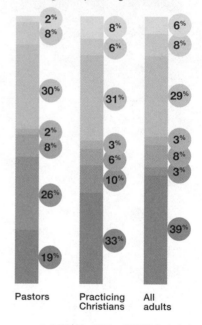

*n=1,001 | May 2017; n=609 U.S. Protestant pastors | May–June 2017*

population (22%) are actually stricter about this religious qualification.

There are signs that pastors, though clearly aware of the needs of the world's poor and their Christian calling to care for them, experience a hope deficit when it comes to global poverty. When presented with a spectrum of emotions one

# Pastors Less Likely to Believe in Their Global Influence

*How much influence do you think you personally can have on these issues?*

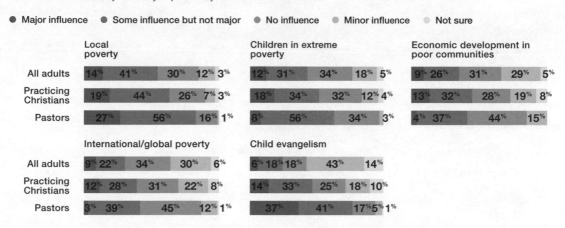

● Major influence    ● Some influence but not major    ● No influence    ● Minor influence    ● Not sure

**Local poverty**

| | | | | | |
|---|---|---|---|---|---|
| All adults | 14% | 41% | 30% | 12% | 3% |
| Practicing Christians | 19% | 44% | 26% | 7% | 3% |
| Pastors | 27% | 56% | 16% | 1% | |

**Children in extreme poverty**

| | | | | | |
|---|---|---|---|---|---|
| All adults | 12% | 31% | 34% | 18% | 5% |
| Practicing Christians | 18% | 34% | 32% | 12% | 4% |
| Pastors | 8% | 56% | 34% | 3% | |

**Economic development in poor communities**

| | | | | | |
|---|---|---|---|---|---|
| All adults | 9% | 26% | 31% | 29% | 5% |
| Practicing Christians | 13% | 32% | 28% | 19% | 8% |
| Pastors | 4% | 37% | 44% | 15% | |

**International/global poverty**

| | | | | | |
|---|---|---|---|---|---|
| All adults | 9% | 22% | 34% | 30% | 6% |
| Practicing Christians | 12% | 28% | 31% | 22% | 8% |
| Pastors | 3% | 39% | 45% | 12% | 1% |

**Child evangelism**

| | | | | | |
|---|---|---|---|---|---|
| All adults | 6% | 18% | 18% | 43% | 14% |
| Practicing Christians | 14% | 33% | 25% | 18% | 10% |
| Pastors | 37% | 41% | 17% | 5% | 1% |

might feel about the possibility of ending global poverty in the next 25 years, pastors are inspired and feel a sense of responsibility but ultimately are not convinced that solving poverty during this time frame is a doable or believable outcome. Though a majority of pastors (56%) are convicted that their congregation should be more engaged with global poverty, pastors are also less likely to view it as absolutely critical for Christian churches to apply their resources toward helping the poor in other countries (19%, compared to 30% of practicing Christians and 28% of the general population). Pastors are also more critical when assessing their own church's involvement in global poverty. One in five (21%) says their church has a "below average" sense of urgency to help the international poor, compared to 5 percent of practicing Christians and 9 percent of all adults who feel this way about their church.

Given the local context and immediate needs that arise in any pastorate, some ministers may struggle to feel engaged in or optimistic about needs beyond their community, let alone outside the country. For example, though 27 percent of pastors believe they could have a major influence on local poverty and 37 percent feel the same about child evangelism (often a part of local ministry), just 3 percent sense this kind of personal influence when it comes to international poverty. By comparison, three times as many practicing Christians (12%) and twice as many among all adults (9%) feel they could have a major impact on global poverty.

Though it seems the realities of a ministry calling temper pastors' hopes of realistically making a dent in global poverty, pastors have tremendous opportunity to provide for and defend the world's poor, as well as to harness the enthusiasm and awareness of those they lead. A majority of U.S. adults says they would definitely (39%) or probably (49%) listen to the opinion of a pastor or faith leader when it comes to global poverty. And despite their doubts about ending poverty in the near future, half of pastors (48%) strongly agree that one person can make a difference in solving poverty, if only for one child.

What might help pastors to better understand poverty? A majority says their efforts would be encouraged by having practical ideas to implement, and more than half say they look for facts and statistics (55%) or biblical perspectives on how the Church is responding to social justice issues (56%). It's vital that church leaders not only experience a Christian compassion for the poor—wherever they live—but also have the education and resources to make informed, effective contributions in the fight against poverty.

*n=1,001 | May 2017; n=609 U.S. Protestant pastors |*

*May–June 2017*

# The State of the Church 2018

*A snapshot of faith in America today*

*n=76,505 | 2000–2016 |*

*See Glossary (page 13) for definitions of terms in* **bold**.

## How Americans Affiliate and Practice Their Faith

*More than three-quarters identify as Christian. Only 13 percent say they have no faith at all.*

**78%** Identify as Christian

**13%** No faith

**7%** Other faith

**2%** Not sure

More than a third of Americans are **practicing Christians,** *though they are still outnumbered by* **non-practicing Christians.** *A plurality qualifies as* **post-Christian.**

**50%** Post-Christian

**36%** Practicing Christian

**40%** Non-practicing Christians

## How Americans Express and Experience Faith

*Church attendance in small congregations continues to be most common, while mega-churches draw less than 10 percent of Americans.*

- attend a church of 100 or fewer attendees
- attend a church of 100–499 attendees
- attend a church of 500–999 attendees
- attend a church of 1,000 or more attendees

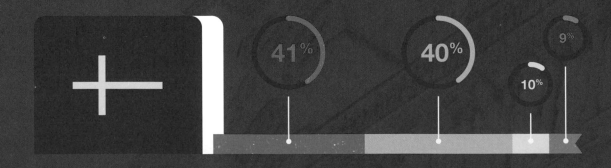

**41%**    **40%**    **10%**    **9%**

*A majority of U.S. adults has made their way to a religious service other than a wedding or funeral in the past six months. Six in 10 have donated money to a church.*

**57%** Churched

**43%**

Unchurched

**60%** % who have donated any money to a church

**20%** % who have donated any money to a nonprofit, other than a church

*What does a week in the (spiritual) life of an American look like? Here are the ways people report engaging their faith in the past week:*

| **78%** | **38%** | **38%** | **18%** | **18%** | **17%** | **18%** |
|---|---|---|---|---|---|---|
| Pray to God | Attend a church service | Read the Bible | Volunteer at a nonprofit | Volunteer at church | Attend adult Sunday school | Attend small group |

## What Americans Believe

*One in four U.S. adults is **Bible-minded** (has read the Bible in the past week and strongly asserts the Bible is accurate in the principles it teaches), and nearly two-thirds have an **orthodox view of God**.*

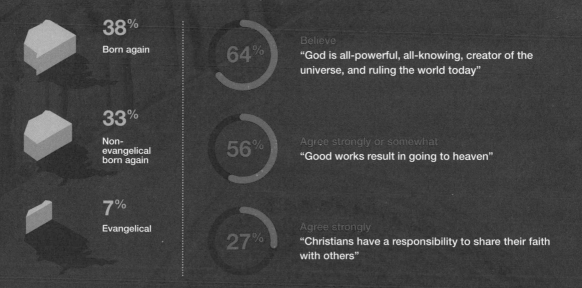

**38%** Born again

**33%** Non-evangelical born again

**7%** Evangelical

**64%** Believe "God is all-powerful, all-knowing, creator of the universe, and ruling the world today"

**56%** Agree strongly or somewhat "Good works result in going to heaven"

**27%** Agree strongly "Christians have a responsibility to share their faith with others"

# Appendix

# Methodology

The statistics and data in this book have been drawn from a series of national public opinion surveys conducted by Barna Group.

Unless otherwise noted, all the studies referenced in the book were conducted by Barna Group, among a nationally representative sample of the population identified. Barna relies on both online and telephone data collection methods, including interviews with cell phone users, in an effort to include people of all ages who no longer have a landline in their home and rely solely on their mobile phones.

To control response error, all telephone studies employ multiple callbacks to households or churches not reached after the first attempt, including a maximum of five callbacks at various times of the day and days of the week. The average length of each survey ranged from 10 to 22 minutes.

The online studies used national consumer panels that are representative by age, gender, region, and socioeconomic class. Respondents were fully verified by the consumer panels and representative sample sources. Additionally, quality control measures checked that respondents were completing surveys at an appropriate pace and paying attention to the questions asked.

Based on U.S. Census data sources, regional and ethnic quotas were designed to ensure that the final group of adults interviewed in each study reflected the distribution of adults nationwide and adequately represented the four primary ethnic groups within the U.S. (those groups which comprise at least five percent of the population: white, black, Hispanic, and Asian). Among pastors, quotas and minimal weighting were used to reflect the distribution of U.S. churches nationwide by denomination, church congregation size, and region.

All percentages reflect the percent of U.S. adults, unless otherwise noted.

| Audience | Data Collection | Dates Conducted | Sample Size | Sampling Error |
|---|---|---|---|---|
| U.S. Protestant senior pastors | Online | May 18–June 5, 2017 | 609 | +/- 4.0 |
| U.S. adults | Online | May 16–24, 2017 | 1,001 | +/- 3.1 |
| U.S. adults | Online | May 15–19, 2017 | 1,019 | +/- 2.9 |
| Practicing Christians | Online | April 14–21, 2017 | 1,020 | +/- 3.1 |
| Active Christians in the U.K. | Online | April 7–11, 2017 May 10–26, 2017 | 1,170 | +/- 2.9 |
| U.K. church leaders | Online + Phone | April 6–May 9, 2017 (online) April 6–May 9, 2017 (phone) | 302 | +/- 5.6 |
| British adults | Online | April 6–9, 2017 | 2,054 | +/- 2.2 |
| Senior pastors and church staff whose church has experienced a transition with the senior pastor | Online | March–April, 2017 | 378 | +/- 4.9 |
| Practicing Christians whose church has experienced a transition with the senior pastor | Online | March–April, 2017 | 1,517 | +/- 2.3 |
| Active or retired service members of all four main branches of the military | Online | February 21–March 27, 2017 | 500 | +/- 4.3 |
| Practicing Christians | Online | March 10–23, 2017 | 1,456 | +/- 2.4 |
| U.S. adults | Online | February 8–14, 2017 | 1,021 | +/- 2.9 |
| U.S. adults ages 18–32 | Online + Phone | January 20–February 2, 2017 | 1,002 | +/- 2.9 |
| U.S. adults | Online + Phone | January 20–February 2, 2017 | 2,030 | +/- 1.9 |
| U.S. Protestant youth pastors | Online | November 14, 2016– January 17, 2017 | 335 | +/- 5.4 |
| U.S. parents of students in ACSI Christian schools | Online | November–December 2015 | 971 | +/- 3.0 |
| U.S. Protestant senior pastors | Phone | October 27–November 17, 2016 | 600 | +/- 3.9 |
| Churched Christian parents of teens ages 13–19 | Online | November 8–16, 2016 | 403 | +/- 4.9 |
| Teens ages 13–18 | Online | November 4–16, 2016 | 1,490 | +/- 2.5 |

| Audience | Data Collection | Dates Conducted | Sample Size | Sampling Error |
|---|---|---|---|---|
| U.S. adults | Online | November 4–15, 2016 | 1,281 | +/- 2.6 |
| U.S. adults, aggregate data | Online + Phone | January 2015– November 2016 | 12,677 | +/- 0.8 |
| U.S. Protestant senior pastors | Online | October 11–21, 2016 | 600 | +/- 3.9 |
| Practicing Christians | Online | September 27–October 11, 2016 | 1,807 | +/- 2.1 |
| U.S. adults | Online | September 12–19, 2016 | 1,023 | +/- 2.9 |
| U.S. parents | Online | September–October 2015 | 400 | +/- 4.8 |
| U.S. interested Christians | Online | July 8–18, 2016 | 1,556 | +/- 2.5 |
| U.S. Protestant senior pastors | Online | May 31–June 14, 2016 | 606 | +/- 4.0 |
| U.S. adults | Online | October 21–30, 2015 | 1,011 | +/- 2.9 |
| U.S. youth pastors | Online | March 15–June 15, 2016 | 352 | +/- 5.1 |
| U.S. senior pastors | Online | March 15–June 7, 2016 | 381 | +/- 4.9 |
| U.S. adults | Online | April 7–14, 2016 | 1,097 | +/- 2.8 |
| Parents of teens who regularly attend youth groups | Online | March 29–April 7, 2016 | 295 | +/- 5.6 |
| Leaders of multisite and church-planting ministries | Online | March 7–April 6, 2016 | 222 | +/- 6.6 |
| U.S. Jewish adults | Online | March 2016 | 1,503 | +/- 2.5 |
| Australian employed adults | Online | February 18–25, 2016 | 1,001 | +/- 2.9 |
| Millennials ages 18–30 | Online | February 2–10, 2016 | 803 | +/- 3.3 |
| Parents of children ages 4–17 | Online | January 25– February 4, 2016 | 1,021 | +/- 2.9 |
| U.S. Protestant senior pastors | Online + Phone | April–December 2015 | 900 | +/- 3.1 |
| U.S. parents of students in ACSI Christian schools | Online | November–December 2015 | 971 | +/- 3.0 |
| U.S. parents | Online | September–October 2015 | 400 | +/- 4.8 |
| U.S. adults | Online | April 29–May 1, 2015 | 1,025 | +/- 2.9 |
| U.S. adults | Online + Phone | February 24–March 21, 2012 | 2,002 | +/- 2.0 |
| U.S. adults | Phone | January 2000 and October 2000 | 3,059 | +/- 1.5 |
| U.S. adults | Online + Phone | 1997, 2002, 2007, 2012, 2017 | ~1,000 per study | +/- 2.9 |

# Barna's Risk Metric for Pastors

In Barna's *The State of Pastors* report, commissioned by Pepperdine University, we examine how many pastors are at risk of burnout, relational breakdown, or spiritual problems. To understand the challenges to pastors' well-being, researchers posed a series of questions. Questions included pastors' self-assessment of their emotional and mental health, their satisfaction with their vocation and confidence in their ability to minister effectively, the strength of their family and friend relationships, and how they feel about the spiritual dimension of their lives. Researchers then used pastors' self-assessments to formulate risk metrics for burnout, relationship problems, and spiritual issues. The items for each metric are listed to the right. Numerical values were assigned to all possible answers.

- **Burnout risk** is assessed using 11 factors from *The State of Pastors* research. A pastor is low risk if they do not meet any of the factors, medium risk if they meet criteria for one of the factors, and high risk if they meet three or more of the factors.

- **Relationship risk** is assessed using seven factors from the study. A pastor is considered low risk if they do not meet any of the factors, medium risk if they meet one or two factors, and high risk if they meet three or more factors.

- **Spiritual risk** is assessed using four factors from the study. A pastor is considered low risk if they do not meet criteria for any of the factors, medium risk if they meet one to two factors, and high risk if they meet three or more factors.

## BURNOUT RISK

- Less confident in their calling today than when they began ministry
- Rate mental and emotional health as average, below average or poor
- Seldom or never energized by ministry work
- Frequently feel inadequate for their calling or ministry
- Frequently feel emotionally or mentally exhausted
- Have suffered from depression sometime during their ministry
- Not satisfied with their pastoral vocation
- Not satisfied with ministry at their current church
- Tenure at their current church has been a disappointment
- Tenure at their current church has not increased their passion for ministry
- Their primary day-to-day tasks do not fit their calling or gifts

## RELATIONSHIP RISK

- Rate their relationship with their spouse as below average or poor
- Rate their relationship with their children as below average or poor
- Rate their satisfaction with friendships as average, below average, or poor
- Frequently or sometimes feel lonely or isolated from others
- Seldom or never feel well-supported by people close to them
- Say it's completely true that ministry has been difficult on their family
- Report a difficult relationship with their board or church elders

## SPIRITUAL RISK

- Rate their spiritual well-being as average, below average, or poor
- Say it is very or somewhat difficult to invest in their own spiritual development
- Receive spiritual support from peers or a mentor several times a year or less
- Say their tenure at their current church has not deepened their own relationship with Christ

# Endnotes

1.  "Mobile Fact Sheet," Pew Research Center, January 12, 2017, http://www.pewinternet.org/fact-sheet/mobile/.

2.  Stephen J. Blumberg, PhD, and Julian V. Luke, *Wireless Substitution: Early Release of Estimates From the National Health Interview Survey* (July–December 2016), https://www.cdc.gov/nchs/data/nhis/earlyrelease/wireless201705.pdf, 2.

3.  Housing Assistance Council, *Rural Research Brief: Race & Ethnicity in Rural America*, April 2012, http://www.ruralhome.org/storage/research_notes/rrn-race-and-ethnicity-web.pdf., 9.

4.  Anh Chih Lin and David R. Harris, eds., *The Colors of Poverty: Why Racial & Ethnic Disparities Persist*, National Poverty Center Policy Brief 16 (January 2009), http://www.npc.umich.edu/publications/policy_briefs/brief16/Policy-Brief16.pdf.

5.  Lin and Harris, *Colors of Poverty*, 1.

6.  Frank Hobbs and Nicole Stoops, *Demographic Trends in the 20th Century* (Washington, D.C.: U.S. Government Printing Office, 2002), https://www.census.gov/prod/2002pubs/censr-4.pdf.

7.  Christena Cleveland, *Disunity in Christ* (Downers Grove, IL: InterVarsity, 2013), 21.

8.  Bernadette D. Proctor, Jessica L. Semega, and Melissa A. Kollar, "Income and Poverty in the United States: 2015," United States Census Bureau, September 13, 2016, https://www.census.gov/library/publications/2016/demo/p60-256.html.

9.  Andy Crouch, *Culture Making: Recovering Our Creative Calling* (Downer's Grove, IL: InterVarsity, 2013), 78.

10. Pete Kasperowicz, "DeVos: Shift Education Policy to What 'Moms and Dads Want'," *Washington Examiner*, January 17, 2017, http://www.washingtonexaminer.com/devos-shift-education-policy-to-what-moms-and-dads-want/article/2612019.

11. "First-Generation Students," Postsecondary National Policy Institute, updated December 2016, https://pnpi.org/factsheets/first-generation-students/#_ftn1.

12. Tamar Lewin, "Most College Students Don't Earn a Degree in 4 Years, Study Finds," *New York Times*, December 1, 2014, https://www.nytimes.com/2014/12/02/education/most-college-students-dont-earn-degree-in-4-years-study-finds.html.

13. Frances Alonzo "Highest Educational Levels Reached by Adults in the U.S. Since 1940," United States Census Bureau, March 30, 2017, https://www.census.gov/newsroom/press-releases/2017/cb17-51.html.

14. Susan Dynarski, "For the Poor, the Graduation Gap Is Even Higher Than the Enrollment Gap," *New York Times*, June 2, 2015, https://www.nytimes.com/2015/06/02/upshot/for-the-poor-the-graduation-gap-is-even-wider-than-the-enrollment-gap.html?rref=upshot&abt=0002&abg=1.

15. "Labor Force Participation Rates," United States Department of Labor, accessed September 3, 2017, https://www.dol.gov/wb/stats/NEWSTATS/latest/laborforce.htm#two.

16. "Fact Sheets—Moderate Drinking," Centers for Disease Control and Prevention, updated July 25, 2017, https://www.cdc.gov/alcohol/fact-sheets/moderate-drinking.htm.

17. Center for Behavioral Health Statistics and Quality, *Key Substance Use and Mental Health Indicators in the United States: Results from the 2015 National Survey on Drug Use and Health* (Rockville, MD: Substance Abuse and Mental Health Services Administration, 2016), https://www.samhsa.gov/data/sites/default/files/NSDUH-FFR1-2015/NSDUH-FFR1-2015/NSDUH-FFR1-2015.htm.

18. Philip S. Wang, Patricia A. Berglund, and Ronald C. Kessler, "Patterns and Correlates of Contacting Clergy for Mental Disorders in the United States," *Health Services Research*, 38.2 (2003): 647–73.

19. Joyce C. Abma, PhD, and Gladys M. Martinez, PhD, *Sexual Activity and Contraceptive Use among Teenagers in the United States*, 2011–2015, no. 104 (Hyattsville, MD: National Health Statistics, 2017), https://www.cdc.gov/nchs/data/nhsr/nhsr104.pdf.

20. "Youth Risk Behavior Surveillance System (YRBSS) Overview," Centers for Disease Control and Prevention, updated August 9, 2017, https://www.cdc.gov/healthyyouth/data/yrbs/overview.htm.

21. "Millennials Outnumber Baby Boomers and Are Far More Diverse, Census Bureau Reports," United States Census Bureau, June 25, 2015, https://www.census.gov/newsroom/press-releases/2015/cb15-113.html.

22. Amy Stuart Wells, Lauren Fox, and Diana Cordova-Cobo, "How Racially Diverse Schools and Classrooms Can Benefit All Students," The Century Foundation, February 9, 2016, https://tcf.org/content/report/how-racially-diverse-schools-and-classrooms-can-benefit-all-students/.

23. "American Time Use Survey—2016 Results," U.S. Department of Labor, Table 12, June 27, 2017, https://www.bls.gov/news.release/pdf/atus.pdf.

24. Courtney Kennedy, Kyley McGeeney, and Scott Keeter, "The Twilight of Landline Interviewing," Pew Research Center, August 1, 2016, http://www.pewresearch.org/2016/08/01/the-twilight-of-landline-interviewing/.

25. Rand Corporation, "Twenty Percent of U.S. Households View Landline Telephones as an Important Communication Choice," news release, November 17, 2016, https://www.rand.org/news/press/2016/11/17.html.

26. Louis Uchitelle and Megan Thee, "Americans Are Cautiously Open to Gas Tax Rise, Poll Shows," New York Times, February 28, 2006, http://www.nytimes.com/2006/02/28/us/americans-are-cautiously-open-to-gas-tax-rise-poll-shows.html?mcubz=3.

27. U.S. Bureau of Economic Analysis, "Real Disposable Personal Income: Per Capita," updated August 31, 2017, retrieved from FRED, Federal Reserve Bank of St. Louis, https://fred.stlouisfed.org/series/A229RX0.

28. Timothy Keller, The Reason for God: Belief in an Age of Skepticism (New York: Penguin, 2009), xvii.

29. George Barna, Today's Pastors: A Revealing Look at What Pastors Are Saying about Themselves, Their Peers, and the Pressures They Face (Ventura, CA: Regal Books, 1993). All 1992 data from this source.

30. Arlene F. Saluter, Marital Status and Living Arrangements: March 1994, U.S. Bureau of the Census (Washington, D.C.: U.S. Government Printing Office, 1996), https://www.census.gov/prod/1/pop/p20-484.pdf.

31. U.S. Bureau of the Census, "America's Families and Living Arrangements: 2014" accessed September 21, 2017, http://www.census.gov/hhes/fami-lies/data/cps2014A.html.

32. "Inflation Calculator," U.S. Inflation Calculator, updated September 14, 2017, http://www.usinflationcalculator.com/.

33. Jaweed Kaleem, "Anti-Semitic Incidents Have Reached Levels Unseen in Recent Years, Anti-Defamation League Report Says," Los Angeles Times, April 23, 2017, http://www.latimes.com/nation/la-na-anti-semitism-adl-report-2017-story.

34. Sean Murray, "'No More Baptism Barrier': Catholic Schools Won't Use Religion as Admission Criteria, Says Bruton," thejournal.ie, June 28, 2017, http://www.thejournal.ie/baptism-barrier-education 3468727-Jun2017/.

35. World Bank Group and the International Monetary Fund, Global Monitoring Report 2015/2016: Development Goals in an Era of Demographic Change (Washington, D.C.: World Bank Publications, 2016), https://www.compassion.com/multimedia/global-monitoring-report-2015-2016-world-bank.pdf.

# Index

# About Barna

Barna Group is a research firm dedicated to providing actionable insights on faith and culture, with a particular focus on the Christian Church. Since 1984, Barna Group has conducted more than one million interviews in the course of hundreds of studies and has become a go-to source for people who want to better understand a complex and changing world from a faith perspective.

Barna's clients include a broad range of academic institutions, churches, nonprofits, and businesses, such as Alpha, the Templeton Foundation, Pepperdine University, Fuller Seminary, the Bill and Melinda Gates Foundation, the Maclellan Foundation, DreamWorks Animation, Focus Features, Habitat for Humanity, The Navigators, NBC-Universal, the ONE Campaign, Paramount Pictures, the Salvation Army, Walden Media, Sony, and World Vision.

The firm's studies are frequently quoted by major media outlets such as *The Economist*, *BBC*, *CNN*, *USA Today*, the *Wall Street Journal*, *FOX News*, the *Huffington Post*, the *Atlantic*, the *New York Times*, and the *Los Angeles Times*.

# Acknowledgments

Barna Group wishes to thank those who partnered with us on the research presented in these pages: Andy Crouch, American Bible Society, Ascend, the Association for Biblical Higher Education, the Association of Christian Schools International, Bible Study Fellowship, Bread for the World, Brotherhood Mutual, Christ in Youth, Compassion International, Cornerstone Knowledge Network, Impact 360 Institute, Jews for Jesus, MJM Entertainment Group, Pepperdine University, Prison Fellowship, Reventure, Summit Ministries, Thrivent Financial, the Tim Tebow Foundation, Youth Specialties, YouthWorks, and World Vision UK.

Roxanne Stone and Alyce Youngblood deserve special recognition for their editorial leadership in pulling together this ensemble of stats and stories. Features were compiled and written by Aly Hawkins, Cory Maxwell-Coghlan, Susan Mettes, Sarah Ngu, Caitlin Schuman, Amy Simpson, June Steckler, and Alyce Youngblood. Brenda Usery provided editorial support. Data were organized and checked by Inga Dahlstedt, Traci Hochmuth, Pam Jacob, and Lisa Schoke. This project would be impossible without those who contributed insights, columns, and Q&As: Sarah Pulliam Bailey, George Barna, Mark Batterson, Katelyn Beaty, Francis Chan, Joyce Chiu, Jeremy Courtney, Andy Crouch, Inga Dahlstedt, Chuck DeGroat, Mark DeYmaz, Shani Dowell, Brooke Hempell, Daniel White Hodge, Sharon Hoover, Cheryl Bridges Johns, Sharon Ketchum, David Kinnaman, Tom Krattenmaker, Stanley McChrystal, Susan Mettes, Latasha Morrison, Jonathan Morrow, Svetlana Papazov, John Perkins, Mac Pier, Gareth Russell, Pete Scazzero, Roxanne Stone, Sara Tandon, Jamie Tworkowski, and Alyce Youngblood. Thanks to Chad Allen, Amy Ballor, Rebekah Guzman, and Baker Books for their collaboration and encouragement. The cover, layout, and multiple visuals were designed by Chaz Russo, with additional charts and infographics created by Annette Allen, Judson Collier, Grant England, Summer Verwers, and Rob Williams. Alexa Mendez provided design support. Many images came from the faith-focused stock collection at Lightstock.

Special thanks to the rest of the Barna team, including Chrisandra Bolton, Amy Brands, Matt Carobini, Joyce Chiu, Inga Dahlstedt, Bill Denzel, Aly Hawkins, Brooke Hempell, Traci Hochmuth, Rick Ifland, Pam Jacob, David Kinnaman, Elaine Klautzsch, Cory Maxwell-Coghlan, Steve McBeth, Elise Miller, Susan Mettes, Josh Pearce, Gareth Russell, Lisa Schoke, Caitlin Schuman, Todd Sorenson, Sara Tandon, Jess Turner, Brenda Usery, and Todd White.

LINCOLN CHRISTIAN UNIVERSITY

**Barna**

# What Can Barna Do For You?

When you need to make a decision, you want good information to guide you. You want a trusted advisor who knows the times. For more than 30 years, Barna has been providing reliable data and actionable insights to the leaders of some of the most influential organizations of our day. Whatever decision you're trying to make, Barna can help.

## Custom Research
Accurate, timely, and affordable research for organizations, faith leaders, entrepreneurs, and innovators

## Barna Polls
Shared-cost research that provides strategic insights about pastors or U.S. adults at minimal cost

## Consulting
Actionable recommendations for your organization, grounded in research and an understanding of your context

## Resources
Published research and insights for leaders and decision-makers

*Learn more about Barna's work at barna.com/services*

**Discover**
Listening to understand your unique needs and expectations

**Design**
Determining the best questions and methodology to ensure meaningful and reliable findings

**Gather**
Ensuring that the data are accurate and representative of your key audiences

**Analyze**
Interpreting results and identifying key patterns, trends, and insights

**Deliver**
Creating custom monographs, reports, or presentations to fit your needs

**Advise**
Applying Barna's decades of knowledge and experience to give you confidence to take action